STRIKE and RETURN

American Air Power and the Fight for Iwo Jima

CORY GRAFF

specialty press
PUBLISHERS AND WHOLESALERS

ISBN-13 978-1-58007-092-8
ISBN-10 1-58007-092-2

Item #SP092

39966 Grand Avenue
North Branch, MN 55056 USA
(651) 277-1400 or (800) 895-4585
www.specialtypress.com

Printed in China

Distributed in the UK and Europe by:

Midland Publishing
4 Watling Drive
Hinckley LE10 3EY, England
Tel: 01455 233 747 Fax: 01455 233 737
www.midlandcountiessuperstore.com

Cover: Late in the war, a General Motors TBM Avenger Cruises over Mount Suribachi at the south end of Iwo Jima. (U.S. Navy via National Archives)

Front Cover Inset: How did perhaps the most famous combat photograph of all time quickly reach the American public from a battle-ravaged island only 750 miles from Tokyo? With no usable land runways, Navy Martin PBM Mariner floatplanes were employed to keep Iwo Jima linked with the outside world. Joe Rosenthal's image, along with thousands of other negatives, stories, and reports, traveled to the Mariana Islands by aircraft, along with a handful of grievously wounded Marines. (U.S. Navy via National Archives)

Title Page: A P-51 Mustang from the 15th Fighter Group, 78th Fighter Squadron cruises over the north end of Iwo Jima. (Nick Teresi via the 7th Fighter Command Association)

Back Cover, Top: A weary-looking Consolidated B-24 Liberator of the 30th Bomb Group, 392nd Bomb Squadron pulls away from Iwo Jima with Mount Suribachi in the background. (U.S. Army Air Forces via National Archives)

Back Cover, Bottom: A formation of 15th Fighter Group Mustangs form up over Saipan before making the trek to Iwo Jima on 7 March 1945. This group of aircraft, lead by Colonel James Beckwith, was the second formation of P-51s to reach the island. (U.S. Army Air Forces via National Archives)

Library of Congress Cataloging-in-Publication Data

Graff, Cory, 1971- Strike and return : flying from Iwo Jima / by Cory Graff. p. cm.
ISBN 1-58007-092-2
1. Iwo Jima, Battle of, Japan, 1945. 2. World War, 1939-1945--Aerial operations, American. 3. Aeronautics, Military--United States--History--20th century. 4. Iwo Jima (Volcano Islands, Japan)--History. I. Title.
D767.99.I9G73 2006
940.54'2528--dc22

2005022966

TABLE OF CONTENTS

FORWORD

The 36-day land battle for Iwo Jima is famous. Nearly everyone has read about the brutal island combat and seen the image of American fighting men raising the flag on Mount Suribachi. The question that is too often glossed over is why the epic battle took place. After the horrific fighting was over, America's aircraft were let loose in the Central Pacific. The U.S. military used air power to defeat Germany and Japan in World War II. And while the England-based flyboys got nearly all the press, another group of equally skilled aviators flew, fought, and died in the Pacific.

These are the stories of the Army airmen, Naval aviators, and Marine flyers involved with the initial attacks on Iwo Jima. Those that used the tiny island as an "unsinkable aircraft carrier" until Japan surrendered. Often, when speaking to these flyers, I could sense their great desire to have their long-lost accomplishments, hardships, and experiences recorded. In many excellent narratives about the bloody battle of Iwo Jima, discussions of aviation activities are limited to a few pages or even a handful of paragraphs.

In this work, I have tried to cover all important aspects and phases of Iwo Jima's air battles from the first day Navy carrier planes arrived to attack on 15 June 1944, until the Japanese surrender more than a year later. The first chapters are written in chronological order. But after the American military establishes itself on the island, each of the chapters discuss a certain portion of Iwo Jima's massive and ambitious air activities in detail—heavy bombers, rescue efforts, day fighters, and night fighters. These chapters overlap during a span of time from April to August of 1945.

Dates were a challenging aspect of creating this work. On an isolated, barren rock where Saturday seemed the same as Monday and this week was exactly like the next, there was often confusion about when certain events took place, even in official military documents. Through personal interviews, written accounts, action reports, and group and squadron histories, I have been able to construct an extremely accurate account of the flying and fighting. But it would be wrong for me to state that every date is flawless.

Much of the slang used by American flyers has been included in the book through my own explanations or through direct quotes. For example, the Japanese Mitsubishi A6M fighter, interchangeably called "Zeke" and "Zero" by pilots, appears in the manuscript as it was discussed by the flyers at the time.

Lastly, a handful of direct quotes from American soldiers and flyers contain derogatory names for Japanese personnel. I have chosen to record these comments without edits or changes in order to give the reader a sense of the times and to maintain historical accuracy. No disrespect is meant.

Cory Graff, Seattle, Washington, 2006

ACKNOWLEDGMENTS

Hardly anyone can create a book alone. I had the assistance of many generous and helpful people. First, I'd like to thank Mark Stevens, historian for the 7th Fighter Command and 20th Air Force. I found his fabulous websites and began asking him questions, not knowing that he was working in a building just a few yards away from my own in Seattle. Mark has been an invaluable resource while creating this project.

Thank you to those who helped field my requests for Iwo Jima images, including Holly Reed and the staff from the National Archives, Edwin Finney, Jr. at the Naval Historical Center, Hill Goodspeed of the Naval Aviation Museum, Dennis Case from the Air Force Historical Research Agency, Jay Graybeal at the Military History Institute, Jim Yuschenkoff of the USS *Hornet* Museum, Stan Piet of the Glenn L. Martin Maryland Aviation Museum, Mike Lombardi from The Boeing Company Archives, and Alan Renga from the San Diego Aerospace Museum.

A special acknowledgment goes to the Iwo Jima flyers and soldiers who were gracious enough to patiently answer my questions and share images from their personal collections. They include P-51 flyers, Paul Chism, Gordon Scott, Jim Van Nada, Frank Rodgers, Jim Tapp, Walter Kreimann, and Leon Sher; the big bomber airmen, Harry Hadlock, Arnie Bader, and Phil Boguch; and flying Navy fighters, G. Roger Chambers; and on Iwo Jima's airfields, Robert Krueger, Frank Saffarrans, Jr., and Hamlin Williston.

Retired Colonel Roy Stanley II fielded my request for information about Iwo Jima aerial photos in a most generous way. Instead of sending me along to some dusty government archive, he broke into his own collection and provided me with everything he had on the subject. I recommend that you find a copy of his book, *To Fool a Glass Eye: Camouflage Versus Photoreconnaissance in World War II.*

Thanks to the late Walt Sandberg, whom I met as we were trying to outbid each other for Iwo Jima articles, books, and maps on eBay. Walt happily shared his unpublished manuscript, a resource book on Iwo Jima. His valuable book, *The Battle of Iwo Jima: A Resource Bibliography and Documentary Anthology*, has since been released.

P. J. Muller of Blue Swan Studios created a pair of Iwo Jima maps especially for this volume. He can be reached at bluseswanstudios@netzero.com. Thank you to Janice Baker and Katherine Williams of The Museum of Flight's marvelous aviation library and photo archives. And my sincere appreciation to Sean and Katherine Martin, who provided my "home-away-from-home" on the East Coast.

Thanks to Jay Miller, Eric Hammel, John Little, Steve Ellis, Tyler Staal, John Lambert, and Barrie Trinkle for helping me get started and keeping me going.

And finally, my thanks to Steve Hendrickson and Josh Brown of Specialty Press.

AUTHOR BIOGRAPHY

Cory Graff is the exhibits research and development manager at The Museum of Flight in Seattle, Washington. In his free time, he works on other aviation-related projects, including writing and research for other museums. He has had articles published in *Air & Space Smithsonian Magazine* and The Museum of Flight's *Aloft Magazine*. *Strike and Return: American Air Power and the Fight for Iwo Jima* is his second book.

INTRODUCTION

A Hellish Scrap of Nothing

"What the heck is *Iwo Jima*?" It was a question grumbled thousands of times by American servicemen as World War II was nearing its final year. In the months before the United States Marines stormed ashore and took terrible casualties in one of the most famous and hard-fought battles of the war, hardly anyone had ever heard of this lonely, wave-battered rock, adrift in the vast Central Pacific Ocean. Before Americans back home viewed the photographs of leathernecks fighting for their lives in a moonscape of volcanic ash in the pages of *Life* magazine, or saw the famous photo of the raising of the American flag atop the shell-battered corpse of Mount Suribachi, Iwo Jima meant nothing.

But in mid-1944, the island came into focus as a target of the American war machine. Navy and Army intelligence experts were tasked with the difficult job of trying to find out what exactly Iwo Jima was. From the little they gathered from dusty textbooks and yellowed sailing charts, they were none too impressed with the answer.

Pre-invasion reports on Iwo Jima's somewhat patchy history were often divided into three sections—the island's geography, its early history (ancient history, as far as military planners were concerned), and its current status under the occupation of the Japanese military.

IWO JIMA'S GEOGRAPHY

Iwo Jima is an infinitesimal rocky dot amidst an island chain called the Nanpo Shoto, which extends southward from the mouth of Tokyo Bay to within 300 miles of the Mariana Islands. The chain is divided into three groups—Izu Shoto (northern), Ogasawara Gunto (middle), and Kazan Retto (southern).

Among the Ogasawara Gunto, also known as the Bonin Islands, was the craggy outpost of Chichi Jima. This enemy-controlled island was large enough to have port facilities, an airfield, and radio station. Chichi was also under the wary eye of the U.S. military as its forces moved toward Japan.

The name "Bonin Islands" was often used by the United States military to describe the entire chain and its three island groups. However, Iwo Jima actually lies in the southern Kazan Retto group, the Volcano Islands. The name for the group is accurate—Iwo Jima was the product of an extinct volcano.

Lying at 24° 47' 40" north latitude, 141° 18' 26" east longitude, Iwo Jima was most often described as "pork chop-shaped" by U.S. flyers and Marines who were unlucky enough to fight there. With Iwo Jima's Mount Suribachi, a 554-

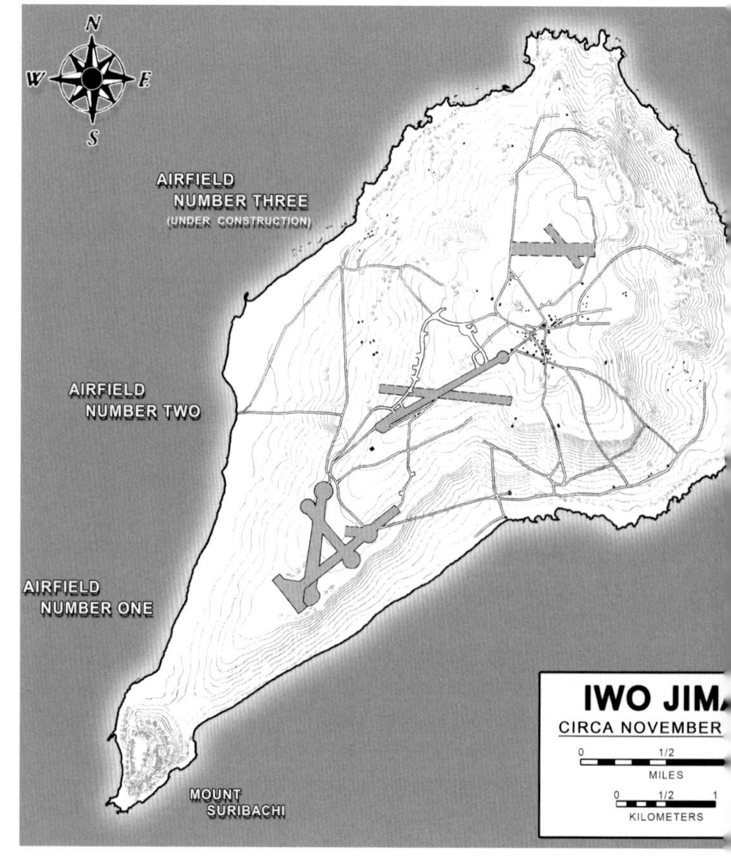

foot volcano anchoring its southern end, and a rough plateau to the northeast, the entire island is approximately 4-1/2 miles long and 2-1/2 miles wide at its widest point. An isthmus, a lower plateau, connects the crater and the northern plateau.

While Suribachi seemed to have died, the entire island was (and still is) laced with lively sulphur springs that occasionally spouted into the air, reeking like rotten eggs and leaving ghostly, putrid clouds in low-lying areas. The springs also kept the rocky landscape too hot to touch in many areas.

Iwo Jima's 4,850 acres were a wasteland of jagged rocks, pumice, sand, cinders, and ash. In most areas, vegetation was sparse with mostly low grass, small scrub growth, and a few gnarled trees. The northern coasts were steep and rocky. The southern beaches, which were along the isthmus, consisted of coarse black volcanic sand. Iwo Jima's beaches would become the focus of much curiosity, concern, and frustration in the early days of the upcoming invasion.

IWO JIMA'S HISTORY

After reporting Iwo Jima's physical basics, military researchers attempted to build a coherent story from the island's spotty past. A "nothing" rock with no sheltered ports and no valuable resources to acquire, Iwo Jima had long been ignored. So it was not surprising that the island's history was difficult to unearth.

Iwo Jima and other islands in the Volcano Group were first sighted in 1543 by Spanish explorer Bernardo de Torres. He didn't even stop. But other visitors followed, including sailors from England in 1673 and Russia in 1805. One report even states that white men, survivors from three-masted Italian merchant ship that had been destroyed by a typhoon, briefly lived on the uninhabited island. An Englishman named Gore gave the strange, ugly bit of land its name in 1673—Sulphur Island, for obvious reasons.

While Spain, England, and Russia each claimed jurisdiction, no one really had control of Iwo Jima or even a serious interest in the island until 1887, when the Japanese arrived. Colonists from Japan stayed on the island. The name Sulphur Island was retained, but translated into Japanese—Iwo Jima. Four years later, the island (and the others in the Volcano Group) came under the jurisdiction of the Tokyo Prefectural Government.

The inhabitants first tried to grow cotton, but were not very successful. At various times, settlers cultivated small crops of coca, coffee, indigo, medicinal plants, bananas, papayas, corn, and vegetables, mostly for local consumption. They also attempted commercial fishing, but that, too, yielded only enough for the locals.

By 1910, sugar and sulphur mining were established as Iwo Jima's primary industries. From February to May, when the sugar cane was ready for harvest, the 500 people working in the sulphur plant switched jobs, assisting at one of the 12 small sugar mills that dotted the bleak landscape.

Most of the colonists lived in the village of Motoyama, with a few populating four other tiny hamlets spread over the small island. Their buildings were simple structures made from wood frames covered with *pandanus* (palm-like) leaves, raised wooden floors covered with matting, and corrugated roofs of tin or steel. Among the dwellings, there were two schools, a tavern, a bar, several cafes, a police station, a gov-

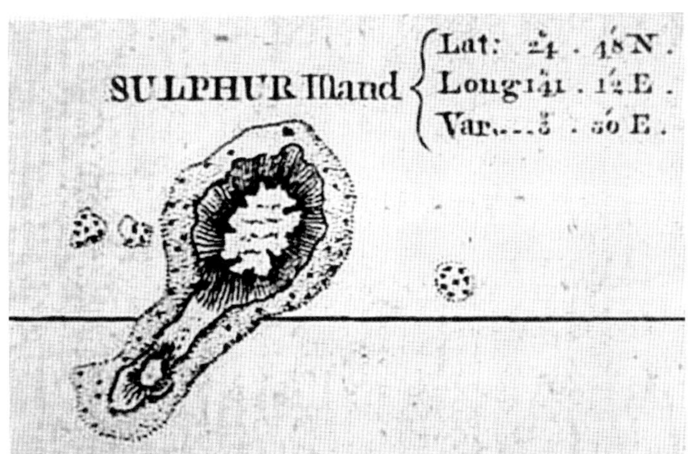

A member of Captain James Cook's third voyage of exploration created this crude illustration of Sulphur Island sometime between 1779 and 1784. The HMS *Discovery* and HMS *Resolution* sailed near the then-uninhabited and uninviting rock on 14 November 1779 while heading west. William Bligh, later of *Bounty* fame, claimed to have drawn many of the maps from the voyage, though he was never formally credited with the works. (Author's Collection)

The U.S. government was able to acquire this rare (and somewhat fuzzy) photograph taken by someone actually on the island of Iwo Jima. Shot in "1931 or earlier," the photographer was standing on Iwo's east beach, facing Suribachi. This area was where American Marines first landed more than 14 years later, in February of 1945. (U.S. Navy via National Archives, Pacific Alaska Region)

One of many signs, in English and Japanese, warning that trespassing or recording of Iwo Jima's details, through "surveying, photographing, sketching, modalling [sic], etc." is punishable by Japan's Military Secrets Protection Law. The fact that visitors were unwelcome on Iwo Jima made it difficult for military intelligence personnel to learn all the details they needed to know about the island before the invasion. (U.S. Marine Corps via National Archives)

ernment survey office, a mail ship warehouse, the sugar mills, and the sulphur refinery.

Clean water was always a problem. Wells sunk into Iwo Jima's volcanic strata rendered hardly drinkable sulphuric brine. Most water came from the skies during the rainy months of April, May, and June. Iwo Jima averaged 60 inches of rainfall annually. In the drier months, January through March, the collected rainwater was drawn from small storage tanks that were prevalent throughout the population centers.

Iwo Jima had a sub-tropical climate, cool from December to April, and warmer from May to November. Temperatures ranged from 63 to 70 F degrees in the former, and 73 to 80 F degrees in the latter. It was not uncommon for temperatures to climb up to 95 F degrees in the summer months. Storms in the Pacific often passed to the north of the island, but from December through June, Iwo Jima was considered to be located in a typhoon danger area.

Iwo Jima's harsh living didn't stop more than a thousand Japanese colonists from settling on the island. Near the turn of the century, Japan imposed a ban on foreign settlement, and Iwo Jima became entirely closed off to the outside world. No white man had been allowed on the island since the early 1900s. After the U.S. invasion, American men found signs, dated August 1937, posted near Iwo Jima's beaches. They were, in essence, no trespassing signs written in Japanese and English. The signs warned that the Military Secrets Protection Law prohibited taking photographs or sketching maps.

IWO'S PRE-INVASION STATUS

The fact that Iwo Jima had been a closed society for 40 years made the last part of the researchers' reports even more difficult. Military leaders had very little interest in Spanish explorers, jurisdictional wrangling, or crops. They wanted to know about the island as it was *now*—in the summer of 1944. Could a tank drive onto the beach? How many airfields were operational? How close could you get to blast the shoreline with battleships? How many Japanese troops were based there?

The researchers patiently fed them what little they had been able to find out. By 1943, there were 1,019 civilians on Iwo Jima, almost evenly divided between male and female. When it became clear that Iwo Jima and Okinawa would become the dual keystones for American activities in the last phases of the war (at least before a possible invasion of the Japanese homeland), the civilians were evacuated. The sulphur plant closed down on 12 July 1944.

The Japanese military buildup had begun months earlier. By May 1944, more than 5,000 soldiers were reported on the island. Iwo Jima's tiny towns disappeared. The raw materials from the simple houses were reused in the military fortifications rapidly being constructed—revetments, bunkers, and gun emplacements. The village of Motoyama was obliterated, making room for the second of Iwo's airfields near the center of the island. The first flying field, which had been completed in the 1930s, was located to the south, near Mount Suribachi. A third field was slowly coming to fruition near the north end of the island.

Overpopulated by fighting men, Iwo Jima became an increasingly unpleasant place. Lack of drinking water was a major problem. Rainfall was enough to sustain 1,000 villagers, but when the numbers enlarged to 5,000 and finally more than

A side-view drawing of Iwo Jima acquired from Japanese sources in the 1920s appeared in many U.S. military reports on the island. Overall, it is a fairly accurate representation of Iwo's layout. However, the plateaus at the northeast end of the island actually only rise to a height of around 360 feet—well below the 554-foot peak of Mount Suribachi at the island's southwest end. (U.S. Navy via National Archives, Pacific Alaska Region)

21,000 soldiers, flyers, and sailors, they had little choice but to consume water from the primitive series of wells. Diarrhea and paratyphoid were rampant among the Japanese forces. And Iwo Jima's normal rainy-season population of bothersome flies, fleas, and mosquitoes suddenly boomed along with the increasing number of human hosts.

Besides being able to dredge up only the bare facts about military forces based on Iwo Jima, American officials were concerned about the beaches. Unlike many of the tropical Pacific islands that had fallen to U.S. forces, this "rock" had no harbors, no anchorage, and no reefs. The black sand beaches dropped off steeply into the depths, and Iwo was exposed to waves breaking very near the shore. Any wind simply aggravated the surf conditions, making the beaches even more precarious. Would Marines have difficulty landing there? There was little other choice.

WHY IWO JIMA?

Then why Iwo Jima? Why not bypass the island and strangle it into submission as was done with another strong Japanese outpost, Truk Atoll? It seems strange that such a tiny and terrible lump of soil would be the site of some of the fiercest fighting of the war. Why would anyone bother to fight over it at all? The answer was that it was not simply a matter of the quality of the land. It was just like any other real-estate equation—it was about location, location, location. This hellish scrap of nothing was just 750 miles south of Tokyo. And as the United States' island-hopping campaign moved rapidly toward the Japanese mainland, Iwo Jima was the critical key to unlocking the Empire.

A report compiled by the U.S. Seventh Air Force explained the situation like this: "Iwo Jima's vital, strategic location, as the center of an air route, guarded the gateway that controlled approaches to the Aleutians, Japan, Korea, China's coastline, Formosa, the Philippines, Palau, Marianas, and the Caroline Island groups."[1]

Locally, Iwo Jima was a nuisance to the massive American air bases that would be built in the Mariana Islands 750 miles to the south. Iwo Jima's airfields were a constant threat to U.S. planes parked at the sprawling island air bases. Raids on the Marianas from Iwo Jima-based Japanese fighters and bombers could cost the U.S. Army Air Forces (AAF) many aircraft and lives.

Iwo Jima's radio and radar stations also meant that, as American long-range bombers flew overhead, enemy forces could give hours of warning to their eventual arrival over Japan. This could have meant the loss of thousands more men and hundreds of machines over time. To avoid detection, the bombers could dogleg around Iwo Jima, but avoiding the island made a very long trip even longer. It also seriously curtailed either the range and/or payload of the Army Air Forces' Boeing B-29 Superfortress bombers.

The advantages of wresting control of Iwo Jima away from the Empire of Japan were many. Besides the elimination of the Japanese presence, the miserable little island offered much more once the tables were turned. The island could act as an unsinkable American "aircraft carrier." With an air base reasonably close to Japan, long-range North American P-51 Mustang fighter escorts could join the U.S. bombers, protecting the heavy aircraft from enemy fighter attack during the most dangerous part of the trip. American rescue planes could range close to the Empire's coast, swiping downed airmen from right under the nose of the angry enemy. Navy patrol bombers could harass shipping at Japan's front door. And perhaps most important, stricken B-29 heavy bombers limping home from Japan with damage, injured flyers, or too little fuel to make it back to base, could land safely at Iwo Jima instead of going missing at sea.

The Americans had to have Iwo Jima, and they were going to take it. They had done it before—on Guadalcanal, Saipan, and at Tarawa. Military leaders figured the fight would last about 10 days.

But on Iwo Jima, the Japanese forces weren't going to stand toe-to-toe and slug it out with the Americans as they had done so many times before. They were going to hide. The attack and eventual takeover of the island was inevitable, but the invading forces were going to pay for every inch of soil with the lives of American boys. The Japanese defenders would fight to the last man.

CHAPTER 1

The Navy Strikes First

Grumman F6F Hellcats on board the aircraft carrier USS *Essex* prepare to launch in June of 1944. Deck crewmen, nicknamed "airedales," await the signal to pull the wheel chocks in the lead aircraft. Others stand at the ready with fire extinguishers while the R-2800 Double Wasp engines warm up. The center Hellcat is *The Minsi*, David McCampbell's fighter. (U.S. Navy via National Archives)

As the United States moved closer to Japan's home islands, Iwo Jima came into focus as an increasing threat to American military activities. The invasion of Saipan, scheduled for 15 June 1944, was the impetus for the U.S. Navy to finally hammer Iwo Jima for the first time.

While the Marines made their final preparations to storm ashore on the western beaches of Saipan, seven aircraft carriers from the Navy's Task Force 58 sailed north on the evening of 14 June to disrupt the flow of Japanese combat aircraft from Chichi Jima and Iwo Jima. The attacking force was put under tactical command of Rear Admiral Joseph J. "Jocko" Clark aboard the aircraft carrier USS *Hornet*.

As the sun set over the Pacific, general quarters sounded among the northbound fleet of American ships as radar detected unidentified aircraft closing from 30 miles distant. The outer ring of vessels in the task group blazed away at the swift-moving shadows as they roared past. The ships reported a pair of Japanese Betty bombers and at least one Zeke fighter coming in fast and low, 50 feet off the deck.

Luminous tracers filled the air on the port side of the armada as crewmen aboard the USS *Essex* saw one of the Betty bombers spark into a brilliant flash, climb slightly, then smash into the sea. Nearby, a destroyer excitedly radioed that their gun crews had shot down the Zeke.

The second Betty turned tail and ran. At only 10 feet above the wave tops, the Japanese bomber disappeared into the shadows, chased by a storm of glowing anti-aircraft shells. The *Essex's* captain, Ralph A. Ofstie, turned to his men, shrugged, and told them, "There goes our chances for surprise at Iwo, gentlemen."[2]

THE OPENING ATTACK

The weather on 15 June was ugly and showed no signs of improving. The USS *Yorktown's* meteorologists reported moderate to rough seas and "a solid, thick blanket"[3] of rain squalls with heavy, broken clouds. Aboard the *Essex*, commanders considered sending a radar-equipped night fighter out to examine the weather over Iwo Jima; flyers were unsure that they would even be able to locate the island in the nasty soup of clouds and rain.

The most famous Japanese bomber of the war, the Mitsubishi G4M typically carried a crew of seven and had a range of about 3,700 miles. Iwo-based G4Ms, code-named Bettys by Allied fighting forces, located the Navy task force before the first attack on "the Jimas" and later harassed the growing U.S. air bases in the Mariana Islands. (U.S. Army Air Forces via National Archives)

However, the idea of dispatching a lone airplane was scrapped. The Betty, which had escaped them the evening before, may have been damaged and crashed or become lost in the worsening weather. No doubt a single American night fighter appearing over Iwo Jima would bring Japanese airmen and gunners on the island to high alert. If the Americans attacked quickly, and in force, there was still a remote chance of catching Iwo Jima's defenses flat-footed.

Seas this far north were unexplored territory for the United States Navy's air arm. The *Yorktown's* Executive Officer, Commander Cameron Briggs, told his men, "Get your shootin' irons ready and maintain a keen lookout. These are the closest bases to Japan proper ever attacked by Naval aircraft."[4] The aviators were understandably nervous as they headed into the unknown.

The task group had made good time steaming north and was in position to strike many hours earlier than expected. The plan was to fly on the morning of 16 June 1944. But at 1330 on 15 June, Grumman F6F Hellcat fighters, loaded down with bombs, were launched from the decks of the *Essex*, *Yorktown*, *Hornet*, and smaller carriers steaming about 130 miles east of Iwo Jima.

The *Yorktown's* fighters arrived at Iwo Jima around 1445, and the pilots could hardly believe their luck—no Japanese fighters had been spotted. They gleefully went to work lobbing bombs onto the operational runways and spraying the parked Japanese airplanes with machine gun fire as the island's anti-aircraft guns crackled away in return.

But it was all too good to last. Moments later, scores of Zeros materialized out of the gray clouds. The men of *Yorktown's* Fighting One (VF-1) and the just-arriving Hellcats of the *Hornet's* Fighting Two (VF-2) joined in a whirling mass over the island.

The leader of the *Hornet's* fighter squadron, Commander William Dean, had accurately predicted that the sky over Iwo Jima would be filled with enemy planes. That morning, he had specifically singled out the pilots from VF-2 who had yet to earn an aerial victory in the squadron's previous engagements and assigned them to fly this mission. He wouldn't be disappointed.

Called "the old man" by his squadron mates, David McCampbell was just 34 years of age when this photo was taken in June of 1944. Before he led his men into battle over Iwo Jima, he had shot down two enemy aircraft. When the war was over, he had become the Navy's leading ace—officially scoring 34 victories—and earned the Medal of Honor. (U.S. Navy via National Archives)

The *Hornet's* Lieutenant Lloyd Barnard arrived over the melee at 15,000 feet and immediately saw Hellcats in trouble below. As he dove, he found himself nose-to-nose with a Zero, took aim, and pulled the trigger. He saw the enemy plane explode as he passed. "Wings and debris went everywhere," Barnard would later report.[5] But the 25-year-old pilot's day was far from over. In the next few minutes, Barnard watched two more Zekes blow up under his gunfire and two others crash into the sea as he twisted his F6F around the wild mass of fighting aircraft. With five enemy planes shot down, he had become an "ace-in-a-day" over Iwo Jima.

The famous Mitsubishi A6M Zero fighter flown by many Japanese pilots stationed at Iwo Jima, including ace pilot Saburo Sakai. Interchangeably called Zero and Zeke by the Americans, the plane was fast and extremely maneuverable—a tough adversary for any Allied opponent. (U.S. Army Air Forces via National Archives)

The *Essex's* fighter contingent was led by Air Group Commander David McCampbell. In the days and months to follow, McCampbell would become known as the Navy's "Ace of Aces," earning the Medal of Honor and shooting down 34 enemy planes (including nine in one day). But at the time of the Navy's first Iwo Jima attack, the 34-year-old aviator had only two confirmed victories to his credit and was universally known by his fellow pilots as "the old man."

McCampbell's fighters left the *Essex* flying at nearly zero altitude and slowly moved up to 8,000 feet as the weather around them worsened. As the radio crackled with the sounds of the nearby dogfight, the *Essex* fighters missed Iwo Jima in the murk and had to double back. When they finally arrived on the scene, they found Hellcats from the *Hornet* and *Yorktown* still battling the last of the Japanese air resistance.

The *Hornet's* F6Fs claimed 17 Japanese fighters and the *Yorktown* 20 more. McCampbell's aviators, arriving late to the party, claimed three Zekes destroyed. While the numbers are most likely high, Japanese records show that most of the aircraft that fought in the clouds over the island that day never came home. For example, the Japanese Navy Air Group 301 put 18 fighters into the air. The pilots of 16 aircraft were killed and one airplane made a forced landing. Only Petty Officer First Class Mitsugu Yamazaki was able to return to Iwo Jima with an intact aircraft.

The *Yorktown's* Lieutenant Paul Henderson, Jr. went missing during the air battle. His comrades later reported that he had shot down four Japanese aircraft in the fight, bringing his final total to five, before they lost sight of his Hellcat.

The *Yorktown's* Lieutenant Paul Henderson, Jr., went missing in the air battle over Iwo Jima on 15 June 1944. But "Pablo's" squadron mates witnessed him shoot down four Japanese aircraft before his Hellcat disappeared. (The Museum of Flight/ American Fighter Aces Collection)

With the enemy fighter threat abated, the Naval aviators once again turned their attention to the two active airfields below, holing the runways and mercilessly strafing scores of parked aircraft. They paid particular attention to any Japanese aircraft that showed signs of life, pouncing on anything that moved as they tried to spot turning propellers in the smoke and shambles below.

One flyer radioed, "Look out for that battery in the volcano crater. It looks like five inch stuff to me."[6] Nearby, an *Essex* F6F flown by Lieutenant (jg) Alfred Jones raced across the south airfield, blasting parked aircraft. The Japanese anti-aircraft guns caught him in their sights and his Hellcat rolled completely over and smashed into the sea at nearly 300 miles per hour.

The *Yorktown* lost another fighter to Japanese gunners defending the island. Ensign Jack Hogue's Hellcat was hit in the starboard wing. A thin line of orange fire and black smoke trailed his plane as he headed out to sea. An *Essex* flyer saw him bail out, radioed the downed pilot's location to a rescue submarine, and then winced as he realized the strike had gone off nearly a day early—the sub wouldn't arrive until the following morning.

As the American fighters headed for home, Commander David McCampbell awaited the carrier's bombers. Now that the aerial threat had been crushed, the bigger, heavier planes of the task group would go to work, hefting 100-, 250-, and 500–pound bombs onto the airfields and buildings.

The weather, it seemed, had worsened. It took nearly an hour's worth of fuel before McCampbell found a "hole in the mattress"—the cloud cover—and led the bombers through. For the TBM Avenger pilots, it was business as usual as they salvoed their bombs on anything that looked like a juicy target. For the Curtiss SB2C Helldiver flyers, the clouds had settled too low for them to effectively dive on the airfields from high above. They quickly adopted the Avenger's style of shallow glide bombing from 500 feet.

The Japanese anti-aircraft gunners found their rhythm by the time the second wave arrived, and more planes were hit. At least one Avenger crashed and another ditched in the sea near the island. As the planes used up their bombs and ammunition, and the clouds closed in, the aviators were forced to abandon the downed TBM crew, floating in their life raft near the shores of Iwo Jima.

Over the task group, the first of the aircraft from the final wave began to appear amidst the squalls. A battle-damaged Helldiver arrived over the *Essex* and could only lower one wheel. The plane was from one of the smaller carriers, but wanted to try for the expansive, albeit storm-pitched deck of the *Essex* in the worsening weather.

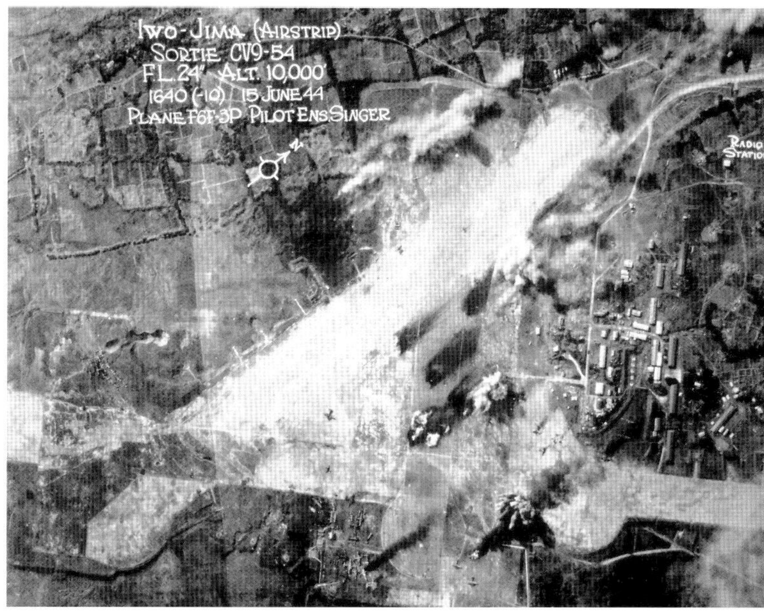

A Hellcat "photo ship" assigned to the *Essex* took this image of Iwo Jima's number one airfield after the American fighter sweep had moved through. The first bombs from the heavier Avenger and Helldivers can be seen exploding near the runway. Note the large grouping of Japanese aircraft in the lower middle of the image. Another concentration of fighter planes can be seen just above the left end of the runway. (U.S. Navy via National Archives)

After an attack mission in June 1944, an aviator waits in a ready room below decks in the *Yorktown*. The photographer captured the young man as he pauses for a moment, listening to radio transmissions, hoping to hear news about his friends and squadron mates who are still aloft. (U.S. Navy via National Archives)

The officers aboard the *Essex* discussed the problem while the damaged aircraft circled overhead. The carrier's own aircraft were all due back momentarily. If this Helldiver crashed on the deck, the *Essex* could be out of commission at the very moment their own fuel-hungry bombers arrived to land.

The pilot of the stricken Helldiver urgently radioed that he was critically short on gas. The men on the *Essex*, who had a reputation throughout the fleet for taking on cripples when no one else would, decided to try to take him aboard.

The one-wheeled plane made its final turn and flew up the wake of the ship. Over the carrier's stern, the landing signal officer gave the pilot the "cut" sign and his Helldiver lurched drunkenly onto the deck, throwing splinters of wood high into the air. The plane's pilot and gunner climbed quickly from the jumbled wreck and, within just a few minutes, the crushed airplane was nudged over to the edge of the ship and dropped into the sea.

Soon after, the Avengers and Helldivers from the *Essex* returned to their roost, with wounded crewmen aboard and showing the terrible scars of battle collected over Iwo Jima. The carrier's crew had gambled by taking the stricken Helldiver—and saved the lives of two flyers. They wondered: would they be so lucky the next time?

Along with stifling the Japanese air response to the invasion of Saipan, the United States Navy had done something else almost as important that day over "Sulphur Island." They had taken pictures. Modified Hellcats with cameras installed battled along the other fighters, dodged the attacking Zekes, and buzzed over the island's interior, snapping hundreds of photographs that would be used by military map makers and strategists in the months to come.

On board the *Essex*, the photo analysts reported 97 Japanese aircraft on the ground at Iwo Jima. They included Zeke and Hamp fighters, Betty bombers, and one L2D, which was a DC-3-type cargo plane nicknamed "Tabby" by the Allies. Most of the aircraft were gathered in tight groups, "as large and tight as what might be expected on the deck of a CVL (an American light carrier)."[7] Only four Zekes were parked in protected revetments.

The positioning and volume of aircraft—along with the absence of a proportional number of adequate hangers, shops, and barracks buildings—led analysts to believe Iwo Jima was being used as a staging point, funneling aircraft to other parts of the Pacific. The Navy pilots' reports of viewing "new-looking" aircraft with fresh and distinctive paintjobs seemed to corroborate this theory.

With tires skidding along the deck of the *Yorktown*, a battle-damaged F6F Hellcat returns home after the 15 June raid on Iwo Jima. The fighter was hit by enemy gunfire and returned to the ship with inoperable flaps. The pilot was forced to land much faster than normal to avoid stalling. When the speeding Hellcat's tail hook caught a landing wire, the force was too great for the tail structure of the aircraft, which pulled completely off. The pilot walked away with no serious injuries. (U.S. Navy via National Archives)

Many of the Japanese aircraft appeared to be de-fueled, with covers over their canopies. Repeatedly hammered by the strafing Americans, the parked planes refused to burn, even when hit so hard their tail collapsed or a wing was torn free. Four Japanese fighters attempted to take off during the attack. Each was spotted and pulverized immediately.

Air combat intelligence officers concluded 62 of the 97 planes on the ground were destroyed in the attack and the runways had taken a number of direct bomb hits. But there was no doubt that more planes would come down from Japan, and the craters in the runways were being filled in at that very moment. A single air raid would not keep Iwo Jima down for long.

ROUND TWO

The veteran Navy flyers had no illusions that they had dealt a death blow to the island. They were up the next morning to return to the scene and give Iwo Jima another sound thumping before their carriers steamed south to help locate the Japanese naval fleet.

The weather, again, was terrible. It was to be a frequent condition in the Central Pacific that Navy and Army flyers would encounter for more than a year to come. The morning missions were cancelled as huge swells and high winds washed floods of foaming seawater over the decks of the carriers. On the *Yorktown*, the ready room tickers hammered out, "Scheduled coverage by planes of this force this morning is cancelled. Oh, what a beautiful morning? To retire once again to the sack!!!"[8]

At 1245, the winds died down and Navy aircraft once again rumbled off into the rain. Over Iwo Jima, they encountered no Japanese fighters in the air. The Navy flyers would later joke that, "Only maniacs would go up in this sort of weather!" A handful of fires from the previous day still burned. Though the Japanese pilots were grounded, the gunners were alive and well, blasting high explosives into the skies.

The rough weather on the morning of 16 June 1944 cancelled the morning air attack on Iwo Jima. Here, the destroyer USS *McCall* steams alongside the aircraft carrier *Hornet* during refueling. Periodically, the bow of the destroyer was almost submerged by waves in the stormy seas. (U.S. Navy via National Archives)

As the fighters dived in from 8,000 feet, an anti-aircraft shell slammed into the canopy of *Essex* flyer Lieutenant John Ivey's Hellcat. Blinded and bleeding from his left eye, Ivey pulled away and jerkily guided his damaged fighter out to sea.

Over the island, the carrier pilots noticed quite a bit of change in only 24 hours. There had been repairs to some facilities and runways and, most importantly, there were new airplanes. Lots of new airplanes!

Loaded with bombs, Avengers from the USS *Yorktown* prepare to take off for attacks on Iwo or Chichi Jima in June of 1944. Designed by Grumman Aircraft Engineering Corporation, most of the Avenger torpedo bomber aircraft in the Pacific were TBMs—built by General Motors. (U.S. Navy via National Archives)

And so the attack resumed. Navy fighters and bombers swarmed the airfields, strafing and bombing anything that looked like it was militarily valuable. One Avenger pilot discovered, as he pulled away from Iwo Jima, that two of his 500-pound bombs had failed to drop. Lieutenant Leonard "Woodie" Wood became the talk of the *Yorktown* when he turned back to the island and laid his remaining bombs squarely in the middle of a group of parked aircraft while every gun in the neighborhood fired in his direction. Observers said that he then circled Iwo Jima, "at treetop level," machine-gunning anything he could find. Not surprisingly, the opinions of the other two crewmen, flying in the Avenger with Woodie, were not recorded!

As the injured Lieutenant Ivey headed back to the *Essex*, two Hellcats, flown by his comrades, pulled alongside. Ivey's radio was smashed and the escorting pilots could see he was bleeding badly. They tried to catch his attention. They frantically tried to signal him to bail out, but Ivey simply flew on. Conversing with each other, Lieutenant George Carr and

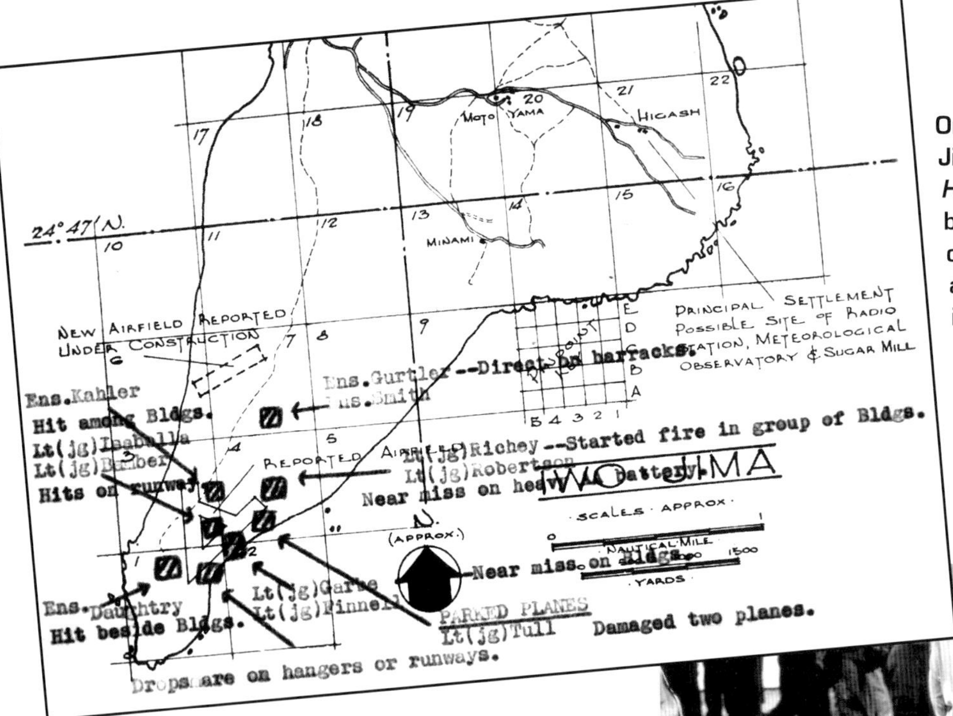

On an attack map for Iwo Jima, members of the *Hornet's* VB-2 report their bombing results for 16 June on the facilities surrounding airfield number one. Note the inaccurate location and size of airfield number two on this early layout. (U.S. Navy via National Archives)

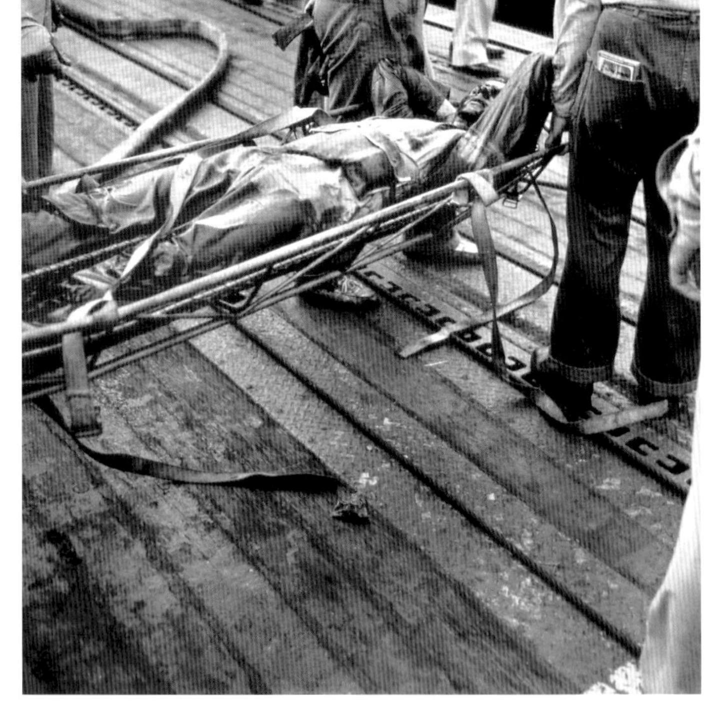

During a duel with Zekes over Iwo Jima on 16 June, Ensign A. P. Morner was hit in the foot and an oil line on his fighter was severed. He was able to make it back to the *Yorktown* and crash-land his Hellcat. While crews prepare to lift his severely damaged aircraft and most likely dump it over the side, the oil-soaked aviator is carried below decks to receive medical treatment. (U.S. Navy via National Archives)

Ensign Glenn Mellon began to suspect that Ivey was only half there—slipping in and out of consciousness and flying simply by reflex.

As Ivey's Hellcat slowly began to bank off to one side in a slight turn, Carr reportedly wrangled Ivey back onto the correct attitude and heading by gently nudging the top of Ivey's wing with his own—an amazing feat of flying skill.

Over the *Essex*, Carr and Mellon circled with Ivey in tow at 300 feet while they tried to think of a viable plan. The weather was still bad and they all knew that John Ivey, even completely conscious and unhurt, had very little chance of surviving a ditching in seas this rough. They also knew that, in the state he was in, he could kill a lot of men if he attempted to land on the deck of the *Essex*.

The Hellcats circled and burned away their fuel reserves. Finally, the captain ordered Carr and Mellon to land. With heavy hearts, they drifted away into the landing pattern and lurched to a stop on the deck of the *Essex*, leaving their wounded fellow flyer above.

Lieutenant John Ivey made a number of half-hearted approaches above the wake of the *Essex*, and then wandered away into the clouds. Word was sent to the picket destroyers and, before the task group turned south toward the Mariana Islands, one destroyer reported encountering a dye marker and fuel slick on the wave-tossed ocean. Ivey was never found.

RETURNING FOR MORE

After the Marine's attack on Saipan, reinforcements of Japanese aircraft were shuttled through Iwo Jima and Chichi Jima in an attempt to shore up defenses on Tinian and Guam. The horrible weather made for slow progress.

In his autobiography, famed Japanese ace and veteran flyer Saburo Sakai described struggling to get to Iwo Jima from the Japanese mainland with 30 Zero fighters for four days, 16–20 June. During four attempts in ugly skies, the inexperience of newly trained flyers forced the group to turn back before reaching the island.

Finally, fighting "violent updrafts and blinding sheets of rain,"[9] Sakai and his Zeros were able to break through to Iwo Jima on the 20th. He was not impressed with what he saw over the island's number two airfield. "I had thought the dusty runway at Lae was bad, but this was impossible!" he wrote. "Landing on the deck of a pitching and rolling aircraft carrier would have been simpler than descending into the monstrosity below us. Two sides of the landing strip were steep rock walls. Even the slightest skid on landing and… a ball of fire. At the end of the runway there waited for any unwary pilot who missed his brakes a towering cliff."[10]

When the group decided to land at the more inviting number one airfield to the south, they found it packed with 90 planes, and no space left for them. Whether they liked it or not, the pilots were destined to finish their journey at the dangerous number two airfield. But now, they would have to do it on the ground. Sakai wrote, "I felt ridiculous as I jockeyed the Zero along the road. This was my first—and my last—experience climbing the side of a mountain in a taxiing fighter plane."[11]

While Sakai and many other pilots settled in to their "dreary, hostile, and uncomfortable"[12] surroundings on Iwo Jima, American language units listened to Japanese radio chatter and coded messages. Using a code book captured near Hollandia, they learned about their enemy's tough experiences with the weather and about the backlog of aircraft stranded on Iwo Jima and Chichi Jima.

Rear Admiral Joseph "Jocko" Clark, who considered the islands his "special property" since he had led the raids of 15–16 June, asked his superiors to hit Iwo and Chichi again. He hoped to prevent this new group of Japanese machines and men from moving farther south and affecting the battles for the Mariana Islands. Permission was enthusiastically granted and Operation JOCKO, named after its creator, went into action.

Curtiss SB2Cs undergo maintenance on the flight deck of the USS *Yorktown* on 24 June 1944. The Helldiver received a mixed reaction when it joined the fleet in late 1943—many aviators believed the Douglas Dauntless, the dive-bomber the Helldiver replaced, was a better combat aircraft. They scornfully called the larger Curtiss plane "the Beast." But by the time the Navy began to attack Iwo Jima, like it or not, most dive-bombing units in the Pacific were equipped with Helldiver aircraft. (U.S. Navy via National Archives)

On 24 June, planes from the carriers *Hornet*, *Yorktown*, and *Bataan* took off to strike Iwo Jima as the fighters of the *Belleau Wood* flew top cover for the fleet. Despite the typical weather, radar-equipped Grumman Avengers were able to lead 51 Hellcats, each carrying 500-pound bombs, around and over the rain squalls from 230 miles out.

They had been spotted. Halfway to the island, the American planes encountered a force of 80 Japanese defenders. Saburo Sakai recalls, "Then the planes were all over the sky, swirling from sea level to the cloud layer in wild dogfights."[13]

Most of the Hellcats jettisoned their bombs and eagerly piled in. Fresh from the overwhelming victories of the "Marianas Turkey Shoot" just days before, the American pilots rushed into the fray with guns blazing, ready to hit the Japanese air forces while they were down and add to their growing scores.

When it was over, they claimed 68 Japanese aircraft shot down. After the war, the number was adjusted to 24 fighters (Zekes and Hamps) and five Judys. Six Hellcats did not return to the carriers that day.

Only four Navy fighters made it to Iwo Jima still carrying their 500-pound bombs. The blasts they created on Iwo Jima's

Rear Admiral Joseph "Jocko" Clark began to think of Iwo Jima and the surrounding islands as his own special property after leading Navy strikes in June and July of 1944. Pilots even began to casually refer to the group of islands as the "Jocko Jimas." (U.S. Navy via National Archives)

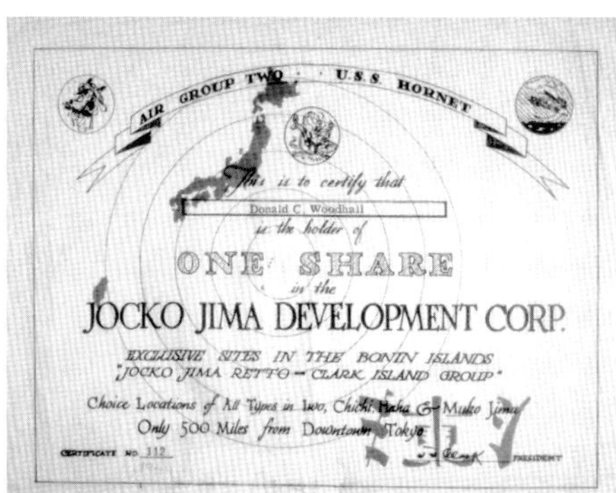

AIR GROUP TWO · U.S.S. HORNET

This is to certify that

Donald C. Woodhall

is the holder of

ONE SHARE

in the

JOCKO JIMA DEVELOPMENT CORP.

EXCLUSIVE SITES IN THE BONIN ISLANDS

"JOCKO JIMA RETTO – CLARK ISLAND GROUP"

Choice Locations of All Types in Iwo, Chichi, Haha & Muko Jima

Only 500 Miles from Downtown Tokyo

CERTIFICATE NO. 312

PRESIDENT

"Jocko Jima Development Corporation" certificates, signed by Admiral "Jocko" Clark, were jokingly awarded to the Naval aviators aboard the USS *Hornet* in 1944. (USS *Hornet* Museum)

runways were not enough to keep a second force of Japanese fighters and bombers from setting out, looking for the American carriers. A group of 20 Kate torpedo bombers found the task force, but none of them survived the onslaught of patrolling Hellcats and anti-aircraft fire from the ships.

Navy fighters attacked another mixed bag of Jills, Judys, and Zekes roaming the clouds before they ever came within sight of the carriers. Fighters from the *Hornet* and *Bataan* claimed seven Japanese bombers and 10 fighters destroyed.

Occasional dogfights continued until 1830 that evening when, after all aircraft were recovered, the American carriers steamed over the rain-streaked horizon. Iwo Jima had been left almost unscathed this time. But the Japanese air armada based on "Sulphur Island" was devastated.

BACK TO THE "JOCKO JIMAS"

The Navy appeared over Iwo Jima again on 3 July. By now, "Jocko" Clark's fixation on hitting "the Jimas" had become well known. Aviators from the *Hornet* created mock "Jocko Jima Development Corporation" stock certificates. Each share smugly claimed, "Choice locations of all types in Iwo, Chichi, Haha, and Muko Jima. Only 500 miles from downtown Tokyo." Share number two was presented to Clark himself. (Share one went to Admiral Chester Nimitz.)

Once again, Avenger and Helldiver bombers took on the airfields as Hellcat fighters buzz-sawed the Zeros that came up to intercept. Saburo Sakai wrote that half the 40 Japanese aircraft that flew that day failed to return to Iwo Jima.

On 4 July, Hellcats bagged 11 more Zeroes and damaged most of the rest as the American bombers again broke through almost entirely unmolested. "Iwo was in incredible chaos," Sakai wrote, "most of its installations wrecked, the field again pitted with bomb craters."[14]

Ensign John Johnson, a Hellcat pilot from the USS *Franklin*, was hit over the island and flew out to sea, clawing to gain altitude. He bailed out only a few miles from Iwo Jima's shore. A call went out to the USS *Archerfish*, a lifeguard submarine cruising nearby. The men in the submarine's conning tower had been enjoying the "air show," counting the Navy aircraft passing overhead to pound Iwo Jima and checking IFF (Identification, Friend or Foe) responders on the planes.

But now, it was their time to really go to work. The *Archerfish* made a dash toward the aviator on the surface at better than 20 knots, a cloud of exhaust smoke trailing behind from the sub's diesel engines. When they arrived, Johnson was quickly plucked from his raft. Leaving the area, a shore battery on Iwo Jima opened up on the submarine. The sub's war patrol report states, "Splash ahead of the bow indicates we are the target. Executed well-known maneuver commonly known as, 'Getting the Hell out of there'."[15]

This oblique of the island was taken on 4 July 1944. While American carrier aircraft went in for the attack, this camera-photo-carrying plane from the USS *Bataan* stood off the shores of Iwo Jima at 5,000 feet, shooting images of the bomb blasts on airfield number one. (U.S. Navy via Roy Stanley II)

The pilot of a Curtiss SB2C Helldiver holds onto the canopy rail tightly as his aircraft nearly turns over on the deck of the *Hornet* during a crash landing after a strike on Iwo Jima on 3 July 1944. The two aviators inside scrambled free as the plane after it caught fire, its engine torn free and fuel lines ruptured. (U.S. Navy via National Archives)

In August 1944, an air crewman, ready for a mission, poses briefly for the camera amid the TBMs parked on the *Yorktown's* flight deck. Each Avenger aircraft carried three aviators—a pilot, a navigator/gunner, and a radio operator/gunner. (U.S. Navy via National Archives)

Grumman Hellcats from VF-1 get ready for takeoff from the USS *Yorktown* in August 1944. Deck space was always at a premium aboard a carrier. Here, only a few feet separating the tail and whirling propeller of the next fighter in line and a third Hellcat's wing fills the void between the two. (U.S. Navy via National Archives)

Later that day, every Japanese plane that was even remotely serviceable was sent out to locate the American fleet. They had been given orders to deliberately crash into the carriers. The event was unusual because this suicide mission was flown several months before organized *kamikaze* attacks on U.S. warships in the Pacific became a common occurrence.

None of the Japanese planes made it close enough to the Navy fleet to perform their dive of death. They were spotted and pounced on by a gang of Hellcats roaming the skies on combat air patrol. Only five of the 17 Japanese bombers and fighters escaped the Americans, many speeding into the clouds with lead-spitting F6Fs hot on their tails. Famous ace Saburo Sakai was one of the survivors of this impossible mission. He and two others, flying Zeroes, returned to the dusty runways of Iwo Jima well after sundown.

Admiral Clark and portions of the fleet visited "the Jimas" for a fourth and final time on 4–5 August. While the attacks netted only a handful of airborne targets in the form of three Zeroes claimed destroyed, other opportunities still existed in the area. Around 25 parked enemy planes were left as burning hulks. The carrier planes caught the destroyer *Matsu* and a pair of destroyer escorts out in the open and promptly sent them to the bottom with gunfire and bombs. They also sunk several Japanese freighters and smaller craft.

The entire operation was judged quite profitable, with one exception—16 American carrier planes failed to come home and 19 pilots and aircrew were killed, all due to anti-aircraft fire. The defenses on Iwo Jima and the surrounding islands, it seemed, were getting tougher.

CHAPTER 2

Enter the Army Air Forces

Stinky was one of the first Lockheed F-5 photo-reconnaissance planes to arrive at Isley Field on Saipan. Similar to a P-38 Lightning fighter, modified "photo ships" carried cameras instead of guns in their nose. The planes were lighter, faster, and could fly longer distances than a standard Lightning fighter. Note the 28th Photo Reconnaissance Squadron emblem located above the plane's nickname. (U.S. Army Air Forces via National Archives)

As the U.S. Army Air Forces arrived and began to set up shop in the Mariana Islands, they took over the task of keeping the Japanese forces based on Iwo Jima on their heels. Elements of the Seventh Air Force were quick to move—not far behind the Marines as they mopped up the remnants of enemy resistance on Saipan. While the Seabees continued to build, scrape, flatten, and repair the runways, and as American fighting men hunted the last enemy soldiers in the jungle-covered hills, the warplanes of the Seventh began to touch down at their new bases of operations.

WATCH THE BIRDIE

On the day that Navy carrier planes finished their third attack on Iwo Jima, another group of American aircraft, soon to become regulars over the bomb-blasted stronghold, flew their first mission.

On the Fourth of July, 1944, from an airstrip still under construction on the island of Saipan, rose a pair of bare metal twin-engine Army fighter planes. Painted on the cowlings was a strange emblem—astride a gray winged comet was a red wolf, focusing an aerial camera on a globe far below.

With Mount Suribachi appearing on the horizon, the Lockheed F-5 Lightnings of the 28th Photographic Reconnaissance Squadron drifted down to low level. Smoke poured from the plane's exhaust stacks as the pilots pushed the throttles forward and slowly built up speed.

By the time they reached the shoreline, the F-5s were roaring along at a terrific rate. Japanese gunfire shot up at them as they hurled forward, straight and level. Cameras in the gun bays in the nose of each aircraft clicked away, recording all of the details of Iwo Jima's landscape. Images of Iwo Jima's beaches, airfields, roads, and gun locations were all imprinted on hundreds of feet of film.

Consolidated B-24 Liberators of the 30th Bomb Group, 819th Bomb Squadron, cruise toward Iwo Jima with a load of bombs on 21 October 1944. The J-model aircraft in the foreground, nicknamed *Curly Bird*, is relatively new—ordered, built, and delivered in 1944. At the time of the photo, the plane has flown twenty combat missions, as indicated by the bomb symbols painted under the pilot's side window. (U.S. Army Air Forces via National Archives)

PHOTO JOES

Prior to the Marine invasion, the American military worked feverishly to collect information about Iwo Jima. The USS *Spearfish*, an American submarine, took photos of the shoreline from the sea. Crewmen practiced the dangerous approach again and again, until they could cruise in close, raise their periscope, and shoot a 12-exposure panorama in less than 40 seconds. The Navy collected additional aerial photos during their attacks in the summer of 1944.

Lockheed F-5 Lightnings of the Army's 28th Photo Reconnaissance Squadron shot the best images of the island. Racing full out at low level, these unarmed "photo Joes" braved Japanese anti-aircraft and small arms fire to steal a look at Iwo Jima's airfields, shoreline, and defensive fortifications. The dangerous photo runs collected a wealth of information used in the invasion of the island.

Pilots of the 28th Photo Reconnaissance Squadron, based on Saipan, replicate an imaginary stack of photographic prints 12 feet tall. The stack is equivalent to the number of photos taken over Iwo Jima in the months before the invasion while flying their modified Lockheed photo aircraft. (U.S. Army Air Forces via National Archives)

On a photo mission to Iwo Jima, an F-5 caught this image of a crashed Betty bomber during an attack on airfield number two. Judging by the amount of vegetation growing amid the landscape, the image was probably taken in the summer or fall of 1944. (U.S. Army Air Forces via Linda Young)

A group of at least 25 Japanese soldiers scatter in all directions, abandoning their truck, as an American "photo ship" zooms overhead at low level. This image was taken near Iwo's east shoreline on 20 February 1945. (U.S. Army Air Forces via National Archives)

This image must have been mildly amusing to the Army photo interpreters on Saipan when they hung the print up to dry. A fully packed clothesline can be seen on the left. On the right is, well, a man. It's a Japanese soldier who appears to be doing ... what everyone has to do now and then. One can only imagine what it was like to be caught by surprise by a 10-ton aircraft, roaring just a few feet overhead on 3 January 1945. (U.S. Army Air Forces via Roy Stanley II)

During this briefing on 10 August 1944, the drape was pulled back to reveal the target of the day—Iwo Jima. This raid was the first of over 2,800 sorties to the island by Marianas-based B-24 Liberators. This attack, by the 30th Bomb Group, was slated to hit Iwo's airfield number one. (Air Force Historical Research Agency)

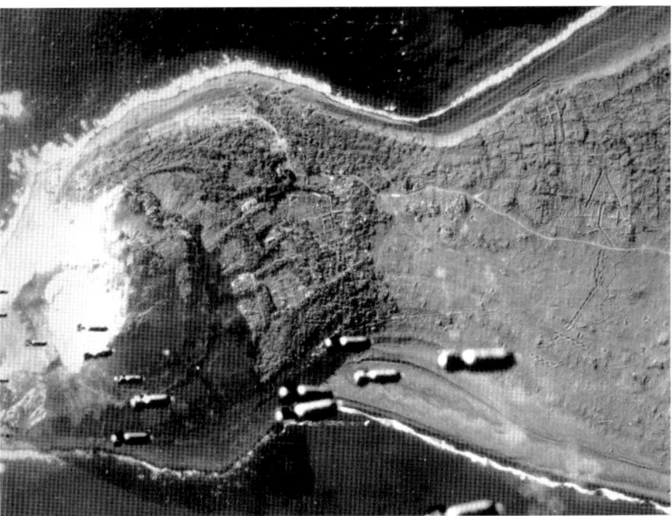

A heavy rain of 500-pound bombs falls near Iwo Jima's Mount Suribachi. Dumped by a Seventh Air Force B-24 Liberator, the high-explosive payload is most likely aimed at the island's southernmost airfield, just out of the frame to the right. Below, Iwo's east beaches can be seen. When the Marines came ashore, this is where they landed. (Military History Institute/Milne Collection)

After a number of high-speed passes, the Lockheed F-5 "photo ships" escaped toward home as fast as they had come. Safe in their camera magazines was a wealth of images. The photos were so clear and detailed that they would become the basis for the Marine invasion plans.

An Army heavy bomber outfit that was in the midst of moving to their new home on Saipan also obtained the photos collected by the 28th. The 30th Bomb Group's Consolidated B-24 Liberators began to arrive from Kwajalein Atoll in the Marshall Islands on 8 August 1944.

Two days later, two of the 30th's three squadrons took off from Isley Field on Saipan for their first bombing missions to Iwo Jima. In all, 143 Liberators dropped 290 tons of bombs on the island during eight missions in August. The 30th lost only two aircraft that month—both while flying missions over Iwo Jima. Quickly, these newcomers developed an intense hatred for the ugly scrap of volcanic rock.

The month of September started much the same as the men of the 30th Bomb Group established a familiar routine—wearing a trail in the skies as they shuttled northward to the target with their bellies filled with bombs. On 3 September a force of 41 Liberators attacked Iwo Jima, spilling 96 tons of explosives on the active airfields. A whopping 74 percent of their bombs exploded within the target areas. The B-24 *Dottie Anne* developed mechanical troubles and the bomber's crew bailed out over the sea. The crews of Navy vessels rescued all but one of the flyers.

THE SAGA OF *THE CHAMBERMAID*

10 September 1944 started like any other day for the crew of the 30th Bomb Group Liberator nicknamed *The Chambermaid*. They would drone up to Iwo Jima, dodge a few bursts of Japanese flak and maybe a fighter or two, dump their payload, and return home. The weather between Saipan and the target was a bit dicey, but it seemed that it almost always was in this part of the Pacific. The 30th's B-24s flew in tight formation as they weaved their way around the worst of the weather. No sweat.

The 10-man flight crew of *The Chambermaid* poses in front of their aircraft. The battered plane was the veteran of many missions in the Pacific before its final flight to Iwo Jima. The men in the top row are the officers: Core, Beatty, Wasser, and Harms, left to right. Below: Harriff, Verescak, Richards, Howard, Shahein, and Martin. Lieutenant Doscher, intelligence officer, who flew along with the crew on their mission to Iwo, is not pictured. (Air Force Historical Research Agency)

As they neared Iwo Jima, someone spotted a string of eight Japanese fighters. They were low, which was unusual, and the fighters were farther out from the island than they normally ranged. But then again, strange happenings were nothing but the norm when it came to attacking Iwo Jima. One day, there might be halfhearted flak and two uninterested Zeros—a milk run. The next day, the Japanese would fight like the devil, throwing everything they had at the formation of bombers.

Today seemed like one of the latter, as the enemy fighters made firing runs at the B-24s from below. The bomber's gunners collectively hammered away, and one of the most aggressive enemy fighters exploded in flames and fluttered into the sea in small pieces.

As the bombers reached the island, the swarm of fighters moved away and let the Japanese anti-aircraft gunners have their turn at hitting the formation. Aboard *The Chambermaid*, the pilot, Lieutenant William Core, had convinced his copilot, Lieutenant Glen Beatty, to fly the plane over the target. Core later told a reporter, "I'd flown over [Iwo Jima] three times before, but each time I'd been at the controls and had never caught a glimpse of the damned place."[16]

The Chambermaid and the other B-24s dropped their bombs into installations and storage areas near one of Iwo Jima's airfields just as the Japanese fighters appeared again to intercept the formation as they turned toward

A montage of aerial images of Iwo Jima taken on 17 August 1944 shows the island bristling with guns and numerous tempting targets. "AW" means automatic weapon. "AA" means anti-aircraft. Photographed early in the bombing campaign, Iwo even appears to have foliage in some areas. Later, the heavy bombing would sweep most of this away, leaving a barren field of jumbled rocks and craters. (U.S. Army Air Forces via Roy Stanley II)

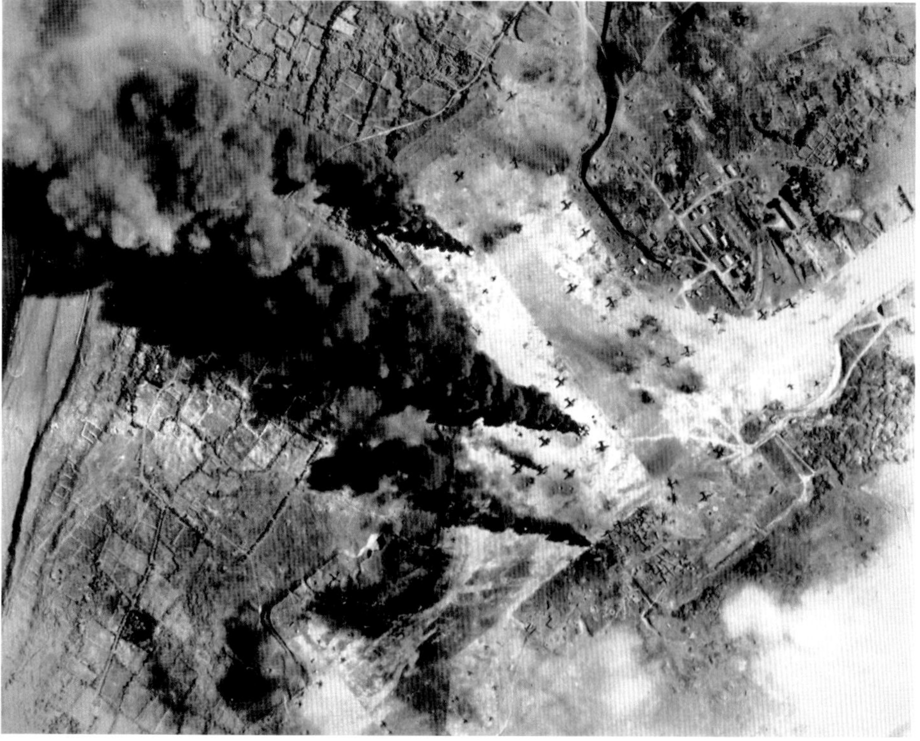

Snapped from an attacking B-24, the burning Japanese planes on Iwo Jima's airfield spew black smoke. Note the two large concentrations of aircraft in the lower part of the frame. (U.S. Army Air Forces via National Archives)

Saipan. Core busied himself being an additional pair of eyes for the gunners, calling out the positions of various threatening fighters as flak still blossomed around the formation.

Then the nose gunner, Sergeant Milton Howard, excitedly asked over the interphone, "Hey, how come my turret has stopped?" And moments later, Staff Sergeant George Shahein reported that something was leaking into his ball turret in the belly of the plane. He said he could hardly see. It was hydraulic fluid—*The Chambermaid* had been hit in the nose by fragments of an anti-aircraft shell. And as the severed hydraulic lines in the faltering bomber bled dry, a pair of Japanese fighters moved in to finish the job.

The Japanese on Iwo Jima often used white phosphorous shells fired from the ground and phosphorous bombs dropped from aircraft. Here, one bursts near a group of Seventh Air Force B-24 Liberators. While such attacks were spectacular, the blasts hardly ever brought down an American bomber over the island. (U.S. Army Air Forces via National Archives)

Core watched the Zekes approach from high above both sides of *The Chambermaid's* nose. He called out the one on the left side first, because it looked closest. The bomber's nose guns remained silent, but the top turret above and behind the flight deck began to blast away at the intruder. Core caught a glimpse of the other fighter, the one on the right side, as it executed a half roll, dropped a phosphorous bomb into the formation of bombers, and dove steeply toward them. He could see smoke belching from the gun bays in the wings of the Zeke as it sped closer and closer. Then he heard the dull thuds of bullets and cannon shells spattering the fuselage of *The Chambermaid.*

A hole appeared in the roof of the flight deck and Plexiglas and shards of metal rattled around the interior. After the Zero dove past, Core figured they'd gotten off pretty easy. Then his copilot, Beatty, took one of his hands off the control yoke and reached around to feel his back. His hand returned to the control column smeared with blood. Beatty turned sideways to let Core have a look. There was a hole in his flight suit and more blood. Core assumed that Beatty had caught a piece of shrapnel from an exploding 20-mm shell. Later, a doctor would remove not a shell fragment from the flyer's back, but a twisted piece of *The Chambermaid's* aluminum skin.

The two flyers argued briefly as Core insisted he take back the flight controls from his wounded copilot. As soon has he did, he knew they were in real trouble. He tried to throttle back the engines, which were still running nearly full out from the bomb run over Iwo Jima. The linkage for the throttle to engine number one was snapped and number two was hopelessly jammed forward. Checking the engines on the opposite side, Core could see that number four was objecting to being run on such a high power setting for so long. It was throwing oil and beginning to smoke.

Core asked the bombardier, Lieutenant Melvin Harms, to make a sweep of the bomber, checking for further damage. The inside of *The Chambermaid* looked like the scene of a murder, with pools of eye-stinging hydraulic fluid in the place of blood. And Harms didn't have very far to travel to find real blood. As he moved aft, beyond Core and the injured Beatty, Harms immediately discovered Lieutenant Clarence Wasser, navigator, and Staff Sergeant Ted Richards, radio operator, lying in a crumpled pile as freezing wind ripped down through the damaged top turret. Wasser, sprayed by shrapnel, had two bullet wounds to the shoulder and three in his right hand.

Richards should have been dead. He was firing the .50-caliber guns in the top turret when Japanese bullets smashed through the Plexiglas bubble. He was covered with small puncture wounds from flying plastic and metal, but what alarmed Harms most was that Richards couldn't speak and was grasping his blood-smeared throat.

With the help of *The Chambermaid's* waist gunners, Harms slowly and carefully managed to transfer Wasser and Richards over the small walkway, more of a beam really, that spanned the now empty bomb bay. It was only a foot wide and slick with hydraulic fluid. One slip meant falling onto the bomb bay doors below. They would never hold a man's weight. Near the waist guns, the injured men were laid on the floor as the able-bodied flyers began to administer first aid.

Harms, unaware that Beatty had been injured, remembered that the copilot had once been a mortician's assistant and went forward to see if he might be available to help with the wounded. The bombardier found Beatty, along with

Lieutenant Robert Doscher, had also been hit in the attack. Doscher, an air intelligence officer riding along as an observer, suffered a deep puncture to his thigh.

News of his wounded comrades made Core even more nervous about the condition of his battered bomber. He had given no thought to flying the plane more than a dozen miles away from Iwo Jima before he figured he'd be forced to ditch at sea. Now, with so many injured aboard, he had to think seriously about milking every minute of flying time from *The Chambermaid's* engines.

The 30th's formation of B-24s slowly pulled away, but the bomb group's flight leader, Captain Robert Valentine, stayed behind with his aircraft and three others. They boxed *The Chambermaid* in, one above, one below, and one to each side. They used their combined firepower to hold off the Japanese planes, which were eagerly circling—waiting for a chance to deliver the *coup de grace* to the maimed bomber.

On the flight deck, Core ordered Beatty to give up his seat and have someone attend to his wounds. In his place, he called the left waist gunner, Staff Sergeant Robert Martin, to come up to the flight deck. Martin had made it much of the way through pilot training before being labeled "unfit to fly" by some instructor back in the States. He had glumly gone overseas as a gunner. But Core had allowed Martin to log time in the copilot's seat whenever he had the chance. He had rightly figured that Martin's abilities and natural interest in flying might be important one day. And today was the day.

Out of fighter range now, Core and Martin went to work on trying to slow down the runaway engines. Throttled to full power, *The Chambermaid* would never have the fuel to make it back to Saipan. After much experimenting, Core and Martin found they could calm the number one engine by pumping in air from the turbocharger. Number two could be slowed by constantly fidgeting with the feathering mechanism button. Core related later that the practice was completely unorthodox, but it helped, and he was desperate.

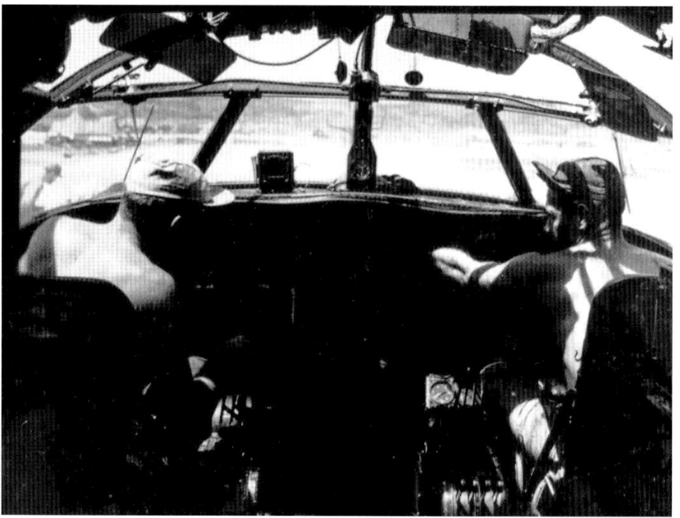

The flight deck of a Seventh Air Force B-24 Liberator—pilot on the left, copilot on the right. It was here that Lieutenant William Core and waist gunner Sergeant Robert Martin (in the place of the injured copilot) struggled to keep the heavily damaged *Chambermaid* aloft during the long flight back to Saipan. (Arvid Johnson via the 7th Fighter Command Association)

The number four engine was the most upsetting. It continued to throw oil and smoke and, every hour, almost on the hour, it would burst into flames briefly, burning all of the oil that had sprayed out onto the cowling.

The Chambermaid slowly made its way over the Pacific at 140 miles per hour—only about 15 miles per hour above stalling speed. Core noted the big B-24 was settling toward the water at around 40 feet per minute. He ordered the crew to dump everything they could. Machine guns, belts of ammunition, flak vests, and helmets went "over the side" out the waist gun windows. The airmen even tried to jettison the plane's 1,200-pound ball turret. But the wrench they were using to twist loose the retaining nuts was soaked with slippery hydraulic fluid and in one second of inattention, it fell from someone's hands, dropped through the gap between the turret and fuselage, and was gone. The flyers tried their best to contain their frustration as their only suitable wrench tumbled into the sea, far below.

Shahein and Harms attended to Wasser in the waist area, but everyone else moved to the front of the bomber to balance the plane as it fought through rough weather. Core would periodically turn in his seat and wink to Richards, settled onto the flight deck floor behind him. Richards, with his neck bandaged and unable to speak, would wink back and give a half-hearted grin.

Core thought now that they just might make it. The notion brought about a whole new set of worries. If they did make it to Saipan, could they bail out? Some of the injured flyers would have a hard time doing that. Could they land? No hydraulics meant no brakes. Core knew that B-24 Liberators had a nasty habit of breaking apart in crash landings. It would be a nightmare to come so far and end up a flaming mess at the edge of the runway.

All they could do was try. And as the sun began to set, the miles drifted by under *The Chambermaid's* nose. The ragged old bomber seemed unwilling to give up, unwilling to let her crew down. By the time they reached Saipan, it would be dark.

The flyers began to try plugging the leaks in the shredded hydraulic lines. When they thought they had the lines suitably patched up, they dumped in more fluid from an emergency tank. The patches blew and slipped, and the last of *The Chambermaid's* lifeblood spilled from her veins. There would be no brakes and if they were going to land, they'd have to crank the gear down by hand.

The right wheel went down, but the cable leading to the left gear had been frayed by gunfire and promptly snapped when the right waist gunner began to crank. They had no way to get the left main down and locked. The men took out their frustration on the nose wheel, viciously kicking it down into position.

Remembering what the crew of a shot-up B-24 had done when returning to Tarawa earlier in the war, the flyers fashioned makeshift brakes from three parachutes. One was secured to each waist gun mount and the third in the tail position. When *The Chambermaid* touched down, and Core gave the signal, the men would pop the chutes in an attempt to slow the big bomber down.

There was nothing left to do but bring the plane into Saipan's Isley Field.

The Chambermaid lies, twisted and smashed, the day after its 10 September 1945 crash landing. B-24s had the alarming characteristic of breaking apart, catastrophically, during forced landings. Here, ground crews swarm over the bomber, stripping away useful parts to be used on other 30th Bomb Group aircraft. Note the pair of bent .50-caliber machine guns from the nose turret sitting in the foreground. (U.S. Army Air Forces via National Archives)

Fuel and ammo are loaded onto a 318th Fighter Group P-47 Thunderbolt. Though they didn't have the range to make it to Iwo Jima, the American planes were once used in an attempt to intercept the Japanese fighters that often followed the Liberator bombers south on the homeward leg of their bombing missions. Pilots say the 318th fighters were tough and powerful, but getting weary and old. (U.S. Army Air Forces via National Archives)

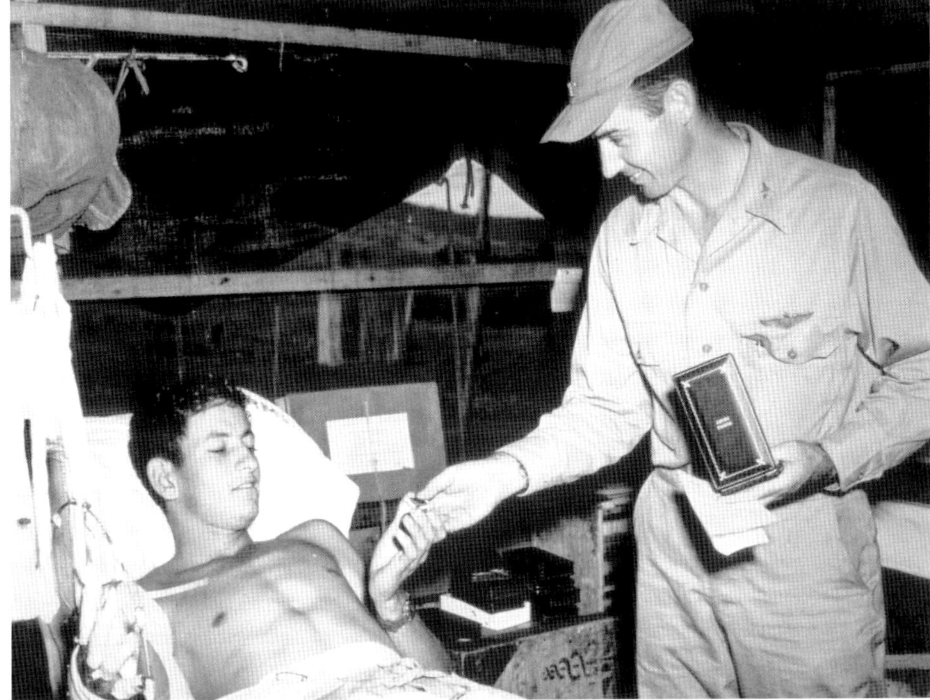

Lieutenant Clarence Wasser, *The Chambermaid's* navigator, receives his Purple Heart while lying in Saipan's station hospital two days after the mission to Iwo Jima. Shot through the shoulder and right hand and sprayed with shrapnel, the bleeding flyer survived the flight back to base and the subsequent crash-landing. (Air Force Historical Research Agency)

When the 318th went out to meet American bombers returning from Iwo Jima, they hoped to encounter a whole gaggle of Zekes. But the only enemy plane in sight was a twin-engine Kawasaki Ki-45 fighter, similar to this one. The P-47 pilots pounced on the plane, code-named Nick by the Allies, sending it down in flames. (The Museum of Flight/Champlin Collection)

Members of the 318th Fighter Group, 73rd Fighter Squadron pose for the camera in their makeshift Officer's Club on Saipan in October 1944. Flying Republic P-47 fighters, their primary job was to protect the Mariana Islands from attack. (Air Force Historical Research Agency)

Ground crewmen prepare fragmentation bombs to be loaded into the belly of a Seventh Air Force B-24 Liberator for a night "snooper" mission over Iwo Jima. The "frag bombs" were dropped on the Japanese-held island to "kill people and hack up equipment" working to repair the runways. (U.S. Army Air Forces via National Archives)

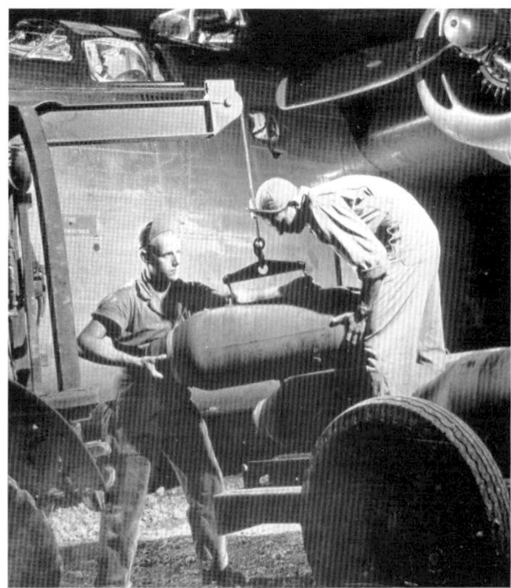

With the help of a lift, armorers manhandle a 500-pound bomb into place. In an attempt to keep the Japanese airfield repair specialists on Iwo Jima as inefficient as possible, some bombs were fused to explode on impact, while others where set to detonate at varying time intervals up to 72 hours after being dropped by the Liberators. (U.S. Army Air Forces via National Archives)

The Chambermaid touched down at 105 miles per hour and almost immediately went over the landing lights off the right side of the runway. The men in the tail let their parachutes blossom, but the big bomber seemed to keep right on going. Martin cut the master switch to the engines as the plane careened over a jeep trailer stacked with floodlights and into the rocky soil beyond. Then the Liberator, completely smashed, slid to a stop against the side of a dirt revetment.

Core could hardly believe it when the plane's entire crew was accounted for. A huge crowed gathered to gawk at *The Chambermaid's* mangled remains. "I saw our crew chief in the crowd," Core later told a reporter. "And I can remember feeling sort of sorry for him. He'd taken care of that plane after every one of her missions, but he couldn't fix her this time." Beatty, the copilot, knew how the crew chief must have felt and, as he was being loaded onto a stretcher, he called out, "I'm sorry we wrecked your plane, Sergeant!"[17]

THE BOMBING CONTINUES

The Chambermaid was gone for good, but there were other B-24 Liberators arriving to take her place. In late October the 11th Bomb Group, based on Guam, began joining the 30th in attacking Iwo Jima.

Japanese fighters from Iwo Jima continued to be a threat to the bombers. In October of 1944 the 30th's historian wrote, "Enemy fighters were encountered on almost every mission over Iwo Jima but because of the excessive distance from Saipan a fighter escort had never been attempted."[18] On 21 October 1944, that was going to change.

Bomber crews had noted that the Zeroes often stuck with them after their attacks, following them south for half an hour or more. In an attempt to eliminate the threat, a deal was struck with the pilots of the 318th Fighter Group, who were handling combat air patrol around the Mariana Islands. Their Republic P-47D Thunderbolt fighters couldn't make it all the way to Iwo Jima, but loaded to the gills with fuel in both wing and belly tanks, they could come to within 50 miles. They coordinated with the bombers to fly up near the island and see if they could catch a few Japanese fighters that ranged a bit too far south and give them a shock.

A group of 16 P-47s left Saipan on 21 October in the usual murky weather to spring their mousetrap. By the time they rendezvoused with the southbound Liberators, the Zekes they so badly wanted to catch had already turned back north to return to Iwo Jima. Only one Nick twin-engine Japanese fighter remained, trailing the formation. The Thunderbolts pounced, making quick work of the lone hunter before returning to Saipan. Though they chalked up only one kill, they found that they had completed the longest over-water fighter mission of the war up to that time. The tired pilots each traveled 1,500 miles and logged six hours and 38 minutes of flying time in their battered and weary Thunderbolts.

The raids on Iwo Jima continued and broadened in scope. Not only were B-24s appearing *en masse* by day to crater the airfields, but they were coming at night, too. Day missions weren't getting the job done—the island's runways were quickly repaired, often bringing the Japanese fighters back up in droves the following day. Trying to throw a wrench in Iwo Jima's works, night missions were undertaken.

Lifting off from the darkened airstrips in the Marianas every 45 minutes, "snooper" Liberators made their way north in the darkness. Nine or 10 on an average night made the eight hour trip, slowing or speeding up so as to arrive over Iwo Jima exactly at their appointed time.

Japanese fighters would often come up to greet the night flyers, but hardly ever attacked. They flew alongside, at a respectable distance, blinking their running lights. Some said they were there to give anti-aircraft gunners speed and altitude information. But hardly any fire came from the island after dark. Others figured they were daring the American gunners to shoot—a burst of .50-caliber at night could be seen for miles. One intelligence officer trying to solve the mystery matter-of-factly told a reporter, "Trying to figure out why the Japs do things would drive anyone crazy."[19]

The overall result of the night missions for the repair crews on Iwo Jima was planes coming and going and bombs falling all through the night. Some B-24s carried bombs that would explode instantly, while others hefted payloads that were time-delayed one to 72 hours to further complicate patching the fields.

After the invasion, captured Korean laborers and a few living Japanese prisoners shed some light on the Liberator groups' futile attempts to put Iwo Jima out of business for good. They explained that 2,000 men were involved in repairing Iwo Jima's airfields. Each crater took about 50 man-hours to repair. Often, seven men were assigned to each fissure blown in the surface by an American bomb. Moreover, one truck was assigned to each group of six holes and one steamroller to every 13 craters. Rocks required for repairs were transported from a nearby quarry.

Even after the most damaging raids, the runways were up and running again in 16 hours. The average was 10 hours. Repairs were most often undertaken at night, unless planes were expected to arrive from Japan that particular day. The American "snooper" raids at night caused the work parties only to lose about 20 to 30 minutes each time one aircraft appeared. Time delay bombs were cause for consternation at first, but bomb-disposal units, nicknamed "death squads,"[20] learned to de-fuse the bombs by boring into their sides. An untimely explosion, workers said, affected only those in the immediate vicinity of the blast. Other crews kept working.

The captured enemy also commented on the overall effectiveness of the raids. Very few aircraft on the ground or fortifications were destroyed. The volcanic soil on Iwo Jima, made of cinder and sand, acted to dampen the explosions and minimize damage. Personnel injuries and deaths due to these attacks were fairly light.

Overall, the bombings didn't kill Iwo Jima's inhabitants or even ruin their will to fight. The Japanese simply moved underground. The airfields had to be exposed, but little else was required to exist on the surface. As months of attacks rolled by, the island's population of Japanese soldiers relied more and more on a growing system of caves, shelters, and tunnels carved in Iwo Jima's soft rock. There, they waited for the day they knew was coming—bomber aircraft could never do the work of infantry soldiers. And when the U.S. Marines did finally arrive on the island, Iwo Jima's elaborate tunnel system would become one of their biggest headaches.

Photographed after the invasion, this is one of the steamrollers the Japanese used to repair the damage done to Iwo's runways almost every day. Work crews labored all night (and sometimes in the daylight hours) to repair craters blasted into the fields. It was important for the Japanese to keep the airfields up and running—to launch defensive fighters and receive more aircraft from the home islands. (The 7th Fighter Command Association)

Top 3 photos: Photographs captured after the American invasion show some of the Japanese soldiers stationed on Iwo Jima. These men waited out the long months of bombing, slowly moving underground and building up defenses for an attack they knew was inevitable. (The 7th Fighter Command Association)

CHAPTER 3

Turning Up the Heat

Scores of combat-ready Boeing B-29 Superfortress heavy bombers dot Saipan's landscape in 1944. Japanese forces on Iwo Jima attacked the new bomber bases many times, hoping to tie up precious manpower and destroy B-29s before they could again reach the Japanese mainland with their explosive payloads. (U.S. Army Air Forces via National Archives)

While the Japanese on Iwo Jima stoutly held on, awaiting the inevitable invasion, American control of the Mariana Islands became nearly absolute. The first Boeing B-29 Superfortress heavy bombers arrived on Saipan on 12 October 1944.

THE SUPERFORTRESS FLEET

The B-29s initially attacked Japan from bases in China. On the same day that Iwo Jima was visited for the first time by the Navy's carrier planes, 15 June 1944, Army Air Forces B-29s took off from Chinese air bases, each loaded with two tons of bombs. They were headed for the Imperial Iron and Steel Works in Yawata. It was the first bombing raid on the Japanese home islands since Lieutenant Colonel "Jimmy" Doolittle's attack more than two years before.

However, the date not only signifies the beginning of bombing from China, but also the end. On 15 June, Marines came ashore on the island of Saipan. The Mariana Islands—of which Saipan, Tinian, and Guam are the largest—were destined to become the new home of the Army Air Forces' very heavy bomber fleet.

Operating squadrons of Superfortress bombers from China posed tremendous difficulties. With Japan holding all available seaports along China's coast, supplies for the B-29 raids were flown in from India. Every single bullet, bomb, spare part, and drop of fuel was carried over the treacherous Himalayan mountain range to forward bases in China before moving on to attack Japan. At best, this mountain flying was inefficient and difficult. And when the weather was bad, it was downright deadly.

The Marianas were different. Supplies could be shipped or flown directly from Midway, Hawaii, or the States. And there were no squabbles with Chinese or Indian officials and very little risk of Japanese forces returning. "We took the Marianas fair and square," airmen quipped. "If the Japs want to come get it back, let them try."

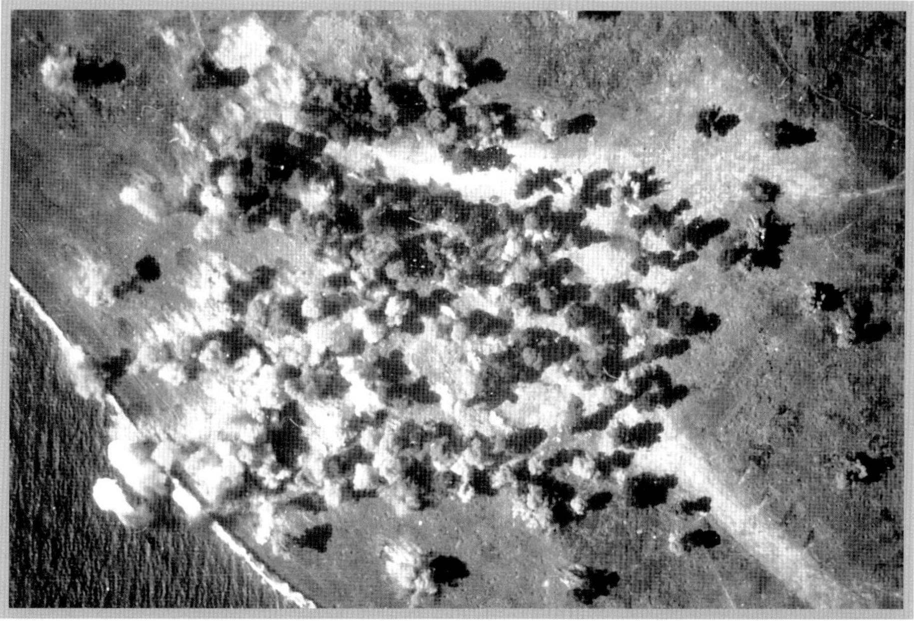

The first Boeing B-29s to be based in the Mariana Islands flew their fourth and fifth missions to Iwo Jima's airfields. Considered "shakedown missions," the bombings were only partially successful. Here, tons of explosives churn Iwo's black soil. (U.S. Army Air Forces via National Archives)

The B-29s flew their first three "shakedown" missions from Saipan to submarine pens at Doblon Island, Truk Atoll. While the third raid was underway, on 2 November 1944, a handful of Japanese Betty bombers, presumably from Iwo Jima, made a surprise low-level visit to Isley Field. They sprayed the B-29 base with bullets and bomb fragments. A Saipan fighter group recorded, "One Betty was shot down by AA (anti-aircraft), one by a P-61 (Northrop Black Widow) of the 6th Night Fighter Group, and a third exploded over East Field, cause unknown." They hardly did any damage, but the message was clear—the Japanese airmen on Iwo Jima were still awake, alive, and not willing to give up. The B-29ers grumbled a bit and then put the tiny island on their "hit list."

The fourth raid for the Saipan-based bombers, three days later, was to Iwo Jima. Planes from the 497th and 498th Bomb Groups, 36 in all, took off to pummel Iwo Jima's airfields with bombs. It was considered a "shakedown mission" to practice daylight bombing and test the night landing facilities at home. The whole affair didn't go very well. While there was no enemy air opposition and anti-aircraft fire was meager to inaccurate, bombing results were deemed poor.

Results were even worse on 8 November when the B-29s returned to Iwo Jima. Eight Japanese fighters came up to sniff out the new bombers but didn't do any damage. One Superfortress had an engine catch fire. And when another engine failed, the bomber was forced to ditch at sea. Only two men out of the crew of 11 were rescued when they were found floating in a life raft the following day.

THE LONG-RANGE FIGHTERS

The P-47 Thunderbolts based on Saipan couldn't quite make it to Iwo Jima. That left the bombers that ventured north to make trouble on the "frustrating little island" open for attack from the seemingly endless stream of Japanese planes and airmen funneling down from homeland air bases. The problem was rectified in a somewhat strange way when the 318th Fighter Group took command of 36 borrowed Lockheed P-38s.

A 318th Fighter Group Lockheed P-38 Lightning nicknamed *The Little Flower* still wears a 21st Fighter Group, 72nd Fighter Squadron insignia on its cowling. The planes were acquired from the group in November 1944. (Fred Erbele via the 7th Fighter Command Association)

Requisitioned from the Hawaii-based 21st Fighter Group, the "new, used" aircraft had the range to get to Iwo Jima, with fuel to spare to do a little damage. The odd part of it was, hardly any of the P-47 flyers of the 318th had any experience with the bigger, heavier, twin-engine machines. The AAF supplied a few 21st pilots, "on loan" to quickly teach them. Shaking their heads, the P-47 flyers told each other that they had no choice but to learn—and learn quickly.

The 318th was now operating a mixture of aircraft types, and the P-38s and P-47s were suited for different jobs. "There are now two distinct significant phases of operation," the 318th Fighter Group reported, "(a) long-range escort and fighter interception, and (b) combat air patrol of Saipan and Tinian, and continued neutralization of the airstrip at Pagan."[21]

At first, the "single-engine guys" had little good to say about their recently acquired P-38s. But after a little flying time, they began to warm to the idea of trading their Thunderbolts for Lightnings. After all, if they were going to spend hours cruising over the endless sea, weren't two engines better than one? And besides, the longer-ranging Lightning put more potential targets within reach of the aggressive young pilots.

This image of Iwo Jima's airfield number one was taken from a low-flying F-5 "photo ship" of the 28th Photo Reconnaissance Squadron. A hopelessly wrecked and picked-over Japanese aircraft stands partially on a 55-gallon drum. In the top right, a 318th P-38, "riding shotgun" for the photo aircraft, can be seen. (U.S. Army Air Forces via National Archives)

Their first mission to Iwo Jima kicked off on the morning of 18 November when 11 P-38s of the 318th joined two F-5 photo aircraft of the 28th Photo Reconnaissance Squadron assigned to fly up and survey the east and west beaches of the island. Four B-24 Liberators, acting as navigational guides, led the formation north.

Southeast of Iwo Jima, the fighters and photo planes dropped to 200 feet and commenced their high-speed runs. A flight of four P-38s escorted one "photo ship" down the west side of Iwo Jima, the F-5 closest to the shore, snapping photos, and the fighters echeloned away from the island off his port wing. The pilots reported, "meager, inaccurate automatic weapons fire emanating from coast positions." What concerned them more was a pair of enemy aircraft they spotted over airfield number two. As they completed their run and turned to the right around the northern tip of the island, they kept a wary eye on the Japanese planes.

On the east side, the aircraft had dropped to 50 feet as they raced along the shore in a mirror image to those on the west. Halfway up the coastline, where the sandy beach faded away into rocky cliffs, the American planes made a slow turn out to sea.

Suddenly, four single-engine Japanese fighters were spotted above the P-38s as they cruised toward the rendezvous point. A phosphorous bomb that dropped from one of the enemy planes exploded well ahead of the formation. And as the American Lightnings swerved around the smoking white tentacles of the blast, two of the Japanese flyers made half-hearted runs at Captain John Ottenstein's P-38. He lifted the nose of his big fighter and returned fire. Not interested in continuing the fight, the enemy planes held steady in their dives, headed in the opposite direction, toward Iwo Jima. The final Japanese fighter encountered a burst of fire hurled in his direction by the Lightnings and joined his comrades, speeding toward home.

The P-38s landed back at Saipan at 1357, after seven hours 55 minutes in the air. The planes completed what was believed to be a new record for the group—1,518 miles round trip. The group's mission report also added that the fighters had expended 420 rounds of .50-caliber and 63 rounds of 20-mm on the fleeing enemy aircraft, and burned 7,315 gallons of gas.

The 318th was back on 27 November, this time escorting a bomber force. It was a frustrating start, as the 318th Fighter Group mission report states, "F/O [flight officer] James (Violet 1-4) bogged down in soft ground while taxiing and did not take off. Capt. Park (Violet 1-1) could not get gas from his belly tank. He returned around 200 miles from base and pancaked [landed] at 1110. Lt. Sullivan (Violet 4-2) began losing power 225 miles from base. He returned, accompanied by Lt. Stephenson (Violet 4-3). They pancaked at 1145. Lt. Wilson's (Violet 5-1) right engine cut out right after takeoff. He pancaked at 0940. F/O Walker (Violet 5-2) turned back at 1120 due to fuel pressure failure. He pancaked at 1305."[22]

But even with six fighters out of the mix, 12 others cruised north. They had many tasks—watching over three navigational B-24s, guarding the Liberators bombing the island, and escorting the lone F-5 photographic plane that had tagged along to focus its cameras on Iwo Jima's eastern beaches.

South of the target, Lieutenants Roy Jacobson and Robert Rickard spotted a Zeke as he made a head-on pass on navigational B-24s. The plane dropped two phosphorous bombs near the bombers but did no damage. As the enemy fighter pulled into a 180-degree turn to re-engage the lumbering Liberators, Jacobson, with Rickard tailing, raced in behind the Zeke. Jacobson squirted out a burst of fire, corrected his aim, and fired again. On the third try, bullets struck the Zeke's fuselage and tail, sending pieces flying. The Japanese fighter rolled onto its back as Rickard fired a short burst as well. The plane smashed into the water below.

As the B-24 bombers pulled away from Iwo Jima, Lieutenants William Loflin and Kenneth Sitton watched a Zeke, returning to the island, with two P-38s close behind. "For some reason

Using an empty fuel drum as a work stand, ground crewman services the cameras in the gun bay of a 28th Photo Reconnaissance Squadron F-5 on 20 July 1944. The "Photo Joes" commonly carried five cameras, which were aimed through the Plexiglas view ports in the nose of the modified aircraft. (U.S. Army Air Forces via National Archives)

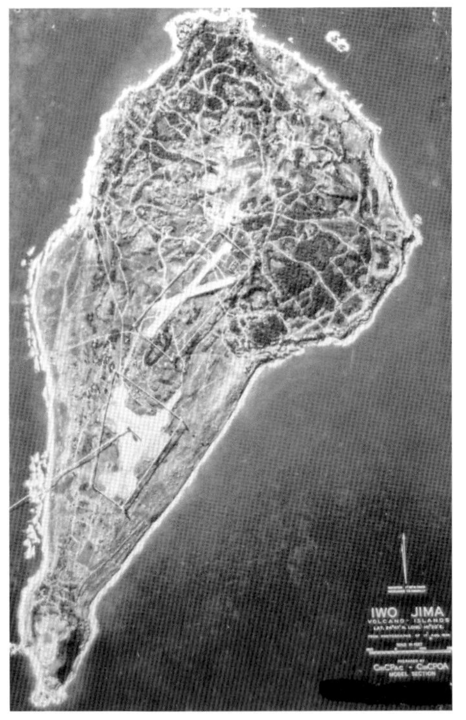

A painted rubber model of Iwo Jima serves as a three-dimensional map for planning 11th Bomb Group attacks. The boundaries of the two operational airfields are delineated with string. Another string shows the day's flight path to the target—airfield number one. (Air Force Historical Research Agency)

A weary-looking Consolidated B-24 Liberator of the 30th Bomb Group, 392nd Bomb Squadron pulls away from Iwo Jima with Mount Suribachi in the background. (U.S. Army Air Forces via National Archives)

unknown to me the P-38s broke off chase," Loflin told intelligence officers later.[23] He eagerly jumped right in, with Sitton covering his wing. The pair pushed their planes over into a 30-degree dive and raced after the Japanese fighter at "better than 450 mph."[24]

Five miles from Iwo Jima, the Zeke came into range and Loflin fired a long burst. The plane took no evasive action as explosive shells crackled over the fuselage and engine. A lick of flame developed from under the plane's cowling and parts of the tail fell away as it heeled over in its back and dove into a cloud. The pair of P-38 pilots searched intently until they spotted an oil slick on the water below. They were convinced that their quarry had not escaped.

Meanwhile, another pair of Lightnings escorted the lone F-5 down Iwo Jima's eastern beach. It was strangely quiet, with no reports of anti-aircraft fire or enemy airplanes spotted.

That evening on Saipan, the "bomber boys" were pleased with their new long-range fighter coverage. In the narrative history for the month of November, the 30th Bomb Group historian wrote, "A fact that is worthy of repetition is the attitude of combat crews toward flying missions with P-38 escorts. It is unanimously felt that escorts are 'wonderful'—combat crews through interrogations are saying, 'more missions of this type would be appreciated'."[25]

SAIPAN ATTACKED

That same day, 27 November, the Superfortress bases on Saipan were the victim of another Japanese daylight raid. Only three days earlier, a large force of B-29s had made the long flight to the Japanese Empire and dropped their bombs on Tokyo for the first time. And, as the Army Air Forces' *Impact* magazine put it, "Anybody who expected that the Japs would hit Saipan in retaliation for our attacks on Tokyo was not disappointed."[26] The Japanese understood fully what the Marianas air bases meant for the homeland and were pulling out the stops to disrupt the Army's bombing plans.

A group of 16 Zekes from Iwo Jima came in low, under the radar, and without warning. They made strafing runs on the parked bombers at around 1200 hours. Many of the attackers were shot down by anti-aircraft guns, but not before the Japanese had destroyed three of the Boeing bombers and damaged many others.

The other portion of the 318th Fighter Group, those still flying P-47 Thunderbolts on combat air patrol in the Marianas area, got in on the action when the island's control ordered Lieutenant Stanley Lustic to investigate a bogey (unidentified plane) south of Saipan. When the stranger was identified as Japanese, Lustic pulled in behind him and fired. The Japanese aircraft took no evasive action and exploded in

This 499th Bomb Group B-29 was one of the victims of the Japanese raid on Saipan on 27 November 1944. Flying under radar coverage and uncharacteristically arriving in daylight, the Japanese Iwo-based aircraft completely destroyed three American bombers and damaged many others. (U.S. Army Air Forces via National Archives)

The anti-aircraft gun crew proudly paints a victory symbol on their "quad-.50." They are credited with shooting down a marauding Iwo-based Betty bomber during a raid on Saipan's air bases in late 1944. (U.S. Army Air Forces via National Archives)

mid-air. In the vicinity, another enemy aircraft was also found, and flamed, by the patrolling P-47s.

Sadly, the 318th also lost a pilot that day. Like Lustic and others, Lieutenant Owen McCaul was on combat air patrol when the raid began. As he dueled with the Japanese fighters, his P-47 was mistaken for a Japanese Zero and fired upon by Saipan's anti-aircraft gunners. McCaul's Thunderbolt dove straight into the ground.

The flyers on Saipan quickly noted that the Zekes couldn't carry enough fuel to take off from Iwo Jima, strike the Marianas, and return. Any survivors of the raid would probably attempt to land on Japanese-held Pagan Island to the north. Additional P-47 Thunderbolts were sent there to see if they could catch any more Japanese aircraft. When the American pilots arrived, they found two Zekes attempting to pick out a suitable landing spot on Pagan's pockmarked north taxiway. The American pilots swooped in and shot them both down.

Like a pair of boxers, the air forces on the islands of Iwo Jima and Saipan continued to exchange blows. On 29 November, Japanese Bettys from Iwo Jima attempted to bomb Isley Field in the dark and missed completely. They were back on 7 December, arriving in daytime and claiming three more B-29s demolished and many others damaged. Superfortress crews nervously joked that a B-29 was more likely to get destroyed sitting at Saipan than it was in the cold skies over the Japanese Empire.

The following day, the Marianas-based B-24s and B-29s took off to try to settle Iwo Jima down. First to arrive were the P-38s of the 318th with orders to take care of any fighters that might be snooping about before the American bombers arrived in force. The pilots were excited because it was the first time they had been cut loose from escorting bombers or photo planes. It was their chance to use their fighters to their full potential and get a few kills.

When they arrived over Iwo Jima, the fighter pilots were disappointed—they found solid overcast. There were certainly Zekes flying about. Periodically, one would bob up through the murk, but as soon as the Lightnings positioned themselves to shoot, the Japanese pilot would dive into the clouds and leave the anxious American flyers cussing to themselves.

Major Warren Roeser's wingman reported engine trouble and the pair turned toward the navigational B-29s orbiting nearby. Just as they did, Roeser spied a Zeke climbing rapidly just above the overcast layer. He eased in behind the enemy fighter and fired a two-second burst from 200 yards. The Zeke exploded and spun though the overcast. It was the only air-to-air victory of the day.

Minutes later, B-24s and B-29s arrived at Iwo Jima on schedule and unceremoniously dumped their bombs through the weather using radar. Their reports dryly stated, "Results mainly unobserved due to cloud cover." From this day until Iwo Jima was invaded, the B-24s came back to Iwo every day and dropped bombs.

On Christmas Eve, the normal pattern was reversed when the B-29s hit Iwo Jima in a mission codenamed ROCK-CRUSHER. Their bombing results were poor, a fact that was brought home to them when Iwo-based Japanese bombers swooped in on them Christmas night.

Dropping metal foil to blur radar, 25 Japanese Bettys appeared. One Superfortress was bombed and then another, fully loaded with 8,000 gallons of fuel and three tons of bombs, exploding in a geyser of flame. Quick-thinking

Hunched over in his seat, an Army engineer bravely works to isolate the fiercely burning wreckage of a B-29 Superfortress that was destroyed when Japanese forces from Iwo Jima attacked Saipan. The men to the left of the bulldozer are attempting to set up a hose to spray the machine and its driver with water. The quick-thinking actions of the soldiers helped save many other bombers parked nearby. (U.S. Army Air Forces via National Archives)

engineers saved the airfield from disaster when they bravely bulldozed the burning wreckage into large heaps and began dumping dirt on the out-of-control fire.

There were a few more minor raids and a number of scares after Christmas, but the offensive air strength on Iwo Jima was dwindling to zero. By day and night, Liberators droned overhead, B-29s disgorged tons of bombs, and the pilots of Lockheed Lightnings attempted to kill anything they could catch out in the open.

FIGHTER SWEEPS

While the Liberator crews were delighted to have the 318th P-38s along for protection, it was painful work for the young fighter pilots. Their planes were too fast to simply fly in formation with the plodding bombers. They had to circle and zigzag for hours upon hours.

Photo missions were a little better. The modified F-5 "photo ships" were even faster than their fighters were. But it was still baby-sitting, pure and simple. They wanted to have some fun. They wanted to catch some Zeroes with their pants down. They wanted to go up to Iwo Jima and raise hell.

On their first chance to "roam free," 8 December, the weather ruined their outing. On 19 December, they came back. Racing in on the deck, 14 P-38s in line-abreast formation, approached Iwo Jima from the west. They spotted a lone Zeke on air patrol at 1,500 feet over the island and Captain Charles Tennant and his wingman zoom-climbed up to intercept. The Zeke was taken by surprise and didn't alter his course until 20-mm shells began smashing into the cockpit behind the pilot. The Japanese plane fell in a left-hand turn and Tennant's wingman witnessed the plane drill into the ground northwest of the number one airfield.

Meanwhile, other 318th pilots located a pair of silver Zekes and a Betty at airfield number two. Major Warren Roeser machine-gunned the Betty and also scored hits on one of the Zekes. The latter, taxiing on the runway, was observed to spin around suddenly "as if in a ground loop," the mission report said.[27]

On 24 December, they came back, and with no airplanes in the air to challenge them, set out to strafe anything they could detect from their speeding aircraft. They hit a number of parked planes, along with gun emplacements, the beached ships on the eastern shore, troops, buildings, a truck, and a steamroller. Lieutenant Marsden Dupuy spotted another truck, filled with troops just east of the runways. "The Japs dismounted and scattered for cover but Violet 34-4 [Dupuy] was pulling up at the time and could not strafe the troops," explained the mission report.[28]

On 27 December, the P-38s bagged a Nick fighter that burned and crashed into the water near Iwo Jima. Many of the fighters concentrated on a Japanese naval APD-type (high speed transport) vessel they discovered off the island's east coast. Lieutenant Curtis Foster's P-38 was hit with automatic weapons fire which tore off a large section of his left outboard horizontal stabilizer.

Foster was lucky to get away, but the 318th's luck changed on the 5 January 1945 fighter sweep. As eight fighters were nearing Iwo Jima at very low altitude, the right engine on Lieutenant Warren Sheneman's P-38 suddenly quit and he plunged into the ocean. It was the 318th's first loss while attacking Iwo Jima.

The American fighters split up, some circling the crash site (only an oil slick and one oxygen container were spotted) and the others pressing on to attack the island. Two P-38s went after a single-engine fighter observed taking off from the number two airfield. The pair followed the enemy plane as he went into a left-hand turn and they opened fire from 800 feet away. The Japanese plane belched flames and went into a gradual dive before hitting the water.

Meanwhile, the other P-38s sped toward airfield number two to hammer ground targets. Lieutenant Fred Erbele's fighter

The 318th Fighter Group acquired 36 Lockheed P-38 Lightnings from the Hawaii-based 21st Fighter Group in November 1944. Though the planes had enough range to make it to Iwo Jima and fight, most of the pilots didn't like the P-38s at first. Hardly any of them had experience flying the large, heavy twin-engine fighter planes. (Lew Sanders via the 7th Fighter Command Association)

Young Lieutenant Fred Erbele sits in the cockpit of his 318th Fighter Group Lockheed P-38, *Ripper*, weeks before his near-death brush with anti-aircraft fire over Iwo Jima. (Fred Erbele via the 7th Fighter Command Association)

was hit almost immediately by anti-aircraft fire near Iwo Jima's shoreline. A large hole was blasted in his right wing and his airspeed dropped to 120 miles per hour. He had no choice but to keep on track, toward the airfield, in his foundering, burning fighter. More enemy fire crushed his left engine, and he struggled out to sea, fighting his crippled aircraft as it trailed a stream of black smoke.

Limping away from the scene on one engine, Erbele jettisoned his canopy and prepared to bail out. "I think I'm going in," he told his companions. "Try to keep an eye on me."[29] In a struggle to climb to higher altitude, he attempted again to start his left engine. It coughed to life and though it was running extremely rough, it pulled the battered P-38 into a climb. As the altimeter needle spun around the dial, the fire in the hole in the right wing sputtered and died. "There was a little man out on the wing," Erbele joked later. "He blew it out."[30]

The other P-38s circled around him as his Lightning painfully crept up to 3,000 feet and flew toward the navigational B-24s waiting nearby. Soon, the left engine was overheating to the point where Erbele felt he had to shut it down. When he arrived at the rendezvous, the formation split up—with the majority of the P-38s and a single B-24 buzzing home at normal speed. A pair of Liberators and Erbele's wingman stayed with the injured airplane and its nervous flyer. He was flying so slow that even the big B-24s had to lower their flaps to stick close by.

Fred Erbele ate up the miles heading south in his windy cockpit. His beloved P-38, nicknamed *Ripper*, was a mess. The left propeller refused to feather and continued to windmill as his battered plane trudged along at only 135 miles per hour. From where he sat, the hole in the rear of the right wing seemed enormous. The plane vibrated so violently that he couldn't see the instruments.

Nearing Saipan, Erbele's spirits rose—until he was drenched in his open cockpit by a pounding rainstorm. Poking out the other side of the clouds, he was delighted to see a formation of Thunderbolts, one of which was carrying a "Josephine" belly tank life raft.

But Fred Erbele had no intention of going into the drink now. He landed at Saipan with "a cup of gasoline to spare," he said.[31] His flight was a new record for the group—a cold and worrisome eight hours and 30 minutes.

Photographed from an escorting B-24, Fred Erbele's blasted fighter makes slow progress on the 750-mile return trip to Saipan. The right wing has a massive hole and the left engine is destroyed. Erbele jettisoned the top of his canopy right after he was hit—thinking he had no choice but to bail out. He eventually made it safely back to Saipan. (U.S. Army Air Forces via National Archives)

SOFTENING UP IWO

Something big was on the horizon. In December 1944, the 30th Bomb Group flew 96 percent of all bombing missions to Iwo Jima. The American invasion was almost certainly going to happen, but when?

Continuous sorties seemed to be wearing the island down. The surface of the "pork chop," as some flyers called the island, was perforated with so many craters it looked like the surface of the moon. But no matter how hard they hit the island, the Japanese below continued to fight back.

There were still a handful of fighters based on Iwo Jima and there was still plenty of flak. On 3 December an 11th Bomb Group Liberator was approaching airfield number one when a phosphorous anti-aircraft shell exploded right in front of the nose. Lieutenant Wilfred Bloom, the plane's

As American bombs rain down, Japanese phosphorous shells come up to meet the attacking B-24 Liberators at Iwo Jima's shoreline. This exchange took place on 11 November 1944. The 30th Bomb Group dropped more than 353 tons of bombs on the island that month. (U.S. Army Air Forces via National Archives)

Dangerous Business

Bomber losses over Iwo Jima were surprisingly light. The Seventh Air Force reported that, when the invasion commenced, only nine B-24s and a single B-29 (and their entire crews) had been destroyed outright while attacking the island. But at times the fighting was fierce. The same report reveals that an attacking B-24 had a better than one-in-10 chance of being damaged on a typical Iwo Jima bombing mission. In October 1944, the chances were around one in six. In total, 243 Liberators returned home with dead engines, a smattering of holes, or wounded crewmen aboard.

Above: *A massive phosphorous burst dwarfs a formation of 11th Bomb Group B-24s as they approach Iwo Jima. Though not particularly accurate or effective at bringing down a four-engine heavy bomber, the sight of the huge bursts was certainly intimidating to flyers in the vicinity. (Arvid Johnson via the 7th Fighter Command Association)*

Left: *The 11th Bomb Group B-24 nicknamed* Tarfu *had a run-in with a Japanese fighter over Iwo Jima on 19 January 1945. The bomber was rammed by a "suicidal Jap pilot" and kept right on going—without the use of one engine. (U.S. Army Air Forces via National Archives)*

Below right: *Private Tony Storment, an armorer and gunner of the 30th Bomb Group, shows off the damage done by a shell fragment over "the Jimas" on 29 October 1944. Working as a photographer on the mission, the offending piece of hot metal tore through his camera mount, an oxygen bottle, and clipped the seat of his electrically heated suit. (Air Force Historical Research Agency)*

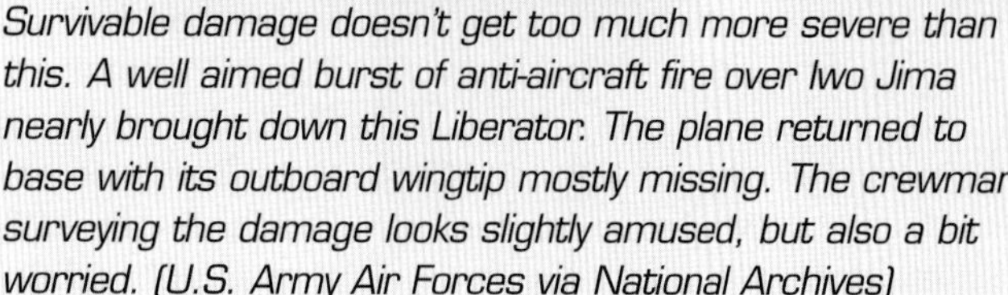

Survivable damage doesn't get too much more severe than this. A well aimed burst of anti-aircraft fire over Iwo Jima nearly brought down this Liberator. The plane returned to base with its outboard wingtip mostly missing. The crewman surveying the damage looks slightly amused, but also a bit worried. (U.S. Army Air Forces via National Archives)

Above middle: *The copilot of* Little Chief *contemplates a flak hole in his side window distressingly close to his head. A reporter mused, "Deep down, every one of us has a sneaking idea that his luck will hold, and that the Nips haven't yet turned out the bullet with his number on it." (Arvid Johnson via the 7th Fighter Command Association)*

bombardier, was knocked backward, hit in the left shoulder. In great pain, he managed to return to his bombsight and toggle the plane's bombs before calling the pilot to report he was injured. Back on Saipan, when they pulled the pellet out of his shoulder, it was still smoking.

A B-24 dubbed *Bird of Paradise* barely made it home after flak exploded a number of fragmentation clusters that had just dropped from its bomb bay over Iwo Jima. "It was a damn freakish thing," pilot Lieutenant James Fagan told reporters after he coaxed the dying plane back near Saipan.[32] Fagan and the other survivors were picked up by a patrolling PT boat after *Bird of Paradise* crashed into the sea. Three of the airmen went missing.

Each carrying eight 55-gallon drums of napalm, B-24s of the 30th Bomb Group, 27th Bomb Squadron unload over Iwo Jima. The new bombing tactic was not particularly effective at burning off the last pockets of growth on the island. (U.S. Army Air Forces via National Archives)

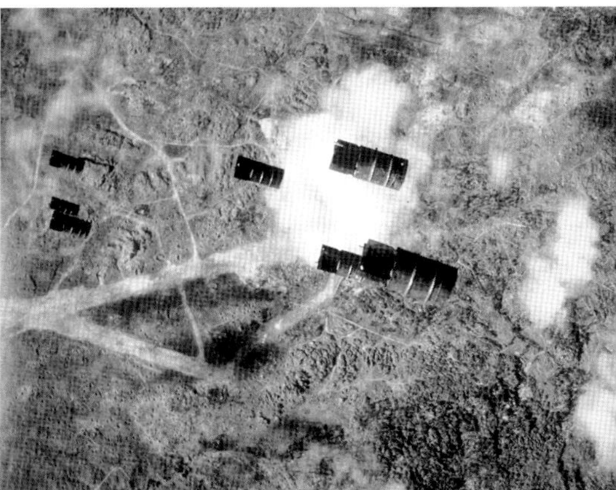

This photo was taken from the bomb bay of a napalm-carrying Liberator over Iwo Jima on 1 February 1945. Each homemade bomb was fitted with crude plywood fins to help with accuracy. Still, many of the drums missed the target area. (U.S. Army Air Forces via National Archives)

After miraculously returning to Saipan, a soldier poses in the hole blasted in the flight deck of a 30th Bomb Group B-24 while it was on a bombing mission over Iwo Jima. The 75-mm explosion blinded the navigator and copilot, leaving the wounded pilot to fly home on his own. (U.S. Army Air Forces via National Archives)

On another occasion, 27 January 1945, a 75-mm shell crashed through the flight deck of a 30th Bomb Group bomber over the island. "It is generally agreed," says the group's history, "that Lieutenant [Herbert] Broemer [the pilot], wounded in the right arm and right eye, did the 'nearly impossible' by flying back a badly mangled plane without the aid of his co-pilot."[33] Lieutenant William Smith, co-pilot, and Lieutenant John Donnelly, navigator, suffered serious shrapnel wounds to their faces and eyes.

Now, every available plane in the Pacific, it seemed, was employed in the job of hitting Iwo Jima. On 24 January 1945, the B-29s joined in again and returned with the news "airfield number one rendered unserviceable." They went back again on 29 January and noted that there were still Japanese planes about.

On 1 February, the 30th Bomb Group tried something new. A formation of 21 Liberators left Saipan carrying 165 napalm-filled 55-gallon drums. Each drum had been made into a "bomb," with plywood tail fins and a fuse set to explode each drum on impact. Only about 50 percent of the unwieldy containers made it from 20,000 feet to their desired impact point. The rest were scattered everywhere, including into the water near the shoreline. "Well," said the crews, "there's not much left to burn anymore on Iwo anyway."[34]

When it was all said and done, the B-24 bombers flew a total of 5 million miles and dropped 5,582 tons of explosives on Iwo Jima—equivalent to 725 tons per square mile. When the Marines went ashore, the airmen wondered, would there be anything left of the Japanese forces at all? "Iwo Jima looks beaten to hell," they told their superiors.[35] How could anything survive that kind of pounding?

A soldier stops traffic while a pair of 318th Fighter Group P-47s rumble into the air from one of Saipan's runways. While the fighters provided protection for the Marianas Islands, Seabees and Army engineers continued to improve and expand the growing bomber bases. (U.S. Army Air Forces via National Archives)

CHAPTER 4

INVASION

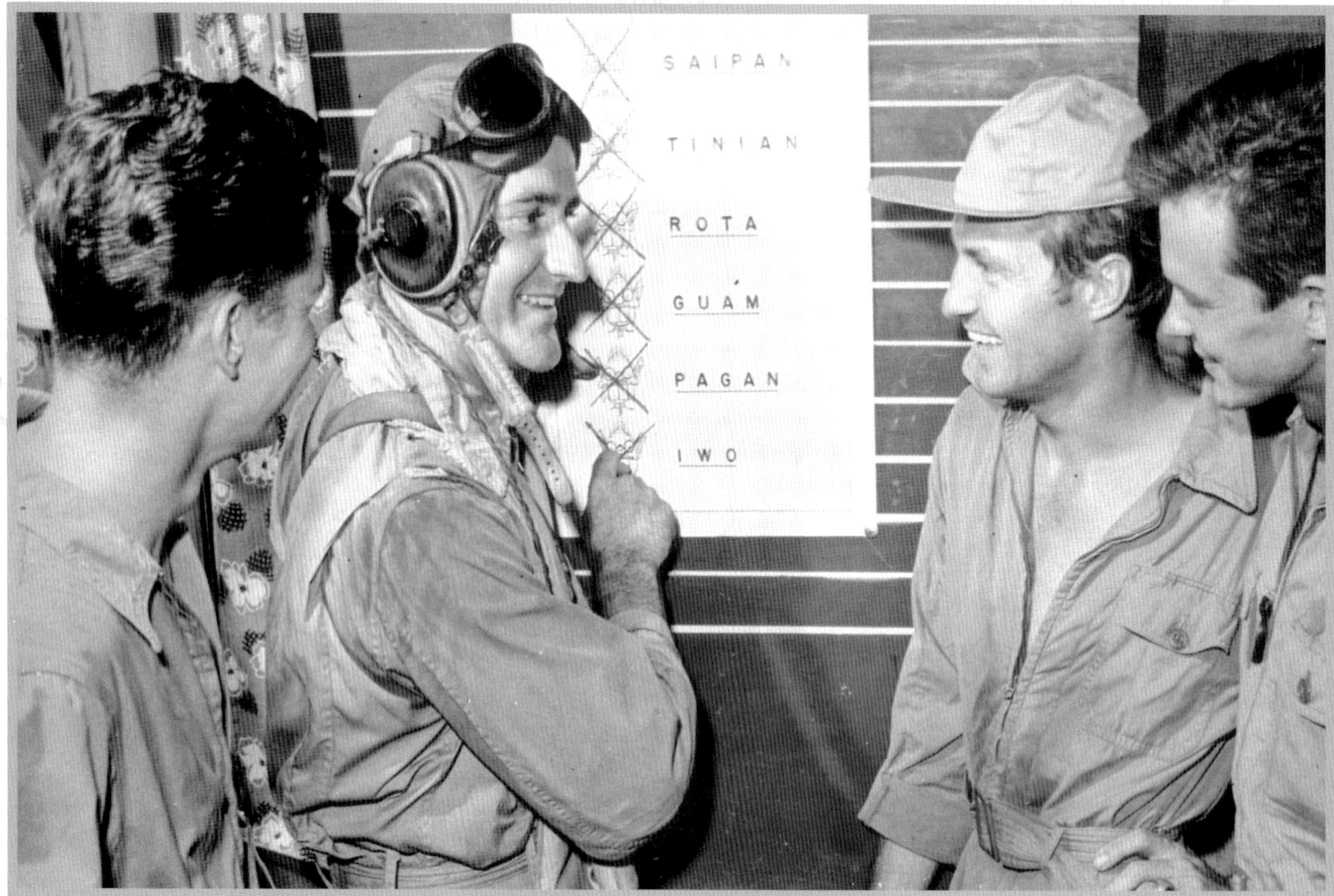

Lieutenant Victor Besche (still in his flying garb) had a close call when the landing gear on his Lightning collapsed upon return from the 318th Fighter Group's final mission to Iwo Jima on 15 February 1945. Here, he proudly crosses Iwo off the long list of enemy strongholds that he and his comrades helped bring down as the U.S. war machine moved ever closer to Japan. (U.S. Army Air Forces via National Archives)

After all the bombings and aerial attacks, the Japanese soldiers on Iwo Jima were still there—more than 21,000 of them. They had seen the Navy planes come and go, lugging over 400 tons of explosives. They had burrowed underground as the Liberators brought even more. And they had patiently waited in their caves as the B-29s on their shakedown missions spilled their payloads onto the now barren soil.

The soldiers had learned to live with the sudden appearance of fighters during the day and the random attacks from snoopers almost every night. The Japanese aircraft were now mostly gone—just twisted hulks in a cratered landscape. The Japanese ships were gone too. Lately, the American battleships and cruisers were coming right up to the coast and their tiny blue spotter planes puttered around in the skies. When they found something of value, the ship's giant shells came thundering down like freight trains.

THE LAST FIGHTER MISSIONS

Five F-5 photo planes came back on 3 February to survey Iwo Jima's now desolate topography. Riding shotgun was a complement of 20 Lockheed P-38s. Still miles from Iwo Jima, the planes eased down to 200 feet above the water and dropped their external tanks. Moments after, Lieutenant David Duket called out, "Mayday, mayday." His P-38 hit the water and nosed over. Later, the other pilots speculated that one of his drop tanks must have come off his aircraft awkwardly and hit the tail of his fighter as it tumbled away. Duket was never found.

Lieutenant Robert Amon looks grimly at the damage done to the tail boom of his P-38 Lightning during an attack mission over Iwo Jima. While some Army Air Forces fighters were lost during the 3 February 1945 sweep, Amon miraculously retuned to Saipan, hoping his Lightning would hold together. (U.S. Army Air Forces via National Archives)

During their flights over Iwo Jima, several planes were hit by automatic weapons fire. The photo pilots cheerily called their high-speed passes over the enemy, "dicing runs"—a gamble every time. This day, one of the photo flyers rolled snake eyes. His F-5 burst into flames, turned onto its back, and plunged into the water about 800 yards off the west coast of the island.

A bombing mission on 6 February turned back due to bad weather and when American aircraft returned on the 10th, they were surprised to find renewed activities on Iwo Jima. The Japanese were apparently attempting to celebrate "Empire Day" (11 February) by launching a night attack on Saipan. The P-38s pounced on several Betty bombers that had just taken off from Iwo Jima's airfields. Four Bettys fell under the guns of the American fighters, as did a single Zeke that appeared to harass the navigational B-24s. The marauding planes also discovered two Japanese destroyers near the island and a pair of unidentified supply vessels already well on their way north. One pilot took the opportunity to strafe the nearest warship before turning toward home.

On 15 February, the pilots of the 318th Fighter Group flew their final mission to Iwo Jima. They intercepted a handful of "aggressive and experienced"[36] Japanese pilots as they worked to protect a formation of B-24s in the midst of bombing the airfields. In the twisting melee, the fighter pilots expended 1,475 rounds of .50-caliber ammunition and 176 of their 20-mm cannon shells, yet could only keep an enemy aircraft in their sights long enough to claim one Zeke damaged.

One pilot's mundane 700-mile return trip came to a most exciting end when his P-38's landing gear collapsed upon landing at Saipan. The first 12 planes landed safely, but the thirteenth—lucky 13—slid to the left side of the runway and clipped a parked P-51 Mustang before coming to rest in a cloud of dust. The pilot, Lieutenant Victor Besche, was not hurt in the crash.

D MINUS 4 TO D MINUS 1

A portion of the Navy's aviation elements scheduled to take part in the Iwo Jima attack force took a long road to their appointment for invasion. Task Force 58 first steamed well north of Sulphur Island to launch air attacks on the Japanese homeland. These strikes were meant to keep Japanese military forces spread thin during the Iwo Jima invasion, eliminating the enemy's ability to respond with aircraft once the actual takeover on the island was underway.

At dawn on 15 February, American carrier fighters and bombers set out through rain, wind, and snow to hit targets in Tokyo and surrounding areas. The expected overwhelming hoards of aggressive Japanese air defenders, for the most part, failed to appear and the American planes mercilessly blasted their assigned airfields.

During the next day and a half, various industrial sites and Japanese vessels also fell to the onslaught. Perhaps most important to the huge collection of American shipping amassed around Iwo Jima days later, the Navy's carrier aircraft claimed 341 Japanese planes destroyed in the air and another 190 caught and demolished on the ground.

Withdrawing south toward Iwo Jima, the carrier group launched fighter sweeps against Chichi and Haha Jima to assure that no threats were there, waiting to strike the island. Meanwhile, other naval forces were already on station surrounding Sulphur Island.

Over Iwo Jima, American escort carriers accomplished 239 sorties on D Minus 3 (16 February). Operating a mixture of TBM Avenger torpedo bombers and FM-2 Wildcat fighters from 50 miles south of the island, the "baby carriers" not only struck Iwo

Near a 40-mm mount on the USS *Essex*, Marines pose for the cameras as the ship heads to Tokyo. The attacks on the Japanese mainland were carried out partly to dampen anticipated enemy air threats during the invasion of Iwo Jima. (U.S. Navy via National Archives)

Two days before the Marine invasion, a Vought OS2U Kingfisher lands among the American Navy ships after a mission spotting gunfire for the USS *Arkansas*. The closest ship, beyond the spotter plane, is the heavy cruiser USS *Tuscaloosa*. (U.S. Navy via National Archives)

Jima in six coordinated attacks, but also harassed the depleted enemy air and surface units nearby. One Wildcat was shot down, its pilot able to bail out. Another Wildcat, spotting for the guns of the battleship USS *Idaho*, simply disappeared.

One Zeke slipped through the curtain of patrolling American fighters and latched onto a Vought OS2U Kingfisher that was busy spotting for the eight-inch guns of the cruiser USS *Pensacola*. When Lieutenant (jg) Douglas Gandy nervously reported the Japanese fighter had found him, everyone around the fleet paused, turned toward their radios, and held their breath. "He's after me. He is on my ass," Gandy reported. Then, as the entire fleet listened in amazement, Gandy excitedly exclaimed, "Boy, I'm going after that son of a bitch."[37]

The slow, cumbersome Kingfisher float plane was no match for a Zero, but somehow, Gandy managed to wrench

A Vought OS2U Kingfisher is hoisted aboard the battleship USS *Arkansas* on D Minus 3. Though aviators sometimes joked that the plane's designation stood for "Old, Slow, and Ugly," Kingfisher pilot Douglas Gandy was amazingly able to shoot down a Zero fighter over the island with his single forward-firing .30-caliber machine gun on the same day this photograph was taken. (U.S. Navy via National Archives)

his aircraft into position and engaged his target with his scout plane's single forward-facing .30-caliber machine gun. "I got him, I got him!" Gandy hollered repeatedly into his radio. The flaming enemy fighter came diving to earth moments later.[38] The Zero—Gandy's Zero—was one of the last to be spotted in the daylight over Iwo Jima.

The Liberators also came up from the Marianas on 16 February. The weather was poor; the island could not be seen through the cloud cover—typical at this time of year, the pilots grumbled. Worried that a blind drop might hit American ships nearby, the Army bombers were instructed to wait. When no holes developed in the overcast, they were forced to return home, without getting a chance to weigh into battle with their payload of bombs.

They returned the following day with good weather. The force of 42 B-24 Liberators came in three waves about five minutes apart. They located their targets and dropped their bombs from an altitude of 5,000 to 6,000 feet "with satisfactory results."

The planes from the carriers also were back on D Minus 2. One of the first tasks of the day was to lay down a smoke screen for the underwater demolition teams (frogmen) assigned to explore the invasion beach. The screen was ineffective, with only one pass placed near the target area. Nearby surface vessels fired smoke shells in an attempt to pick up the slack.

When the American LCIs (Landing Craft, Infantry) came near the shore, it seemed every Japanese gun on the island opened fire on them. Each of the 12 landing craft was

As underwater demolition teams near Iwo Jima's shores on D Minus 2, Navy aircraft attempted to lay down a covering smokescreen to protect the landing craft and divers from Japanese fire. The screens were not as effective as expected, and many of the vessels were ravaged by the defending forces. (U.S. Navy via National Archives)

hit; many were completely ravaged by gunfire. The Japanese had mistaken the small force for the beginning of the true invasion. American surface vessels took the opportunity to fire at previously unseen enemy gun emplacements that gave away their position in the premature skirmish. The frogmen, slathered from head to toe with cocoa butter to protect them from the cold water, were only too glad to slip into the sea and move away from the gun battle raging on the surface.

Searching for hidden mines and rocks in the depths near the shoreline, some of the swimmers said later that spent bullets and shrapnel were drifting down on them like snowflakes. Most made it to the beach and scooped up tobacco tins full of Iwo Jima's black sand for later examination. Their mission complete, they swam hurriedly back out to sea.

Meanwhile, the carrier airmen were setting up for another day of combat in the clear skies over "the pork chop." Some were assigned defensive roles, searching for submarines or flying combat air patrol over the ships. Others were assigned to attack missions. Lieutenant G. Roger Chambers of VC-86 launched from the USS *Bismarck Sea* during one such sortie. Flying the assigned compass course, straight and true, he waited to see the telltale brown cloud over Iwo Jima. During the days of heavy air and surface activity before the invasion, the island was constantly wrapped in a veil of dust and smoke that rose hundreds of feet into the air.

The Wildcats droned on and Chambers strained to see a brownish smudge. But nothing appeared on the horizon. He was checking his plotting board when another group of fighters from one of the other carriers pulled alongside. The lead pilot looked Chambers over, a strange expression on his face. Then, he waved his arms, shook his head, and frantically pointed.

A Navy Avenger, hit over Iwo Jima, trails smoke as it struggles away from the island. An alert Army Air Forces photographer captured this image while he was aboard the APA (attack transport) USS *Lenawee*, awaiting orders to go ashore. (John Whitcomb via the 7th Fighter Command Association)

Chambers tapped his head and pointed to the other flyer. It was a hand signal Navy pilots learned in flight training, meaning, "You've got the lead." The division of planes banked off to the left, following a course perhaps 50 degrees off the course Chambers was flying. Chambers and his aviators followed.

Soon, the dust cloud over Iwo Jima came into sight and the Wildcats went about their attacks. Somehow, someone aboard the *Bismarck Sea* had recorded the carrier's location incorrectly, relative to the island. Chambers took it all in stride. He figured, wrong course or not, he would have turned his planes around when his fuel got low, flown the opposite heading, and eventually found his carrier again.

On D Minus 2, Navy pilots concentrated on neutralizing the dual-purpose and anti-aircraft guns they spotted. Repeatedly, fighter and bomber pilots located and dove on these gun emplacements with their bombs, rockets, and machine guns. Two flights carried canisters of napalm, a relatively new type of weapon. The jellied gasoline mixture had been used with some success elsewhere in the Pacific, but the pilots over the island reported their attacks were, for the most part, ineffective due to a large number of the firebombs failing to ignite on impact. Later, flyers speculated that the igniters tore loose from the tanks as they tumbled through the air.

As the carrier planes went about their work, they did so with only light anti-aircraft fire from the island. When they flew directly over the main defenses for this island at altitudes from 500 to 2,000 feet, the aviators reported that they "received very little ground fire and nothing larger than 40-mm."[39] Their attacks on Iwo Jima's system of guns seemed to be working. But when the higher-flying groups of AAF bombers caught a much larger barrage of heavier-caliber blasts, the carrier pilots had to reconsider their success. Some speculated the Japanese gunners held their fire to avoid observation. Other pilots thought perhaps the carrier planes were moving too fast and too low for the Japanese gunners to quickly depress and traverse their larger guns.

Not all aircraft made it through the day unscathed. An Avenger torpedo bomber attached to the USS *Petrof Bay* was hit over the island. The plane ditched near a destroyer and all three crewmembers were later transported back to their carrier. As the sun set, the Navy planes had tallied 336 sorties for the day.

On D Minus 1, all American surface and air units stepped up the tempo of their attacks. Landing forces had requested 10 days of bombardment before the Marine invasion, but they received only three. As a result, this final day of "softening up" took on heightened importance.

Carrier planes were pressing their attacks but still breaking away above 500 feet in most cases. Almost all pilots reported receiving small arms fire from the island, and many returned to their carriers with bullet holes in their wings and bellies. Another Avenger, from the USS *Makin Island*, was lost during the bombings, but the three-man crew was rescued. As before, the planes received little large caliber anti-aircraft fire from the island.

In the afternoon, 36 B-24s from the Marianas came up to join in the battle. They carried 500-pound bombs set to burst in the air after falling 3,000 feet. The overcast hung at between 1,500 and 1,900 feet, and the Liberator pilots were wary of dropping their payload from that height. They had seen the day before that some heavy guns remained operational. The bombers waited for a break in the weather. It never came, and the planes returned to base without making a drop.

D-DAY

Frustration reigned for the Liberator crewmen who had come up to Iwo Jima numerous times during the last phase before the attacks and often left the area without hitting the island.

After their TBM Avenger was hit and brought down by Japanese gunfire over Iwo Jima on 17 February, the crew safely ditched their plane at sea. The lifeguard destroyer USS *Halligan* picked up the three unharmed men. Now, they reluctantly await the next step in their journey—a return trip to their escort carrier, *Petrof Bay*, via the breeches buoy chair. (U.S. Navy via National Archives)

On D-Day (19 February 1945), they were back again to participate in one final all-out clobbering of the east beaches in the early morning.

With the Marines in their landing craft, Navy vessels laid down one last pounding before the ground units came ashore. It was the beginning of the heaviest pre-landing bombardment in history. The carrier planes appeared too, adding a storm of bombs, rockets, and gunfire to the beach. To allow both aircraft and surface units to attack simultaneously, Navy gunfire was to have no trajectory over 1,100 feet. And the aircraft attacked from altitudes above 1,500 feet.

Included in the complement of Navy planes were two squadrons of Marine Corps F4U Corsairs. They had been encouraged to "drag their bellies on the beach," during a lull in the Naval fire. The Marine fighter pilots did their best to comply. Under the watchful eyes of the cheering leathernecks in the attack boats, the Corsairs came down low and fast parallel to the beach, dropped napalm, fired rockets, and strafed furiously.

The B-24 Liberators arrived overhead slightly later than their appointed time. They dodged the scattered clouds to make their bomb runs near the beach. An entire squadron of the 30th Bomb Group moved into position moments too late to add to the pummeling. The lead bombardier saw that the Marine boats were dangerously close to the shore and decided not to drop.

"It seemed a shame to have dispatched 44 planes and have only 15 of them drop their bombs on the target," wrote the 30th's historian, "but there were inevitable circumstances with which the crews could not cope. They did everything within their power to drop their bombs on Iwo in a final endeavor to help the Yank boys making the assault."[40]

A Curtiss SB2C Helldiver from the USS *Hancock* circles the skies near Iwo Jima on D-Day, 19 February 1945. Soon after the order was given on 27 January 1945, aircraft from each large carrier were assigned a unique "G Symbol" (Geometric Symbol) to aid in identification. The white diagonal stripe assigned to the *Hancock* can be seen on the tail and hastily painted on the wing of this aircraft. (U.S. Navy via National Archives)

Marines stack up on the sandy terraces of Iwo Jima's east beach as heavy and accurate Japanese gunfire and falling mortars begin to take their toll on the fighting men. Behind them, more waves of Marines are arriving. (U.S. Marine Corps via National Archives)

When the landing craft neared the shoreline, the low-flying Navy fighters switched their focus 200 yards inland and to the flanks of the invasion beaches. Below, the lead landing craft were reaching the beaches and the first Marines were slogging through Iwo Jima's black sand to take cover behind the first terrace, just 10 yards from the water's edge. They looked out onto a desolate landscape. Stray bullets whizzed by and a few mortars thumped down, but for the most part, it was almost like a dream. The Navy fighters again eased their attacks another 300 yards inland, to keep their fire away from the shore, which was rapidly filling with American troops.

"Something's screwy," the Marines commented back and forth. The fanatical resistance they had expected at the water's edge had failed to appear. Maybe all the bombings *had* killed the Japanese. Maybe, just maybe, this was going to be a cakewalk.

Behind them, waves of assault craft kept bringing in tanks, guns, jeeps, and more Marines. In the relative calm, with very few Japanese soldiers to fight, the men began their battle with another enemy—Iwo Jima's beaches. As the carrier planes hovered overhead, awaiting new targets, American vehicles sunk axle-deep in the deep, volcanic sand.

Then all hell broke loose. The fire from the plateau on the Marines' right, all the way around to Mount Suribachi, on the left, suddenly intensified and men began to get hit. Many Marines were grouped tightly on the beach behind the first terrace when officers like Lieutenant Colonel Chandler Johnson goaded them forward. Johnson's famous words to the Marines around him were, "Okay you bastards, let's get the hell off this beach!"[41]

On D-Day, a TBM Avenger stands off Iwo Jima's east beach and records the action. Suribachi is covered in smoke as landing boats shuttle to the landing zones near a Cleveland class cruiser stationed close to shore to provide heavy firepower. (U.S. Navy via National Archives)

Marines set up a 37-mm gun in the black sands near airfield number one. In the background, a TBM Avenger pulls away after a bomb run near Mount Suribachi. (Naval Aviation Museum)

The War Below

While aviators fought in the skies over Iwo Jima, thousands of Marines took on the nightmarish task of combat amid the island's unforgiving beaches, valleys, and hills. Japanese defenders were pried out of their fortifications by brute force—a terrible trial that few flyers could even imagine.

The fighting was some of the worst of the Pacific war and gains were often measured in yards, feet, or even inches. Most Japanese soldiers had no intention of surrender and American casualties climbed into the thousands as each cave and fortification was discovered and overcome. Reports say that 6,821 Americans died in the fighting; the majority, 5,931 young men, were Marines. Another 19,217 leathernecks, soldiers, and sailors were wounded. Of the approximately 21,000 Japanese on Iwo Jima, it is believed that around 20,000 were killed in combat or sealed forever in their caves. The Marines took 216 prisoners. In later months, the Army rounded up 867 more Japanese soldiers.

The final barrage had just moved inland as this photo was taken from an orbiting USS Bunker Hill *aircraft on D-Day. Below, waves of landing boats are heading for the beaches along Iwo's eastern shore. (U.S. Navy via National Archives)*

Weary Japanese soldiers emerge from underground, ready to surrender. The event was a rare occurrence—defenders on Iwo hardly ever gave themselves up to American forces, even when hopelessly trapped in their caves. Japanese warrior culture considered the act of surrender a fate worse than death. (The 7th Fighter Command Association)

Assisted by their comrades, wounded but ambulatory Marines are helped along Iwo Jima's east beach. Battle ravaged American fighting equipment scattered nearby gives a sense of the ferocity of the fighting in this area days earlier. (U.S. Navy via National Archives)

Landing boats brought in tons of supplies urgently needed by fighting men on the front lines. Here, Marines move an endless mass of boxes by hand over Iwo Jima's treacherous black sand. (U.S. Marine Corps via National Archives)

A Japanese sniper's nest falls under completely new management as the Marines move in. The walls of the makeshift hovel are made from the wings of long-gone Japanese aircraft. The wings keep sand from collapsing into the hole. As the Americans said, digging in Iwo's slippery sand was like trying to burrow into a barrel of wheat. (U.S. Marine Corps via National Archives)

On a makeshift work table made from soon-to-be-used grave markers, Sergeant Roland Tigett sorts through the dog tags collected from dead Marines on the island. (U.S. Marine Corps via National Archives)

Off the beach they went, moving quickly from the east side of Iwo Jima, along the narrow isthmus to near the west beaches in 90 minutes, almost cutting off Mount Suribachi from the rest of the island. When a troublesome spot held up the advance, the soldiers called upon the Hellcats and Corsairs orbiting overhead to strike. The Marines took refuge in the thousands of craters that dotted the landscape. The scattershot B-24s hadn't hit just the airfields in their months of bombing, they had hit everything. And now the holes they had created made for excellent hiding places for the Marines. Soon the Americans had advanced as far as the south end of airfield number one.

As the day wore on, they were not taking nearly as much ground as they had first hoped for. Military planners had drawn a line along Iwo Jima's midsection on their maps—the planned boundary for advancement for D-Day. Except for a thin peninsula of American forces jutting north along the island's eastern shore, the Marines were nowhere near the line as the sun set over the Pacific. Around 566 Marines had died and nearly 2,000 were injured in the first day of fighting.

Most of the airplanes returned to the carriers after flying more than 700 sorties, and the ships steamed away from the island in the darkness. The Marines were left in their holes as brilliant star shells, fired from destroyers, slowly drifted to earth beneath parachutes, casting the island in a ghostly glow.

On the beach, the supplies continued to flow. It seemed everyone needed some sort of "hot cargo"—tanks, bulldozers, steel matting, doctors, radios, and most of all, ammunition. The empty landing craft filled with injured Marines returned to the vessels surrounding Iwo Jima.

Crewmen prepare high velocity aerial rockets on the deck of a Navy carrier. Used extensively in the invasions of Iwo Jima and Okinawa, the weapons streaked unguided after they were aimed and fired from carrier aircraft. The five-inch (127-mm) projectiles were particularly effective against Japanese bunkers and pillboxes on Iwo and gave Navy aircraft the firepower equivalent to a destroyer salvo. (U.S. Navy via Author's Collection)

BUSINESS AS USUAL

Carrier pilots conducted business as usual in the days after the invasion. The offensive might of the Navy planes was still focused on Iwo Jima. As the Marines made agonizing progress, tons of bombs, rockets, and bullets were called in to batter the honeycomb of Japanese bunkers, pillboxes, and caves that were discovered seemingly every few yards along the way. The carrier planes were especially helpful in neutralizing low-lying areas that remained unseen from the warships offshore.

Communications between the Marines and the Navy aircraft were a source of some frustration during the battle. The men on the ground would sometimes attempt to adjust the carrier planes' aerial attacks by reporting, "A hair to the left," or "a teeny-weeny bit closer." The directions meant very little to a pilot speeding along in the skies over the island at several hundred miles per hour.

The Marine units used 30-by-36-inch fluorescent panels to indicate their most forward positions along their lines. Red panels were used to indicate the 5th Marine Division and yellow for the 4th. (Later, alternating red and yellow panels were used for the 3rd Marine Division, which landed on Iwo Jima on 24 February.)

An exhausted leatherneck looks to the skies as Navy aircraft fire rockets into Japanese positions along the front lines, just ahead of his platoon. (U.S. Marine Corps via National Archives)

With the Marines sometimes only a few hundred yards away, the aviators were concerned with making their drops a bull's-eye every time. Some of the *Yorktown's* aircraft flew so low that they began to return to the carrier with dents and small holes created by the explosions of their own ordinance.

Other Navy airmen from the escort carriers USS *Tulagi* and USS *Anzio* were assigned to comb the seas at the fringes of the fleet, looking for signs of underwater intruders lurking near the surface. It was no secret that a massive force of American ships was now gathered near Iwo Jima. It was critical to keep them safe from enemy submarine attack. The anti-submarine planes, in conjunction with surface vessels, nervously shuttled back and forth, looking for signs of trouble and occasionally finding an intruder. Though difficult to confirm in the cat-and-mouse game of underwater warfare, records indicate the aircraft helped sink two Japanese submarines and chased others out of the area.

CONFIDENTIAL

IWO JIMA

AIR ANTI-SUB PATROL DARK

The night anti-sub patrol routes assigned to planes from the USS *Anzio* radiate out in all directions from Iwo Jima like the spokes of a wheel. It was a sure bet that Japanese submarines would be ordered into the area, and Navy planes had the difficult task of keeping the massive American fleet out of danger. (U.S. Navy via National Archives)

Another group of aviators, assigned to combat air patrol, dutifully watched and waited, expecting large waves of Japanese planes from the home islands. Droning in endless circles around the sprawling armada of American ships, they hoped a radar operator would spot a gaggle of bogeys and give them a vector to investigate. Late on 21 February, a handful of the air patrol pilots got their chance.

A flight of rocket-equipped TBM Avengers from the USS *Tulagi* roam over Iwo Jima on 2 March 1945. Part of the time, planes from the escort carrier were involved in patrolling for enemy submarines near the fringes of the U.S. fleet. (U.S. Navy via National Archives)

THE *KAMIKAZE* ATTACK

That evening, the amphibious assault command ship USS *Estes* detected a mass of aircraft heading in from the north on radar. They estimated a formation of approximately 35 aircraft about 150 miles from Iwo Jima.

A flight of Grumman F6F Hellcat fighters let their bombs fall on Iwo Jima's narrow isthmus north of Mount Suribachi. This photo was taken on D Plus 2, 21 February 1945. The planes were bombing Japanese positions in front of the advancing 4th Marine Division. (U.S. Navy via National Archives)

On one of the many cargo and supply ships arrayed around Iwo Jima, Army Captain Robert Krueger of the 386th Air Service Group was awaiting orders to go ashore. The heavy fighting on the island had delayed his unit's entry. He spent much of his time aboard his AKA (Attack Cargo Ship) nervously watching and waiting.

When the alert came, the command ship ordered the cargo and personnel ships to "make smoke." Almost simultaneously, the smoke generators on the sterns of hundreds of blacked-out ships began to belch artificial clouds into the night sky.

Krueger watched, horrified, as the generator on the stern of his AKA caught fire, lighting up the deck and superstructure for all to see for miles around. He imagined what it would look like from a Japanese pilot's perspective, far above the fleet—one flickering, beautifully lit cargo ship in a sea of blackness. It didn't matter though. The force of 50 Japanese aircraft of the 2nd Milate Special Attack Unit had located more lucrative targets farther north.

Northeast of the island, the USS *Saratoga* was steaming toward Chichi Jima to launch a single-handed strike. A load of rocket-armed Hellcats waited on the carrier's forward deck. Overhead, two F6Fs hurried away to investigate the mystery planes headed their way. An escort carrier nearby told the *Sara* that the bogeys were friendly—their own American aircraft "coming back to roost."

When the Hellcats met them, the pilots excitedly reported that the bogeys were anything but friendly. Each American aviator latched on to one Zeke and downed it as the large formation of Jills, Judys, and Zekes roared past.

Below, the first Japanese fighter came out of the clouds, plunged through the *Saratoga's* wall of anti-aircraft fire, and smashed into the bow among the parked Hellcats. Moments later, a second crashed into the aft end of the ship. Another Zeke was caught by the *Sara's* guns, but went tumbling into the side of the carrier and set off a furious fire in the hangar deck. The fourth aircraft missed the carrier in its death dive, but planted its bomb abeam below the waterline. Another Japanese fighter smashed into the *Sara's* starboard gun gallery, spraying flaming gasoline over the gunners stationed there. A sixth Zeke dropped its bomb through the carrier's side.

Sailors work frantically to extinguish the fires on the bow of the USS *Saratoga*. When the *kamikazes* hit, fully fueled and armed Hellcat night fighters were spotted on the deck, readied to launch an attack on Chichi Jima. (U.S. Navy via National Archives)

In three minutes, the *Saratoga* was a wreck. Other carriers in the task unit were warned to be prepared to take the stricken ship's airborne planes. As darkness fell, the *Sara's* escort destroyers pulled in close to the flaming carrier and helped fight off nine more attackers. One Japanese bomber broke through and loosed a huge bomb on the middle of the *Saratoga's* flight deck.

The carrier lost 123 men, either killed or missing in the attacks. Amazingly, the *Sara's* surviving crew had the fires under control and the ship was able to recover aircraft only an hour and 15 minutes after the final bomb hit. But the carrier was out of action for the duration of the war, sent back to the United States for repairs.

Elsewhere in the fleet, Wildcat pilot Lieutenant G. Roger Chambers was returning from a strike on Iwo Jima. His planes had been machine-gunning areas near Mount Suribachi when they began to run low on ammunition, fuel, and daylight. As the planes turned back toward the escort carrier USS *Bismarck Sea*, the fleet signaled they were under enemy air attack and warned the returning American fighters to steer clear or run the risk of being shot.

Lieutenant G. Roger Chambers poses in the cockpit of his FM-2 Wildcat aboard the USS *Bismarck Sea* in January 1945. Less than a month later, he would jump overboard as his carrier exploded, rolled over, and sank near Iwo. (G. Roger Chambers)

While Chamber's Wildcat pilots loitered, they spotted a Japanese fighter making its way toward an American battleship and decided to give chase. It turned out to be a big mistake; the battleship lit up like Christmas, throwing everything they had not only at the Japanese fighter, but also at the tailing Wildcats. The Naval aviators quickly vacated the area.

Soon after, Chambers heard a radio call from a night fighter that had just departed from the *Saratoga*. "He had just taken off and his engine was running rough," Chambers related, "and he told the *Saratoga* that he was going to have to land. They said, 'Well, you can't come back here because we've just taken *kamikazes* on the flight deck.' And that's when we knew all hell was breaking loose there someplace."[42]

"Pretty soon, they called up and said, 'Okay, the attack is over, come on in,' so we did."[43] When he landed, Chambers saw not only the *Bismarck Sea's* aircraft on the flight deck, but also a refugee aircraft from the stricken *Saratoga*. By that time, the sun had just slipped below the horizon. Some of the Japanese planes bypassed the fleet, turned, and were heading back, looking for the silhouettes of the American warships against the evening sky.

Three Japanese aircraft appeared out of the darkness headed toward the USS *Lunga Point*, about 1,000 yards away from the *Bismarck Sea*. The combined guns of the two escort carriers and a nearby destroyer brought one of the aircraft down as a second roared just 15 feet overhead. The wing of a third attacker, identified as a Jill, hit the *Lunga Point* at the base of the carrier's island and sprayed flaming debris over the deck.

Another aircraft came in just off the wave tops and singled out the *Bismarck Sea* as its target. Lieutenant Chambers was down in the carrier's wardroom with the men from his flight when the enemy planes returned. "There was a big shuddering noise and the lights all went out, just like you see in the movies, then they blinked a few times and went back on again."[44]

Sailors on the USS *Lunga Point* view the pieces of a Japanese Jill that exploded over their vessel during the *kamikaze* attack near Iwo Jima. The wing of the Japanese plane hit the carrier's island and the gear came to rest entangled in a catwalk nearby. (U.S. Navy via National Archives)

Flames roll over the flight deck of the USS *Lunga Point* as parts of a Japanese torpedo plane strike the base of the escort carrier's island. A fraction of a second before, the plane was hit by anti-aircraft fire and began to disintegrate. Flaming debris peppered the deck, while the bulk of the airplane plunged into the water. (U.S. Navy via National Archives)

The Japanese plane had buried itself in the starboard side of the escort carrier in a ball of flames. It is thought that the *kamikaze* was carrying a bomb with a fraction-of-a-second delayed fuse. It penetrated into the *Bismarck Sea's* hanger deck, which was filled with planes, before exploding. With a critical water main in the aft section of the ship severed, the *Bismarck Sea*'s firefighters could do very little as the blaze spread, over-running parked planes and stored ammunition with booming secondary explosions. Chambers said he waited near a hatchway until he heard a big explosion and then sprinted through the hangar deck and up to the flight deck. "Maybe if I run now, the next one won't get me," was his logic, as torpedoes, depth charges, and rockets were randomly cooking off in the superheated fire.[45]

Chambers and many others had thankfully made it topside when the second *kamikaze* plunged, almost vertically, into the deck near the carrier's aft aircraft elevator shaft. "And then, just a minute or two later, the captain [John Pratt] called on the squawk box and said, 'Prepare to abandon ship,' and then immediately, 'Abandon ship'."[46]

Chambers took a large raft from the belly of an Avenger bomber spotted on the deck and made his way to the starboard side—the side of the ship lowest to the water as it began to list. He pulled the inflation handle on the raft and jumped overboard. Moments later, Chambers climbed into the raft and pulled another man from the dark water. The pair struggled to push the raft free but the wind kept pushing them back against the hull of the burning *Bismarck Sea*. "We were just going right along the side of the ship and airplanes were falling off and people were dropping off and there was just no way to move out from it."[47]

Near the stern, there was a tremendous explosion and "the whole damn side of the ship looked like it was coming out." Chambers lost hold of the raft and came to the surface of the cold, dark water nearly deaf from the blasts. He then watched the *Bismarck Sea*, "heading off, with fireworks going out in every direction."[48]

After Chambers and the burning carrier were separated, the *Bismarck Sea* turned over and sank. Lieutenant Chambers spent a short while in the cold water near Iwo Jima before being rescued by a destroyer escort moving through the area. More than a third of the men aboard the ship—318 sailors and aviators—were never seen again.

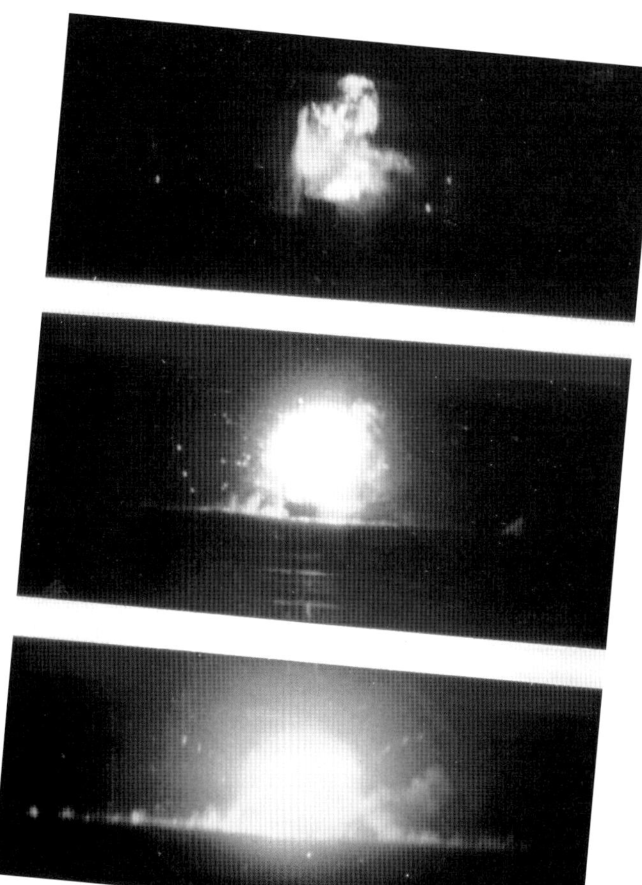

Seen from the USS *Lunga Point*, the *Bismarck Sea* is wracked with a series of fatal explosions on the night of 21 February 1945. The escort carrier was hit by two *kamikazes*. The suicide planes set off a chain reaction among the ship's own stores of rockets, bombs, torpedoes, and depth charges. (U.S. Navy via National Archives)

CHAPTER 5

SETTING UP

The "press PBM" is readied to be loaded onto the deck of the seaplane tender USS *Hamlin* after it suffered damage during a landing in the rough seas near Iwo Jima. This photo was taken just one day after the invasion, 20 February 1945. (U.S. Navy via National Archives)

Ashore, the Marines continued to fight their toughest battle of World War II. The expected *banzai* charge from the Japanese forces, encountered on other Pacific islands, never materialized. Instead of massing in the open, where the American's superior weaponry could function, the enemy stayed frustratingly hidden.

The leathernecks were forced to go after the Japanese in their caves the old-fashioned way—with small squads of men, rifles, satchel charges, grenades, and flame throwers. Places along the front lines were reminiscent of a World War I battlefield, with Marines and Japanese soldiers viciously fighting for a few yards of cratered, lifeless soil. American casualties climbed even higher.

By 22 February 1945, the Marines began to scale the sides of Mount Suribachi. After bitter fighting, the first units reached the top the following day. When a small American flag was raised at the top of what some Marines spitefully called "Mount Sonofabitchi," most everyone fighting on Iwo Jima, those aboard the ships surrounding the island, and the men flying nearby, stopped what they were doing and paused to watch, just for a second.

Another, larger flag from an American LST (Landing Ship, Tank) was put into place a few hours later. Associated Press photographer Joe Rosenthal was on hand to capture the historic moment with his camera. Before Rosenthal climbed down from Suribachi, he most assuredly looked out to the northeast, where all of Iwo Jima was laid out before him. Between the battered airfields, he could see the Marines fighting their way through the jagged rocks and sand.

Bravely springing into the air in a clear spot amid a fleet of Navy ships, a Martin PBM Mariner begins its flight back to the Marianas on 28 February 1945. The heavily loaded floatplane used JATO (Jet Assisted Take Off) rockets to shorten its run. This image was taken by the curious crew of a Navy Avenger from the USS *Makin Island.* (U.S. Navy via National Archives)

THE SEADROME

The Americans loosely controlled one of Iwo Jima's two functional airfields but it would be days, perhaps weeks, before they would be serviceable or safe for any type of aircraft. Meanwhile, a link was established with the nearest bases in the Marianas using the Navy's Martin PBM Mariner amphibious patrol planes.

Soon after the Marine landing, the giant flying boats began to appear, flopping down into the rough seas among the fleet. One of the first, from Saipan's Patrol Bombing Squadron 26, nearly collapsed its tail while performing a full stall landing in the high swells. Lifted aboard a tender, the aircraft would not fly again from the waters around Iwo Jima.

Other PBMs, belonging to VPB-19, were not far behind. They delivered fresh blood that had been airlifted from the States, brought mail, shuttled VIPs and the press, and carried other high priority cargo. On the return trip, the Mariner aircraft often carried some of the most critically wounded Marines to medical facilities on Guam. Four-engine Consolidated PB2Y Coronado flying boats, converted to carry 25 stretchers, were also involved in evacuations off Iwo Jima.

Joe Rosenthal's negatives, including the one that was to become arguably America's most famous wartime image of all time, was among the thousands of reports and pictures flown out of the battle area aboard the flying boats.

As time passed and the bulk of the fighting moved north, the Navy patrol aircraft established a seadrome off the southeast tip of Iwo Jima. Always on the lookout for the smoothest seas, arriving PBM pilots would sometimes radio nearby cruisers and try and convince them to slide through the area in a hard turn to calm the waves before their landings. And there were many more difficulties besides the rough water—a spattering of Japanese gunfire and mortar rounds still hit the seadrome area with regularity.

PBM pilots discovered another hazard almost immediately. The ocean around Iwo Jima was filled with every kind of detritus, including empty oil drums, ammo boxes, lumber, and bodies. While the seadrome was patrolled to try to keep the area clear of floating debris, Mariner pilots were often forced to taxi several miles out to sea before finding an open area in which to take off.

THE SEABEES

Attempts to make Iwo Jima's airfields work to the Americans' advantage began as soon as the Marines passed through. Naval Construction Battalions—Seabees—landed on shore just minutes after the first wave of troops. The jobs to which they were assigned were many and varied, from struggling with pontoon barges in the treacherous surf, to unloading tons of supplies, to exploding stranded landing craft that clogged the beachhead.

Other Seabees worked to open pathways for vehicles and rescue trucks and jeeps that had mired in Iwo Jima's troublesome black sand. Their jobs often left them exposed to gunfire and meant working around heavy machinery—a favorite target for the Japanese. Upon seeing a Seabee bulldozer working near the shore, one Marine deadpanned that he didn't know whether it was best to hide behind it, or move as far away as possible. The hazardous nature of their work caused the Seabees to take terrible casualties on the island.

By 20 February, the Marines had fought their way along the runways of airfield number one. But the front lines bogged down nearby. No matter, the Seabees worked as the battle raged no more than 1,000 yards away. Men of the 31st Battalion had the ugly job of clearing the runways. The task was supposed to be undertaken by the 133rd Seabees, but too many of them had been killed or wounded. So men of the 31st lined up two feet apart and crawled on their bellies down the whole length of the dusty surface, collecting debris, shell casings, and pieces of shrapnel. They said that they lost all respect for the Japanese snipers, who shot at them the whole way but only managed to hit one Seabee, Seaman First Class Emanuel Steed, in the leg.

Soon after, the 62nd Battalion brought in their heavy equipment to fill in the holes and push the countless hulks of wrecked Japanese aircraft out of the way. When mortars fell or rifle bullets cracked too close, the Seabees hunkered down next to a steamroller or truck and waited it out, almost as casually as the way someone would take refuge from a passing rainstorm. When former Chicago resident and Seabee Chief Commissary Steward Henri Dupre was asked what he thought of Iwo Jima, he merrily replied, "The crowds are worse here, but the gunfire is more accurate in Chicago."[49]

Members of the 62nd Seabee Battalion were the purveyors of heavy equipment when it came to repairing airfield number one. Here, a power shovel scoops a load of rocks to fill one of many craters blasted in the runway. (U.S. Navy via National Archives)

When the shooting gets to be a bit too heavy, Seabees and Army engineers hunker down next to their equipment and wait out the storm. The need to have airfield number one up and running as quickly as possible forced the brave men into action as heavy combat was taking place dangerously close by. (U.S. Army Air Forces via National Archives)

THE MAYTAG MESSERSCHMITTS

On 26 February, the first American airplane touched down on Iwo Jima. It was a small Marine observation plane, piloted by Lieutenant Harvey Olson. A Stinson OY-1 Sentinel (built by Consolidated Vultee) from Marine Observation Squadron 4 bounced to a stop on airfield number one as the engineers and Seabees still worked feverishly. They paused only for a moment to cheer their first aerial visitor. Mortar fire fell around the little plane as a Marine climbed on the strut of the aircraft and directed Olson to a safe place beyond the reach of the Japanese guns.

The small green planes had been nicknamed "grasshoppers" by American troops. They were used to spot for the Marine artillery that had been recently hauled ashore. Some of the little planes had been transported to Iwo Jima aboard escort carriers (including two that were lost in the sinking of the *Bismarck Sea*). The first to land on Iwo Jima flew from the USS *Wake Island*.

A Marine OY-1 soars into the skies off the deck of the USS *Sargent Bay* on 28 February 1945. Many of the planes were delivered into the battle zone aboard escort carriers. A pair of the "Maytag Messerschmitts" went down with the *Bismarck Sea* a week before. (U.S. Navy via National Archives)

Mortars fall near the first American aircraft to land on Iwo Jima as it taxies to safer ground. The OY-1 Sentinel of VMO-4 arrived on 26 February and was directed to the south end of the field by the Marine riding on the strut. (U.S. Army Air Forces via National Archives)

Others arrived over Iwo Jima in a most unusual fashion. They were loaded aboard LST-776 and launched from an experimental rig called Brodie Gear. The strange "high-wire act" was named for its inventor, Army Lieutenant James Brodie. A jumble of beams and cables were used to launch the little Sentinels into the air—"like a peanut in a slingshot" one flyer explained—and could recover them at the end of missions. Most pilots considered the practice a little too strange and risky for their liking.

The fighting men called the OY-1s "Maytag Messerschmitts" and their pilots "low-budget sky Marines." But they respected what the tiny green planes could do. The unarmored Sentinels roamed the skies at a few hundred feet, often rocking in the propeller wash of attacking Navy aircraft. When a grasshopper appeared, the Japanese soldiers "buttoned up" and hid. If they didn't, the pilot would use his radio to bring down a rain of American artillery.

LST-776 stands off Iwo Jima's shoreline carrying its strange array of Brodie Gear launching equipment and a flock of Marine "grasshopper" aircraft. Most pilots felt that being launched from such a weird contraption simply seemed unnatural. (U.S. Army Air Forces via National Archives)

At the height of the fighting, 14 to 16 of the small planes flew from the number one airfield. Scuffed, dirt-spattered, and repeatedly patched from bullet damage, the OY-1s flew more than 600 missions in 19 days.

Many observation pilots were shot down, including Major Ray Dollins of the 5th Marines who was reportedly singing his own mangled version of "Oh, What a Beautiful Mornin'" over his radio when he was hit. He was killed when his plane crashed into the water among the assault boats. Marines on every part of the island mourned the loss of the little grasshopper—their friend and helpful ally.

NAVY OPERATIONS

The larger carriers of Task Force 58 moved away from Iwo Jima on 22 February, heading for a second strike on the Tokyo area. The *Saratoga* was to be detached from the group to stay behind, but when the carrier was seriously damaged by *kamikazes*, the USS *Enterprise* was chosen to fill in.

The "Big E" and a group of smaller escort carriers remained on station near Iwo Jima to help the Marines. Since many of the small "jeep carriers" were named after bays, (*Natoma Bay*, *Petrof Bay*, *Sargent Bay*, and the like) sailors jokingly assigned a new name to the only large flattop still supporting the Iwo Jima assault—"Enterprise Bay."

The *Enterprise* primarily launched night fighters over Iwo Jima and the surrounding "Jimas." But her large deck and nighttime operations clock made the carrier the ideal place for

It didn't take too long for the "unarmed" Marine observation flyers to scrounge some weaponry to haul into the dangerous skies over Iwo Jima. The Sentinel in this image, nicknamed *Lady Satan*, now sports a trio of bazooka tubes under the wing for some real "punching power." (U.S. Marine Corps via National Archives)

Preparing to launch Avengers over Iwo Jima on 28 February 1945, the "jeep carrier" USS *Makin Island* steams under sunny skies. After the bigger carriers had departed the area to strike Japan proper, it was largely up to a group of escort carriers like this one to keep the invading Marines supported from the air. (U.S. Navy via National Archives)

An FM-2 Wildcat rumbles off the deck of the *Makin Island*, headed for Iwo Jima. A closer look at the plane reveals some interesting details. The canopy slid open—for easy escape if something goes wrong. And the rudder cranked far over to the right to counteract the torque from the fighter's 1,350-horsepower Cyclone engine and propeller. (U.S. Navy via National Archives)

landing damaged aircraft and stragglers from the daylight missions conducted by the escort carriers. From 23 February to 2 March 1945 (174 hours), the Big E launched and recovered aircraft 24 hours a day.

For the escort carriers, the ugly, dirty job of assisting the Marines on the ground and hunting down Japanese guns, soldiers, and fortifications continued. Marines later said that they felt the quality of their air support lessened when the larger carriers left. There were a number of reasons for this. First, fewer aircraft were on hand to respond to their needs. Second, the fighters from the escort carriers were equipped to carry relatively small 100-pound bombs. Finally, the invasion of the island lagged behind schedule, the escort carriers ran short of bombs, rockets, and ammunition as February turned into March.

A pair of 100-pound bombs is carted along the deck of the USS *Sargent Bay*. After the larger carriers departed the scene of the invasion, Marines on Iwo Jima complained that fighters from the escort carriers could not carry the larger 500-pound bombs helpful in assisting them in blasting enemy bunkers and caves. (U.S. Navy via National Archives)

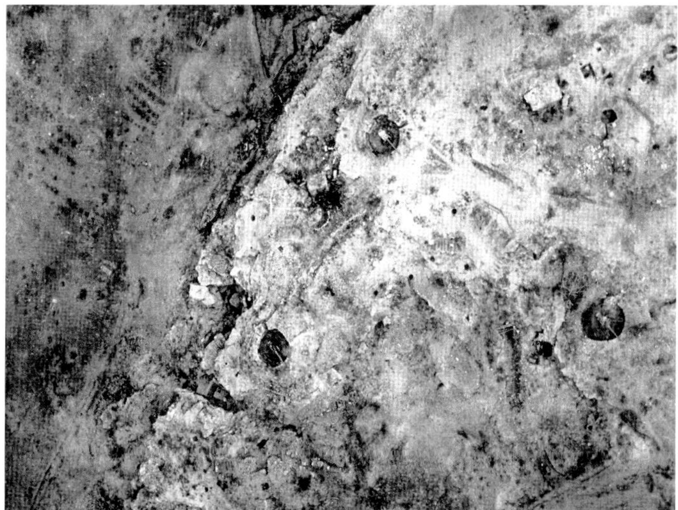

As the crew of a carrier plane from the USS *Sargent Bay* looked for targets over Iwo Jima, they spotted three Japanese heavy anti-aircraft emplacements from an altitude of 850 feet. Within minutes, the guns were erased by marauding Navy aircraft. (U.S. Navy via National Archives)

The escort carrier pilots proved their bravery time and again. Lieutenant Commander Robert O'Neill came back to the USS *Steamer Bay* in his flak-damaged Wildcat with one aileron blasted. He crunched to a stop, skidding his right wingtip on the deck. O'Neill jumped from the cockpit of his fighter in a rage and said, "I know where it is and I'm going after it!"[50] He found another FM-2 on the deck, ready to go, and took off—hoping to revisit the anti-aircraft gunners who had shot his Wildcat.

On the *Lunga Point*, another drama took place as Lieutenant "Bud" Foster came back to the carrier with a napalm bomb that had failed to drop. He'd tried everything to shake it loose—hard dives, snappy rolls, violent jerking maneuvers—but the canister of "liquid fire" refused to budge.

Foster wanted to land on the carrier and the *Lunga's* captain wanted to retain the use of Foster's plane, so instead of bailing out, it was decided to risk taking the Wildcat aboard. When the FM-2 fighter caught a landing wire and came to a

sudden stop, the napalm canister kept going, bouncing forward along the deck and settling near a group of parked aircraft. Aviation ordnance officer Lieutenant "Max" Palena straddled the bomb and quickly worked with a wrench to remove the fuse. Everyone watched, waited, and prayed until Palena extracted the critical portion of the bomb and tossed it aside. Only then was the bomb gingerly carried over to the side of the ship, given a loving pat on the top of its casing, and dumped into the sea.

On 1 March, four Wildcats from the *Natoma Bay* found a Japanese Frances bomber headed for the carriers and made

Above: As a Wildcat catches a landing wire after returning to the *Petrof Bay,* the right landing gear collapses. The Landing Signal Officer, above, steps around his blind to observe the plane's condition as it comes to rest. Sailors on the catwalk off the fighter's right wing warily watch, ready to scramble away if necessary. (U.S. Navy via National Archives)

Navy aviators speculated that the napalm they were dropping was often ineffective because the fuses attached to the tumbling tanks tore free. To rectify the problem, crewmen on the *Petrof Bay* began to rig their tanks with sets of hastily made plywood fins. (U.S. Navy via National Archives)

Stripped down to its bones, an Avenger gets a last catapult launch from the *Sargent Bay* and will make its final landing on the sea floor near Iwo Jima. Hit over the island on 25 February 1945, the torpedo bomber was too damaged to fix. Crews have certainly given it a good once-over before the "deep six"—doors, guns, Plexiglas, the engine, the wings, and other reusable parts are long gone. Sailors have punched holes in the plane's skin and left the bomb bay doors open to hasten its trip to the bottom. (U.S. Navy via National Archives)

Loaded with six rockets, external fuel tanks, and .50-caliber ammunition, a pair of General Motors FM-2 Wildcats are ready to depart the deck of the *Sargent Bay*. (U.S. Navy via National Archives)

quick work of the enemy aircraft. The air-to-air mission was a rarity for the escort carrier pilots and the victory was roundly celebrated.

Another rare mission took place on 28 February and again on 4 March. The green bottle flies on Iwo Jima were becoming almost unbearable. There were hundreds of bodies left unburied as the battle continued to rage. To help with the problem, Avengers from the *Makin Island* flew over Iwo Jima spraying gallons of DDT from belly tanks.

DDT was the new "miracle chemical" for killing the disease-carrying pests of the Pacific. A wartime article on the "harmless" liquid in an Army publication gleefully opens with the sentence, "Saipan dogs have no fleas."[51]

The DDT sprayer pilots had to keep a sharp eye out as they droned slow and low over the island—the skies over Iwo Jima were a busy place. Often, even when there was no strike in progress, there were 10 or 11 American Wildcats, Sentinels, and Kingfishers all jockeying for position and looking for targets near the front lines. As the big naval shells came rumbling in, the planes would scatter to get out of the way.

This dangerous job finally caught up with one of the Vought OS2Us. A sailor loading cargo aboard the attack transport USS *Lowndes* tuned in to a radio in a jeep that was parked on the ship's deck while he was waiting for the next wave of landing barges headed for the island. He idly listened as the spotters deftly went about their work and the huge shells crashed down.

Suddenly, one of the spotter plane pilots calmly called out on the radio, "So long fellows, they just shot off my tail."[52] The sailor looked up to see the flaming Kingfisher—minus its entire tail—plummeting down. It crashed in the water between the *Lowndes* and the adjoining ship, sending a geyser of water into the air. The pilot had stayed with the mortally wounded plane all the way down.

"It is believed that the loss of one OS2U can be laid to causes other than enemy action," an evaluation board report later coldly explained. "An observer saw the actual accident from 1,000 yards with the aid of binoculars and from appearances it had its tail shot completely off. The cause of this appears to have been a hit in the tail by a large caliber shell from one of our own surface units."[53]

In February 1945, a TBM flies over the deck of the USS *Makin Island*—a little too high. The wartime caption affixed to this Navy photo reports that the torpedo bomber is taking a "wave off," meaning the pilot has applied power and will circle around again for another try. Note that another plane can be seen in the landing pattern, just forward of the Avenger's left tire. (U.S. Navy via National Archives)

THE ARMY AIR FORCES COMES ASHORE

Among the Navy ships, groups of men slated to fly from Iwo Jima were impatiently waiting. On D-Day, they had witnessed the terrific bombardment of the island and there was talk among the flyers that not even a mouse could have survived the once-over dealt out by the American ships and planes.

They watched in fascination from the rails as the Marines went ashore and witnessed, firsthand, their struggles along the beaches. Then the assault boats started coming back with the wounded. For most Army Air Forces men, it was the first time they had seen the terrible impact of the fighting from ground level. For many, it was shocking.

Elements of the Army's 386th Air Service Group went ashore on D-Day Plus 5. The group was assigned to initiate operations at airfield number one as soon as possible for the 15th Fighter Squadron's North American P-51 Mustangs. The 386th would supply everything the fighter group needed to operate—including 500 55-gallon drums of 100-octane gasoline, endless belts of ammunition, 700 500-pound bombs, tons of food, generators, tents, tanker trucks, jeeps, weapons, and thousands of spare parts from nuts, bolts, and rivets up to complete crated Merlin engines.

Now that the first airfield had been wrestled away from the Japanese, the 386th was readying itself to transport literally more than a million crates from the beach to the south edge of the airfield—enough supplies to keep the entire fighter group going in combat conditions for six months.

Army Captain Robert Krueger of the 386th came ashore at sunset. The beach was "a horrible madhouse," with tons of debris and blasted boats bouncing in the surf. Yards away, the beach was littered with smashed jeeps, stranded trucks, and men and equipment of all types.

The Navy beachmaster zeroed in on Krueger as he crouched down, sizing up the situation. He yelled, "Hey, it's bad. It's hot here. You've got to dig a foxhole." Krueger told the sailor that he wanted to get to the south end of airfield number one to meet with the rest of his squadron. The beachmaster said, "Well, I don't know. I don't know if you'll make it." But it only took a second or two of arguing before the dirty sailor shrugged and pointed the way. As Krueger got moving, the man yelled to him one last piece of advice. He shouted, "When the flares come over, get down, be quiet, and don't move or you'll get shot."[54]

Krueger began to pick his way through the battlefield, up the hill toward the runways. He carefully followed the designated pathways cleared by the Americans through minefields and marked with ribbon. He quickly hit the dirt whenever a brilliant white flare drifted down overhead. "I've never been so scared in my life," Krueger said. "There were bullets flying everywhere and shells going off."[55] With a new flare being launched from the Navy destroyers offshore every five minutes or so, it took him the entire night to travel approximately half a mile.

At daybreak, the 386th men worked to move the bodies of five Japanese soldiers who had been buried where the unit was supposed to establish its headquarters. The area, in general, held a mass of smashed and twisted Japanese airplanes. "Welcome to Iwo Jima," they ribbed each other as Marine artillery boomed nearby.

Periodically, Marines would pass by on their way to and from the front line and ask, "Who are you?"

"The Air Force."

"What the hell are you guys doing *here*?"[56]

The landing beaches of Iwo Jima were a frustrating mess of hazards, obstacles, and chaos. It was over this disaster area that men like Army Air Forces Captain Robert Krueger had to move literally millions of boxes in order to get American aircraft ready for battle. (U.S. Navy via National Archives)

Left and below: The area slated to be occupied by the 386th Air Service Group would serve as the site for a fully functional repair and maintenance grounds for aircraft on airfield number one. Needless to say, it required a little work before they would be open for business. In the left photo, there are at least three Americans picking through the pile of Japanese wrecks, looking for souvenirs. The below image shows the cleanup efforts of the 386th when they were a little further along. (The 7th Fighter Command Association)

Before an aircraft control tower of any type was erected on airfield number one, Marine Sergeant Randall Craley and others coordinated flying activities from their radio-equipped jeeps. With the fighting only a few hundred yards away, it was a dirty and dangerous job. (Arvid Johnson via the 7th Fighter Command Association)

Above right: The tower originally built near airfield number one was a little rickety and a prime target for enemy soldiers hiding nearby. In the foreground lies one of hundreds of Japanese aircraft wrecks that littered the ground. (U.S. Marine Corps via National Archives)

OPEN FOR BUSINESS

The answer, of course, was the airfields. Army air controllers came ashore on 28 February and spent the night hunched in their foxholes as an American ammunition dump exploded for hours nearby. At sunrise, they went out to survey airfield number one.

For the first week, they shared operations with Navy and Marine air controllers. They ran the field with the help of two radio jeeps, a "biscuit gun" blinker light, and a signal mast for flags. A few days later, a half a dozen Seabees arrived and built a rickety 17-foot control tower.

The signal men soon learned that an airplane approaching airfield number one was an invitation for every Japanese unit on the opposite end of the island to open fire. Trying to outguess the curtain of mortar and rocket shells and bring the airplane in safely became somewhat of an art form among the men.

They also became the lead contenders in what they dubbed the "All-Island, All-Services Foxhole Diving Championship." Army Lieutenant Robert Vickery half-seriously told reporters, "In all classes and styles—the jack-knife, the double

Iwo Jima's first tower gang, with signal light, field glasses, and logbook, became experts at diving into their foxholes. Arriving aircraft always attracted Japanese gunfire, mortars, and rockets. Army reporters claimed, "Shells landed oftener than planes." (U.S. Army Air Forces via National Archives)

flip, the swan dive, the standing or sitting starts—we have some talent in our club that can handle any league."[57]

Sometimes, alone and exposed in the tower, the controllers remained on duty until the plane was safely on the ground. The nervous men said they often felt like "a carrier pigeon that has accidentally wandered into the National Skeet Finals."[58]

One particularly troublesome character was known by the AAF men as "Pistol Pete." They guessed Pete was a Japanese artilleryman operating a 12-centimeter piece hidden somewhere northwest of the runway. The rouge gunner would regularly lob a few shells at

An FM-2 Wildcat from the USS *Petrof Bay* had an external fuel tank come partially detached and turn sideways in flight, causing a severe vibration. The fighter became the first carrier plane to land at Iwo's airfield number one. In this image, Marines come out to have a look at the little fighter, which was piloted by Lieutenant (jg) Noah Butt, Jr. (Naval Aviation Museum)

Parapacks litter the runway at airfield number one as a Douglas C-47 rumbles through with another load. While the area was still too "hot" for planes to land and unload, ammunition and other critical supplies were dropped. Note the B-29 in the foreground—it's probably the first to land on the island. (The 7th Fighter Command Association)

the big planes as they came into the airfield and then he would disappear. Soldiers suspected his gun was on rails and after his attacks, he'd button up in a cave and wait out their searches.

Despite the frequent interruptions, the airfield began paying dividends for the Americans. After the early-arriving OY-1 spotter planes, most other landings were of an emergency nature, including damaged Marine and Navy carrier planes, a crippled B-24, and a photo ship.

AIR TRANSPORT ACTIVITIES

On the day before the Army controllers began operations at the airfield, a critical need for 37-mm gun barrels, carbines, whole blood, and plasma brought a group of Douglas C-47 cargo planes of the Army's 9th Troop Carrier Squadron up from Saipan. They were the first cargo planes to appear over Iwo Jima and the first in the Central Pacific to deliver supplies by parachute.

The planes zeroed on Iwo Jima's beaches to make their drops. They kicked out a string of parapacks from low level and dodged over the crest of Suribachi at the last second. On the beach, Marines quickly rounded up the canisters amid the falling Japanese mortar shells.

On 1 March, Marine transports flew five times over airfield number one with more canisters filled with mortar shells, machine gun parts, more blood, and mail. Leathernecks of the 4th and 5th Marine Divisions were saddened to learn that all the letters dropped in the containers were only for the men of the 3rd Marine Division. Army cargo airplanes returned the next day and dropped 35 more packs of mail to the fighting men.

On 3 March, the Army's cargo planes came back and almost ran out of fuel awaiting a break in the shelling of the runways. Finally, they dropped their 250-pound packs filled with 81-mm mortar shells and two special canisters containing radio equipment.

That same day, Navy and Marine cargo aircraft began to brave the Japanese attacks and come in to land at airfield number one. The first down was a Navy Douglas R4D hospital plane nicknamed *Peg O' My Heart*. The plane carried the first American woman to set foot on Iwo Jima—reporter Barbara Finch of Reuters.

Days later, a young flight nurse, Ensign Jane Kendliegh, became the first military woman to arrive on Iwo Jima. Described as "108 pounds of green eyed charm and efficiency"[59] by the press, Ensign Kendliegh was a pleasant sight to the wounded Marines being loaded aboard the hospital aircraft. Kendliegh would also become the first woman to land on Okinawa.

After their chutes have been removed, Army Air Forces men work to gather and organize the padded parapacks that have been delivered by transport aircraft. With the beaches overloaded and the runways too dangerous, parachute drops brought some of the most urgently needed items to the front—blood, radios, gun parts, ammunition, and mail. (Arvid Johnson via the 7th Fighter Command Association)

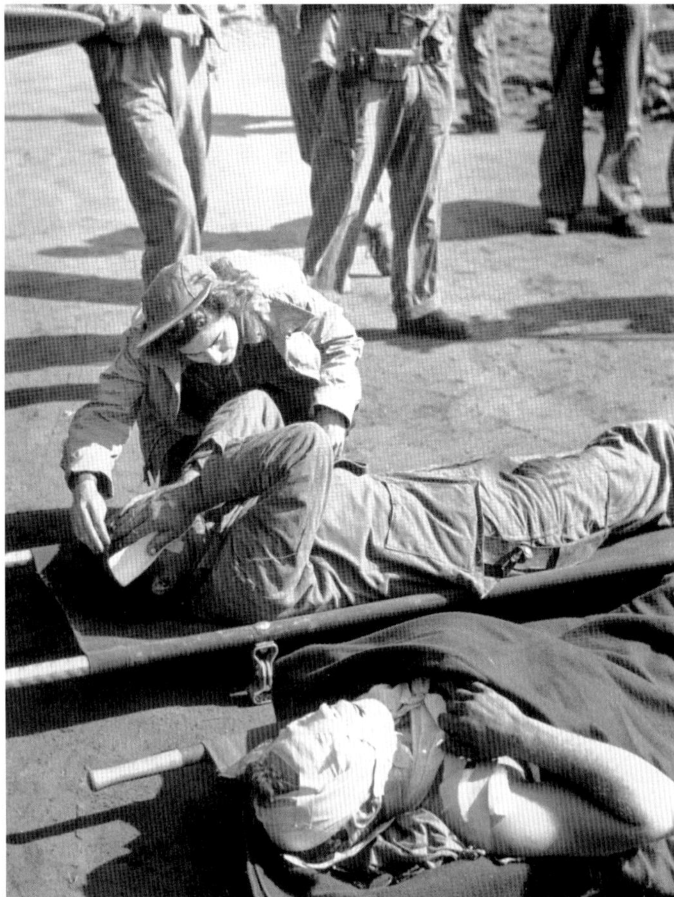

Ensign Jane Kendliegh comforts a seriously wounded Marine being evacuated by air from airfield number one. The Ohio-born farm girl was the first military woman to set foot on Iwo Jima. (Naval Historical Center)

The second cargo plane to arrive was a Curtiss R5C piloted by Lieutenant Colonel Malcolm Mackay, the commanding officer of Marine Transport Squadron 952. The Commando transport carried 5,500 pounds of mortar shells and ammunition. The aircraft of three Marine transport squadrons came in soon after and followed suit—doling out bullets and blood and taking the most critically wounded away to the Marianas.

THE FIRST OF MANY

The biggest test for airfield number one came the next day. The first of many B-29 bombers to use Iwo Jima as an emergency airfield was a 9th Bomb Group aircraft returning to Tinian. *Dinah Might* had helped bomb the Nakajima Musashina Aircraft Plant near Tokyo on 4 March 1945. When its bomb bay doors failed to close in the icy skies high over Japan, the B-29 consumed more fuel than normal on the flight home. By the time *Dinah* neared Iwo Jima, a stuck fuel valve had worsened the problem. The flight engineer told the pilot, Lieutenant Fred Malo, that they could go no farther. Their race between gallons and miles was almost over, and they were

Amid a sea of curious Marines stands the first of many B-29s to arrive at Iwo Jima. In serious trouble on 4 March 1945, the crew of *Dinah Might* voted to land on the island, even though it was strictly against orders. (U.S. Army Air Forces via National Archives)

only halfway home. Malo could ditch in the ocean or try for Iwo Jima—against orders.

The B-29 groups had been ordered to not consider Iwo Jima as an emergency landing site at the time for two reasons. First, the battle for the island still raged. Nowhere on the island was really safe, and a big Boeing Superfortress was an almost irresistible target. Second, airfield number one's runway, the longest and best on the island at the time, was still no place for a 37-ton bomber. U.S. Army and Navy troops had been feverishly working on it, but the pock-marked dirt strip was only 3,000 feet long and 150 feet wide—theoretically much too small for a Superfortress. But with his engines sucking the last available fuel from *Dinah's* tanks, Malo had to commit to a plan of action.

Malo explained the situation over the bomber's interphone and asked the crew to vote. After a few minutes the men began to chime in, "Tail gunner to pilot—it's Iwo for my dough." "Left gunner—hell's bells, make it Iwo. Always wanted to have a look at this war…" "Iwo… Iwo… Iwo… Iwo…"[60] It was nearly unanimous.

The Superfortress came in from the south, passing west of Mount Suribachi and touching down in the first few feet of hardened dirt. Applying the brakes immediately, *Dinah* skidded and slid, stopping only feet from where the north end of the strip faded into the twisted landscape of the battlefield beyond.

The controllers were not ready for such a big aircraft and had misestimated its size. As *Dinah* landed, the B-29's wing bashed over the airfield's lone signal mast and clipped the antenna of two radio jeeps parked too near the runway.

The crews busy unloading the Marine cargo planes nearby paused to watch while Japanese mortar explosions chased the Superfortress as it retreated to the south end of the field. The bomber made it through unscathed and was soon parked in a reasonably safe spot.

As Malo and his crew climbed from their craft, Army engineers and Navy Seabees peppered them with questions

The 11-man crew of *Dinah Might* poses for a Marine cameraman after they landed on Iwo Jima. Sadly, all but one of the men in the photo would be killed before the end of the war—some perished in a takeoff accident and others were lost when their aircraft was hit over Japan. Only one gunner, left on Iwo to care for the B-29 when it returned months later, made it back to the States. (U.S. Marine Corps via National Archives)

about the quality of the runway work they had been able to complete so far. The big bomber also attracted the attention of a bunch of Marines, curious to see this clean, silver machine that had descended into their war-ravaged world. The flyers told them, "Boy, you should have been with us over Tokyo this morning, it was hot!" The Marines responded, "Well, you should have seen it right here buddy!"[61]

Soon, the valve was fixed and enough fuel had been scrounged to get *Dinah* to Tinian. Unprepared for such a job, the ground crew reportedly passed gasoline for the state-of-the-art bomber up to the plane's fueling ports inside steel combat helmets. Those on the ground assured *Dinah's* crew that things would change for the better for the bomber crews coming into Iwo Jima in the months to come.

Dinah took off from south to north, using most of the runway and quickly swerving out to sea to avoid the most intense ground fire from the Japanese soldiers arrayed at the northern end of the island. The sacrifices of thousands of Marines on this remote rock in the far reaches of the Pacific began to pay dividends—Iwo Jima had saved its first Superfortress in trouble.

Dinah Might and the bomber's crew came back to the island with damage one more time, more than a month later. While one gunner was left on the island to guard the plane during repairs, Malo and the rest of his men departed on a "Gypsy Rose" cargo flight to the Marianas to fly missions in other craft. Soon after, some of *Dinah's* crew died in a takeoff crash on Tinian, and others perished on a mission over Kawasaki. In the end, only one crewmember of the first B-29 to land on Iwo Jima survived the war—Sergeant Robert Brackett, the lone gunner who had been left behind to care for *Dinah* on Sulphur Island.

CHAPTER 6

THE FIGHTERS

A formation of 15th Fighter Group Mustangs form up over Saipan before making the trek to Iwo Jima on 7 March 1945. This group of aircraft, led by Colonel James Beckwith, was the second formation of P-51s to reach the island. (U.S. Army Air Forces via National Archives)

A Japanese dog wandered into a Marine command post on D Plus 8. The gaunt animal, part German shepherd, seemed friendly enough and, "after being fed some of our more delicious C rations," said one report, "evidently decided to transfer."[62] The leathernecks said that the dog had the yellowest eyes they had ever seen. The Marines adopted him and named him "Iwo."

The dog survived the months of bombing raids and, "every time a plane flies overhead; he crouches down, snarling."[63] Things were about to get much worse for the mangy dog named Iwo. The first North American P-51 Mustangs arrived on the island on 6 March 1945.

THE 15TH FIGHTER GROUP

The Army's 15th Pursuit Group formed in November 1940 and was assigned to Wheeler Field in Hawaii on the island of Oahu. During the Japanese attack on Pearl Harbor on 7 December 1941, many of the group's aircraft were destroyed and they suffered significant casualties. But several pilots from the group struggled into the air in their Curtiss P-36 and P-40 fighters and scored the first American air-to-air victories of the war.

Later reorganized as the 15th Fighter Group, they remained part of the Hawaiian defense system, transitioning to newer versions of the P-40, then the Republic P-47, and finally to the North American P-51 Mustang in April 1944. With its pilots itching to get back into the fight, the group and its planes moved to the Marianas aboard Navy ships in the early days of February 1945.

The 15th cooled their heels on Saipan as the battle for Iwo Jima began. On 6 March 1945, Iwo's airfield number one was judged safe enough to begin to receive the fighters, and the pilots were anxious to oblige. The planes of the 15th Fighter

Not everyone had a great day when the first P-51 Mustang fighters arrived on Iwo Jima. Captain Raymond "Whitey" Betner was the third man to land that day and his fighter found a soft spot in surface of the island's partially finished runway. Though embarrassed, the pilot was not hurt in the accident. (U.S. Army Air Forces via National Archives)

Group's 47th Fighter Squadron were first to make the hop from Saipan to Iwo Jima.

Pilots with less seniority didn't fly fighters to Iwo Jima, but wrangled their way aboard transport planes headed to the island. Some of the men who climbed onto an Iwo Jima-bound Curtiss cargo plane were amazed to find that their pilot was none other than movie star Tyrone Power, Jr. After filming *Crash Dive* in 1943, Lieutenant Power joined the Marine Corps and flew with Marine Transport Squadron 353, supporting combat operations on the island and later on Okinawa.

The more experienced pilots of the 47th took off for Iwo Jima in their fighters on the morning of 6 March and arrived over the island around 1130. The Army and Marines living and fighting on Iwo Jima remembered the day well—the distinctive rumble of the Mustang's Merlin engines drowning out the sounds of battle for a few fleeting minutes.

A reporter for the Seventh Air Force's *Brief* magazine described their arrival like this: "The Seabees driving the cats that were forcing their way up Mount Suribachi, the aviation engineers on the strip, the Marine mortarmen—all stopped. Even the ping of Jap sniper bullets from the northern tip of Iwo appeared to quiet down, and you could imagine the doomed garrison peering from their caves and holes, watching and understanding, realizing in the silence what this moment meant."[64]

The P-51 piloted by the chief of the 7th Fighter Command, Major General Ernest "Mickey" Moore, landed first. The commander of the 47th Fighter Squadron, Major John Piper, was next. The third man down was Captain Raymond "Whitey" Betner. His Mustang hit a soft spot on Iwo Jima's less-than-perfect runway and a tire exploded. His plane ground looped in front of what must have seemed like everyone on the entire island. Red-faced and unhurt, Betner climbed from his fighter to watch the rest of the squadron's planes come in to the dusty airfield. The 15th's two remaining squadrons, the 45th and 78th Fighter Squadrons, flew into Iwo Jima the following day.

The arrival of fighters overhead gave a member of the 386th Air Service Group an idea. "See those planes?" he hollered to the men on the beaches who were unloading LCTs (Landing Craft, Tank). "Well they are due out tonight on a raid. But we gotta get a lot of this equipment up to them before they can take off. Let's get going." What normally would have taken two days to complete was done in three hours.[65]

Captain Jerome "Jerry" Yellin, a 78th pilot, wrote about his first impression of Iwo Jima in his memoir years later. After he parked his Mustang and cranked back the canopy, Yellin was shocked by the alien landscape that stretched out in all directions. "The island was ravaged by bombs and heavy shells; fires were burning; smoke was thick in the air. On the side of the runway, piles of Japanese bodies were barely covered by mounds of earth.[66]

"The air was filled with the sickening, heavy, unbearable smell of death," Yellin wrote. "It was overwhelming. I have lived with that smell every day of my life since then. You never get rid of it. It's like having cigarette smoke embedded in a wool jacket; you put the jacket on, and you smell it. The smell of death rarely leaves me."[67]

Home sweet home on Iwo Jima was far from a Pacific paradise. It was more like living at the dump. This photograph shows typical Army Air Forces accommodations on the island, with a generous helping of shattered trees, battlefield garbage, and wall-to-wall black sand. (U.S. Army Air Forces via National Archives)

The men settled into life near the battlefront by digging deep foxholes and eating C rations that they boiled in garbage cans filled with sulphur water. The labels came off during the cooking process and the airmen never knew what they were getting. If they were lucky, it was chicken or spaghetti. More often than not, it was pork and beans. "I've never eaten so many cans of pork and beans in my life," said 47th Squadron pilot Lieutenant Leon Sher.[68] Another man jokingly tried to convince his buddies that his rations contained turnips and

A member of the 15th Fighter Group works to start his stove, made from an old gas can. With a little patience, he'll be able to heat up a few dented tins of "god-knows-what" outside his sandbagged living quarters. (U.S. Army Air Forces via National Archives)

In the days after arrival on the Sulphur Island, an Army Air Forces man was allowed two canteens of water a day—for drinking, bathing, and shaving. Here, Staff Sergeant William Mausling, Jr. pours out a day's ration for Corporal Arthur Brown. (Sam Smith via the 7th Fighter Command Association)

billy-goat meat. The initial allotment of water among the men was two canteens a day—for drinking, shaving, and bathing.

Hunkered down at the end of the runway, the men experienced a dust storm every time a plane lined up to take off. "One B-24, mistaking our area for the runway," wrote the 15th's historian, "barely braked his plane in time to avoid running over the entire area."[69]

As night fell, the airmen learned that the Marines were close to pushing to Iwo Jima's north shore and dividing the remaining Japanese soldiers into two pockets. But even well to the south, things were far from safe. Everyone carried a gun. Pilots of the 15th were saddened to learn that, even though their crate of spare .45-caliber pistols had been carefully camouflaged to make it look like something more mundane, it had been discovered and stolen on Iwo Jima's beaches. The grumbling Army pilots suspected the Marines.

Most airmen barely left their holes even to go to the bathroom after the sun went down. If he did move around, it

With a crate for a desk and a ration box for a chair, AAF Staff Sergeant Thomas Cowgil is writing a letter to his sweetheart or folks, no doubt telling them about the "swell time" he's been having so far on beautiful Iwo Jima. (Sam Smith via the 7th Fighter Command Association)

Iwo Jima's aircraft were an attractive target for the surviving Japanese fighting men pushed into the north end of the island. Bullets and explosives continued to be a part of life (and death) at airfield number one. Here, a Marine points to a spot in the hardened soil where a Japanese rocket landed. Mustangs of the 15th Fighter Group are parked yards away in the background. (U.S. Marine Corps via National Archives)

was usually while doing something flamboyant and characteristically American—like loudly singing "Yankee Doodle." If a flyer had his head above ground between seven at night and seven the next morning, there was the risk he'd be shot at by a Marine, a foraging Japanese soldier, or some trigger-happy Seabee. It was a running joke that the Seabees standing guard seemed to lay down a constant barrage of fire—just in case.

On the afternoon of 8 March, Marine units at the front requested air support, and eight Mustangs of the 47th Fighter Squadron took off from airfield number one. In the first days of flying, Japanese rockets and mortars were still regularly hitting the end of the runway nearest to the front lines. Lieutenant Leon Sher said that it was not uncommon for pilots to fire their .50-caliber guns midway through their takeoff roll in an attempt to keep everyone's heads down as they became airborne. Once flying, the Mustangs would veer off to starboard, out to sea and away from the fighting, to gain altitude.

That night, five Japanese soldiers were spotted near the camp. A Marine killed one of the men, but the other four scattered and disappeared into the darkness. Lieutenant James McDermott was standing guard when he saw a strange shadow moving near him. Crouching down, the nervous airman whispered the password, "Lovely," to which another American was supposed to respond with the countersign, "Lady." When McDermott heard nothing, he clicked off his rifle's safety and again voiced the word, "Lovely" much louder, into the darkness. The mystery figure froze, crouched, and after a long pause, finally snarled, "Come here."

No way. Lieutenant McDermott fired at the shadows and the figure fired back with his Arisaka rifle. A grenade exploded between them, and McDermott buried his face in the black sand. Moments later, another grenade exploded. When the sun came up, the nervous airmen nearby went out to have a look. They discovered that the Japanese soldier had saved his last grenade for himself. The incident confirmed the flyers' suspicions that they were not in a safe environment. Many of the men doubled the row of sandbags protecting their foxholes.

By 9 March, all three squadrons of the 15th Fighter Group hammered pockets of remaining Japanese to the north on Iwo Jima. The Marines complimented the AAF flyers for their effective and accurate air support. This was partly because the Army planes could carry larger bombs than the Navy fighters from the escort carriers. Also, the Mustang pilots seemed to press their attacks at lower altitude—a characteristic that endeared them to the Marines fighting and dying on the front lines of battle.

The 15th's pilots were frustrated that they had no access to napalm. Deemed perfect for clearing out fortifications and caves, they experimented with the liquid firebombs in Hawaii months before. They had been ordered to leave their supplies of the weapon behind because the fighting on Iwo Jima was supposed to have been over by the time they arrived.

They collaborated with the 386th Service Group to make their own, filling 110-gallon wing tanks with a mixture of gasoline and diesel oil. An M-3 fuse was seated in a phosphorous grenade to make the igniter. The home-brew fire cocktails were used twice against Japanese forces on Iwo Jima.

On 17 March, the 15th Fighter Group moved to a more suitable location on a high terrace overlooking the ocean on

The pilots of the 15th Fighter Group had become well trained in the effective use of napalm against typical Japanese fortifications. While based in Hawaii, they had run extensive tests with the new "liquid fire" bombs. (Here, a Navy photo Hellcat trails one of the group's P-47s during an experimental drop.) However, the 15th was told to leave their napalm behind for their assignment to Iwo because the fighting was to have been over for weeks by the time they arrived. (Air Force Historical Research Agency)

the western shore near Mount Suribachi. Here, they began anew the process of disposing of dud shells and abandoned Marine fighting equipment and the ugly job of moving the bodies uncovered by the Seabees' bulldozers. By now the 15th had struck up a friendship with the Seabees that was mutually beneficial for all involved. The Army pilots had whiskey and beer and the Seabees had access to heavy equipment and tons of supplies. It was a perfect match. Supplies that couldn't be acquired from their own stocks or from the alcohol-starved Seabees were obtained by means colorfully called, "moonlight requisition."

The Army flyers put up a few tents, but the importance of their foxholes was reinforced when nightfall came and the skies on the southern half of the island were filled with tracers, machine gun, and rifle fire. Someone jogging through the compound said a large group of Japanese had emerged from caves in Mount Suribachi and were trying to fight their way north. Nobody knew for sure, and it seemed crazy to climb from a safe hole and try and find out. Lieutenant Paul Chism of the 78th Fighter Squadron recalled taking refuge under the tracks of a large bulldozer. The fact that the bulldozer was an International Harvester was a bit disappointing to Chism because he'd worked for Caterpillar Tractor Company before the war. But he found even the competitor's brand of machinery seemed to stop bullets just the same.

Later, the airmen learned that a pair of bored Americans (some said Marines, some said Army soldiers) had started the false rumor that Germany had surrendered. The gunfire that thundered all over the island had all come from American weapons—including anti-aircraft artillery. "Flak was so dense that the AW [Air Warning] radar unit on the summit of Suribachi had to go off the air. Planes on landing approaches were hung up off the island," wrote an Army reporter.[70] Several men were seriously wounded in the wild celebration. Finally, the desperate island command announced an air-raid alert to get everyone back into their holes. "Although the celebrants began firing with good intentions," wrote the 15th's historian, "it developed into tragical results."[71]

Combat cameramen were amazed to find the entire fuselage of a Japanese Betty bomber buried 12 feet underground on Iwo Jima. They wrote, "Presumably the Japs who cooked up the idea in the first place used to sit in the hatch, look at the latest raid on Iwo, then stumble downstairs and get off another communiqué to the Emperor informing him that Iwo's gallant defenders had just repulsed another attempt." Now, it made a comfortable and safe place for the lens men to call home. (Arvid Johnson via the 7th Fighter Command Association)

CHICHI JIMA

In the air, the three squadrons of the 15th fell into an ambitious routine of flying air strikes on one day, combat air patrol the next, and maintenance on the third. As the pockets of resistance grew smaller and smaller on Iwo Jima, aircraft attacks could no longer be employed without the risk of hitting Marines. The Mustang squadrons promptly turned their attention to the islands to the north. Haha Jima was 120 miles away, and Chichi Jima was less than 30 miles farther north. On their designated "attack day," if there was nothing happening on Iwo Jima, a Mustang squadron would load up and fly north.

The sprawling, rocky island of Chichi Jima became a target for the marauding Mustangs once the fighting on Iwo Jima was in hand. Approximately 150 miles from Iwo, the island was an outpost for the Japanese with a radio and radar stations, an airfield, and a port facility. (U.S. Army Air Forces via National Archives)

Besides Iwo Jima, Chichi Jima garnered the most attention from the Americans because of its deepwater port (Futami Harbor), a seaplane base, docks, barracks, and Susaki Airfield. Planes moving down from the Japanese Empire could easily be staged there and fly in to attack Iwo Jima under cover of darkness.

Pilots of the 15th Fighter Group, 47th Fighter Squadron gather for the camera before their first attack on Chichi Jima on 11 March 1945. Though they called the bombing raid "lots of fun" when it was over, most understandably look a bit nervous in this pre-mission image. (U.S. Army Air Forces via National Archives)

Another concern on Chichi Jima was the radio and radar installations. If left unmolested, the Japanese on Chichi could warn of B-29 attacks as the formations of bombers passed overhead.

The 47th Squadron made the first strike on Chichi Jima on 11 March. Each of the 17 Mustangs carried two 500-pound bombs. Over the target, the American planes swooped low, holed the airfield, shot up buildings, and a cargo plane. They also went after ships anchored nearby. On the way back, they stopped by Haha Jima and hammered away at the two villages on the island with their .50-calibers. The planes collected a few small holes from anti-aircraft, but the mission report said, "All pilots agreed was lots of fun." [sic][72]

The 45th Squadron went north the next day and laid their bombs on Haha Jima. This time, the Mustangs collected a bit more damage, but again, everyone returned to Iwo Jima safely. The next day the target was again Chichi Jima, flown by the third squadron, the 78th. All of the planes came back unharmed.

On 26 March, the 15th Fighter Group's luck finally ran out. Lieutenant John Shuler was hit during a strafing run over Chichi Jima. With his plane losing oil pressure and coolant, he managed to pull up to 4,000 feet and set a course for Iwo Jima. But soon it became apparent that his plane wasn't going to make it back. Smoke filled the cockpit and Shuler was forced to roll his Mustang over and bail out about 10 miles south of Chichi.

While Shuler parachuted into the water, he disappeared before anyone could get to him. Later, a Navy destroyer found only his life jacket, with its straps broken, floating in the waves. The flyer was the first combat casualty of the 15th since arriving at Iwo Jima.

P-51 pilot Lieutenant Gordon Scott recalls Chichi Jima as a frustrating place, where the marauding Mustangs would often draw fire from upwards of 60 machine guns and 90 automatic weapons. It was a senseless little outpost that claimed the lives of many of his comrades. "They'd have a bunch of derelict Betty bombers up on stilts," says Scott. "We'd go up

Weapons and Fuel

The farther Iwo Jima's Mustangs roamed from their base, the less weaponry and more fuel they needed to carry. "The Jimas" were close enough to be on the receiving end of heavy bombs from the P-51s, but the long flight to mainland Japan was another matter. During the early missions, pilots said it seemed like a shame to travel 1,400 miles over seven or eight hours only to pull the trigger on their machine guns for a few seconds. Over time, larger fuel external tanks were put into service and the Mustangs could carry a load of rockets to Japan as well.

The fighters certainly couldn't carry a large amount of armament to Japan, but they could be a bit more precise with their big brother bombers. Flying low and fast, a Mustang pilot could pick out a lone Zero fighter hidden under camouflage netting and eliminate it from the Japanese inventory in one pass—something B-29 bombers could rarely do from high aloft.

External fuel tanks—"drop tanks"—were used to extend the range of the P-51 Mustang. The tanks pictured here hold 110 gallons. When approaching a ground target or encountering enemy aircraft, the tanks could be jettisoned, leaving the Mustang aerodynamically clean. (U.S. Army Air Forces via National Archives)

Left: *A pair of 500-pound bombs could be installed, one under each wing, for short trips. Mustang pilots dropped them in support of the Marines at the far end of Iwo and carried them north to attack "the Jimas." Here, an armorer tightens the sway brace to keep the bomb from oscillating during flight. (U.S. Army Air Forces via National Archives)*

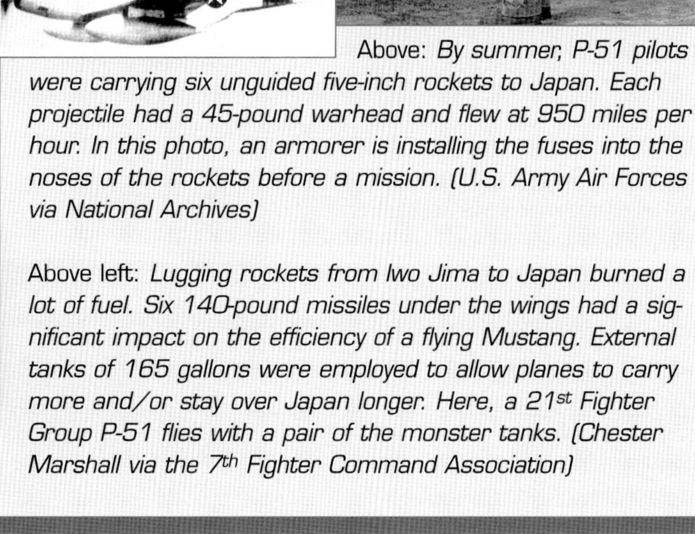

Right: *Ground crewmen reload a 15th Fighter Group P-51 after an attack mission on the north end of the island in March 1945. The Mustang's six .50-caliber machine gun usually fired around 550 bullets a minute, each traveling at 2,900 feet per second. (U.S. Army Air Forces via National Archives)*

Above: *By summer, P-51 pilots were carrying six unguided five-inch rockets to Japan. Each projectile had a 45-pound warhead and flew at 950 miles per hour. In this photo, an armorer is installing the fuses into the noses of the rockets before a mission. (U.S. Army Air Forces via National Archives)*

Above left: *Lugging rockets from Iwo Jima to Japan burned a lot of fuel. Six 140-pound missiles under the wings had a significant impact on the efficiency of a flying Mustang. External tanks of 165 gallons were employed to allow planes to carry more and/or stay over Japan longer. Here, a 21st Fighter Group P-51 flies with a pair of the monster tanks. (Chester Marshall via the 7th Fighter Command Association)*

and shoot at them and they'd blow up. The Japanese would have traps of explosives,"—bombs set to be touched off as a Mustang raced in to strafe at low level.[73] One booby-trap blast claimed the life of Lieutenant Lee Bargaehar on 31 March. After flying through the explosion, Bargaehar's P-51 hit the ground at more than 400 miles per hour and tumbled into a fireball.

Most frustrating of all seemed to be Chichi Jima's radio station and antenna. The radio system weathered numerous attacks by the Mustangs and Navy carrier planes and came through virtually unscathed. "It's still there today," the pilots say.[74]

By June of 1945, one fighter group would report that, "It was becoming embarrassingly obvious that the tactical significance of the bombs that were plowing up the ground on Chichi, Ani, and Haha, or killing the fish in Futami harbor was exceedingly dubious."[75]

But that was months away. In March, as the 15th's pilots took off day after day from airfield number one to risk their hides over "the Jimas," many of them would dip their left wing and crane their necks to check on the progress being made on improving air field number two. Slated for another P-51 group, the field's completion would mean a bit more rest and relaxation for the flyers and a break in their hectic and dangerous schedule.

THE *BANZAI* ATTACK

The 21st Fighter Group's complement of Mustangs began arriving at airfield number two on 23 March. With the fighting well to the northern end of Iwo Jima, the flyers of the 21st laughed at the men of the 15th—still clutching their rifles and huddled in deep holes every night. The new airman proudly announced that they were moving directly into tents. They set up camp near the western shoreline, northeast of the 15th, nearby airfield number two.

Under a cover of darkness in the early morning hours of 26 March, approximately 300 Japanese soldiers from various units joined for a final attack directed at the hated American airmen. They emerged from their caves and tunnels and moved down the island's western shore. Their assault couldn't have been better timed—the Marines were on their way out and Army infantry units were moving in to replace them. Also, because of an air raid, the star shells that normally illuminated the night landscape had stopped falling. In the darkness, the Japanese slipped into the loosely guarded compound.

Near the tents of the 21st, only a few men were out of bed—moving through the area to wake pilots and crew chiefs for combat air patrol over the island scheduled for dawn. Soon, Iwo Jima's usual din of gunfire built to a thunderous roar, with small mortars bursting, grenades exploding, and the crackle of hundreds of rifles.

Men of the 21st Fighter Group celebrate one of their first meals in a war zone near Iwo Jima's northwest shore. Appropriately, a pyramidal style tent stands in the background. The group moved straight into tents, passing on the idea of digging foxholes in Iwo's tricky sand. In the dark hours after this photo was taken, the men of the 21st would find out that Iwo Jima was not so secure. (Jim Van Nada via the 7th Fighter Command Association)

The day before the *banzai* attack, the 21st Fighter Group's beautiful new P-51 Mustangs stand in rows near on airfield number two. All 21st aircraft were marked with a horizontal stripe on the vertical stabilizer, wings, and tail tips. The three fighter squadrons within the 21st Fighter Group had different colors—blue (46th Fighter Squadron), yellow (72nd Fighter Squadron), and white (531st Fighter Squadron). The aircraft in the foreground of this image are 531st Mustangs. (Military History Institute/Crossley Collection)

The 21st Fighter Group's officer's area was the center of the fighting when Japanese soldiers slipped through the lines and launched an early morning attack on the camps near airfield number two. Interestingly, the angular shape of the tents tended to shed the grenades thrown into the area and lessen their effectiveness. (U.S. Army Air Forces via National Archives)

Japanese soldiers methodically walked down the rows of tents, carved long slices in the canvas with swords, and tossed in hissing grenades. A whizzing shrapnel fragment clanked against Captain Harry Crim's mess kit as it was hanging on the central pole of his pyramidal tent. He asked his tentmate, "What the hell are you doing stumbling around in the dark?" The other pilot answered, "I'm in bed not doing anything."[76]

All over the compound, men in blackened tents lunged for their clothes and their .45-caliber pistols. A few of the lucky pilots had bartered with the departing Marines and now "owned" M-1 rifles.

Major Lloyd Whitley, one of the pilots due to fly that morning, was awake and dressed when the attack came. He scrounged a rifle from a nearby truck and fired into the shadows at the onrushing Japanese troops. As he aimed, a rifle bullet hit him in the throat, killing him instantly.

At a guard post on the northwest side of the compound—more of a hole than anything else—a grenade dropped in, killing one man and wounding two others. The soldiers in the northeastern post saw a Japanese soldier come sprinting out of the darkness and flop down just 10 feet away. Two of the Americans jumped up and ran. The third man, Corporal Carlton Bailey, was hit by bullet fragments in the neck, chest, arms, and legs. He later estimated the Japanese threw nearly 50 grenades in his direction, trying to get one to drop cleanly into his hole. At one point, an enemy soldier crawled into the

Posing in a hole slashed in a tent by a sword-wielding Japanese attacker, enlisted men of the 549th Night Fighter Squadron mug for the camera. The men are credited with killing eight of the enemy during the chaotic morning on 26 March. Sergeant Harry Hamilton can be seen at the top of the slit. (U.S. Army Air Forces via National Archives)

hole beside him. Bailey played dead. The blood from his wounds must have looked convincing enough because the Japanese rifleman ignored Bailey and soon moved on to another part of the compound.

Several grenades were thrown into the tent of Lieutenant Walter Miller. There were six men housed in the five-man tent but one was already gone—up early for the flight. Of the remaining five, two were killed outright and Miller and the other two men were seriously injured. Groans from the wounded pilots attracted the attention of the Japanese. They burst in and slashed the throats of Miller's tentmates with their sabers.

The horrified pilot was able to roll behind his bunk and feign death as the Japanese officers set up a makeshift command post in his tent. During the next three hours, Miller bled from his wounds and stared at his service pistol, which was lying on the ground just beyond his reach.

Elsewhere, men pulled together B-4 bags, water cans, and duffle bags to construct firing positions within their own tents. Others quickly scooped holes in their sand-covered floors and climbed in. The four flyers in Lieutenant John Galbraith's tent each covered a canvas sidewall—one in the back and one on each side. Galbraith himself hefted three sandbags, a flight bag, and a metal water can into the front doorway and waited with his carbine.

"It was starting to get light," he related. "I saw two Jap officers brandishing huge Samurai swords over their heads, walk up to a tent, two over from mine. Before I could fire they had slashed long rents clear to the ground in the canvas side."[77] Galbraith and his men fired on the Japanese. They

Men come to look at the carnage surrounding the 21st officer's tents on the late morning of 26 March. Two dead Japanese soldiers lie just outside this tent's entrance. Another enemy fighter was killed just inside the doorway. His body can barely be seen in the shadows on the floor of the tent. (U.S. Army Air Forces via National Archives)

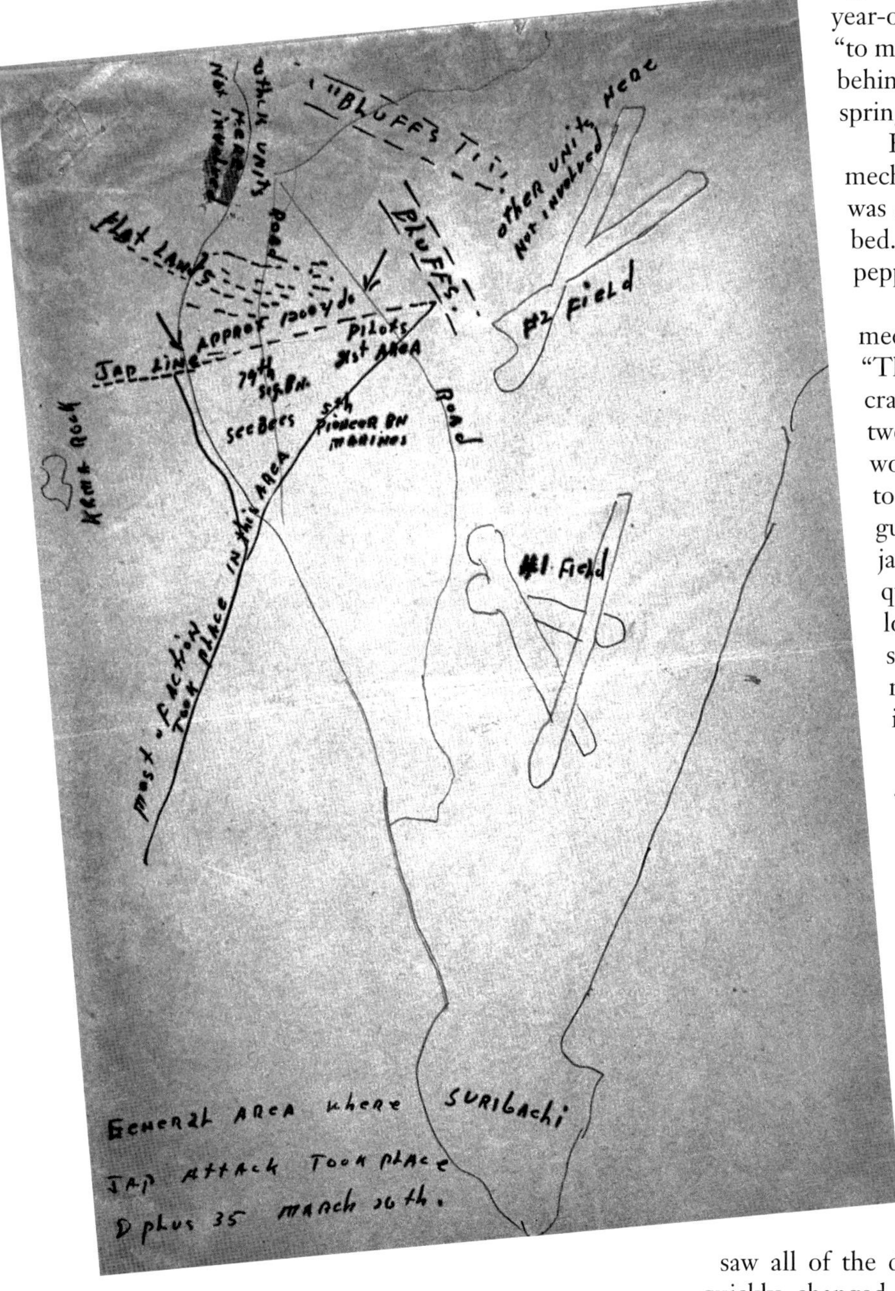

A map drawn by a soldier who was there shows the wedge of Iwo Jima where most of the fighting took place on the morning of 26 March. The location of units, including the 21st Fighter Group, "Seabees," 79th Signal Battalion, and 5th Marines Pioneer Battalion are designated, relative to the battle area. (U.S. Army Air Forces via National Archives)

both went down, one of them fell through the hole he had just sliced in the side of the tent.

Three more Japanese soldiers walked between shell holes as Galbraith watched from about 20 yards away. He waited until they were together and in the open and then rapid-fired a group of shots at them. They fell, but the 22-year-old Mustang pilot shot each of them again, "to make sure they were dead." Then he hunched behind his makeshift battlement and waited to spring his trap once again.

Elsewhere, Sergeant Harry Hamilton, a mechanic for the 549th Night Fighter Squadron, was awakened when a grenade blew him out of bed. Rifle barrels poked into his tent and bullets peppered the room at waist level.

Hamilton gagged a wounded fellow mechanic for fear he would attract attention. "There was no time to be gentle," he said.[78] He crawled to the south end of the tent and saw two Japanese soldiers talking to a fatally wounded comrade. Hamilton put his carbine to his shoulder and pulled the trigger. The gun jammed. He grabbed another one and it jammed too. As the pair of Japanese troopers quickly ran from the area, Hamilton cussed loudly. The dying soldier outside the tent stirred. "Don't talk like that," the Japanese man surprisingly exclaimed, in English. "It isn't nice."[79]

In another direction, a group of Japanese soldiers were crawling up to Hamilton's tent. He fired at an officer who raised to his knees to toss a grenade. The man fell, dropped the grenade, and it exploded. The other Japanese soldiers laughed loudly, as if this was all some big joke. "It was cockeyed. The whole affair," Hamilton later said.[80]

Meanwhile, Lieutenant Galbraith still defended his area with ruthless efficiency. Two more Japanese had fallen from his bullets. "One was wearing large horn-rimmed spectacles and looked exceedingly scholarly," observed Galbraith.[81] A third came by and when he saw all of the dead soldiers sprawled around the tent, he quickly changed direction. Galbraith fired blindly at him through the canvas.

"Then one tall Jap... at least six feet two... walked up to the entrance to the tent next to mine about 15 feet away." Galbraith took him down with three bullets. "The big Jap was followed by a regular issue Jap," he said later.[82] Galbraith killed him just the same.

Around the compound, those who could walk made a break towards the south, sometimes dragging their wounded buddies. The injured men were treated in a bulldozed depression that was being used as a garbage pit. Though many of the men were barefoot, none of them complained as they walked over the piles of discarded cans—they considered themselves lucky to be alive. The AAF flight surgeons, used to

The bodies of Japanese soldiers killed in the attack were thrown into a pit bulldozed later that morning. One captured man claimed that General Kuribayashi, the commander of Iwo Jima's defenders, was among those killed in the attack, but the General's body was never identified. (The 7th Fighter Command Association)

Lieutenant Joseph Coons compares a Japanese grenade (right) with an American one after the *banzai* raid. The Japanese soldiers who attacked Iwo's northwest camps had scavenged a large assortment of U.S. government-issue equipment, including grenades, rifles, clothing, and even a bazooka. (U.S. Army Air Forces via National Archives)

treating nothing more than earaches and sore throats, really had their hands full now.

At 0630, a captain named Monroe and five or six of his men from the 5th Marine Battalion joined the flyers. Under his direction, the ragtag group of pilots, mechanics, Seabees, anti-aircraft men, Marines, and others formed a skirmish line and began to push back through the encampment.

Moving slowly, they evacuated the wounded and fought the Japanese soldiers they found along the way. The veteran Marine captain that appeared from nowhere became a standout personality among the flyers as he led the charge. "Captain Monroe," the 21st Fighter Group's historian would later report, "jumping aside a few feet as a grenade would land near him, would laugh loudly when it exploded and he wasn't hurt. As one of his men, a Sergeant Wilson, got hit in the leg with fragments, he yelled, 'Not you, Wilson, you lucky devil! Now you get to go back to the States.' [It] was the greatest performance of Marineism, if there is such a thing, which probably any of these P-51 Air Corps men will ever see." [83]

The Army's 147th Infantry Regiment and a tank with a flamethrower appeared around 0800, but by then the battle was all but over. The tank rumbled through the compound, torching tents suspected of having Japanese inside and machine-gunning those who ran.

In the daylight, the Americans counted 262 Japanese bodies, many with American M-1 rifles, Browning automatic rifles, carbines, grenades, and Marine-issue field jackets—even a bazooka. Many dead soldiers had bandaged wounds, partly healed, from earlier fighting in the weeks before. One prisoner told the Americans that Lieutenant General Kuribayashi, the Japanese commander of Iwo Jima, was among those killed in the battle, though his body was never identified. "The statement, being that of a prisoner of war," wrote the 21st's historian, "cannot be accepted as fact."[84]

Lieutenant Miller's tent was spared from the flamethrower. He was soon discovered and rushed to the hospital. Lieutenant Galbraith, who had defended his doorway all morning, sustained injuries from grenade fragments in the final phases of the attack and was briefly in the hospital as well.

Sergeant Hamilton wanted more than anything to get his hands on a Samurai sword. When things cooled down, he ran out to retrieve the one from the officer he'd killed, but found he was too late. "Some souvenir hunter had got there ahead of me."[85]

Americans from many units were affected by the attack. Pilots, Seabees, mechanics, signalmen, gunners, Marines, and infantrymen were among the injured or killed. The hardest hit was the 21st Fighter Group, with 15 men killed and 50 wounded. They began to refer to themselves as "the most Purple-Hearted group in the Pacific."

"The most distressing sight of all," wrote the 21st's historian, "was a small brown and white Cocker Spaniel named 'Frisco' that belonged to Major Whitley. His favorite pastime had been that of grabbing Major Whitley's pants leg as he walked along. Frisco couldn't understand why the Major wouldn't get up and play when he tugged on the blanket covering the killed pilot. The dog was finally tied up."[86]

Even though a full-fledged battle went on outside his tent door, Sergeant Harry Hamilton could think of nothing other than getting his hands on a Japanese officer's Samurai sword. He didn't have any luck. The lad in this photo was more successful. Captain Raymond Kessler retrieved a coveted saber the hard way—he killed the Japanese officer using it to slice into his tent. (Sam Smith via the 7th Fighter Command Association)

The 21st was one of very few Army Air Force units to fight in a land battle during the war. The pilots half-jokingly asked about getting infantryman's pay along with their flight pay. As the sun rose on 26 March, the Americans gathered the bodies of the Japanese and buried them in a pit. Though Admiral Nimitz had announced the end of organized resistance on Iwo Jima days before, it was on this day that Major General Harry Schmidt, Commander of the Fifth Amphibious Corps, declared the Iwo Jima operation complete and ended the Marine Corps' combat presence on the island.

The brass may have declared Iwo Jima safe, but the men of the 21st knew better. They set about creating a new living area about 200 feet from their old one—with "de-luxe foxholes." "No infantry was better prepared for an attack than our camp," wrote Captain Harry Crim. "Everyone had a hole. It seemed that six feet was about minimum depth. Our camp bristled with weapons of all kinds and no one slept much the next few nights."[87]

CHAPTER 7

VERY LONG RANGE

A flyer trudges to his Mustang loaded down with 85 pounds of gear, including helmet, goggles, gloves, parachute, life vest, survival seat pack, and raft. (U.S. Army Air Forces via National Archives)

Lieutenant Clyde Decker sits in the cockpit of a North American P-51 Mustang. Pilots spent hour after hour in these cramped surroundings on a typical mission to Japan. The strap around Decker's neck holds a throat microphone. (U.S. Army Air Forces via National Archives)

Around trip flight from Iwo Jima's airfields to landfall near Tokyo covered more than 1,400 miles—farther than a flight from London to Berlin and back. And, unlike flying the European runs, the Iwo to Tokyo route had hardly anything but vast ocean in between. To prepare themselves for escorting B-29s on the VLR (Very Long Range) missions ahead, the P-51 pilots of the 15th and 21st Fighter Groups decided to fly a practice mission of approximately the same distance, but in the opposite direction. During the flight, the pilots would study navigational problems, gas consumption, weather conditions, and fatigue.

On 30 March 1945, the mock target for the day was Saipan, and 90 Mustangs of the two groups were scheduled to participate. After briefing, the flyers rode out to their planes, settled into their cockpits and strapped in for the long haul.

Trouble started almost immediately. A Mustang's engine cut out on takeoff and another accidentally dropped an external fuel tank. More pilots once airborne discovered disappointing readings from their gauges, including low fuel and oil pressures, and immediately turned back to Iwo Jima to land.

On a normal VLR mission, an additional group of "spare" P-51 pilots would wake, dress, and attend the briefings along with those men actually slated to fly the mission. They would take off too, alongside the mission aircraft. As flyers dropped from position with mechanical problems, spares would pull into place to fill the formations.

But on this practice sortie, the ranks of fighters were already shrinking as the Mustangs climbed to link up with the navigational B-29s orbiting nearby. Small groups of Marianas-based Superfortress aircraft and their crews were assigned on a

Navigational bombers were assigned on a rotational basis from the Mariana Island's bomb groups to Iwo Jima's fighter. Here, a navigation B-29, *Joltin' Josie* from the 498th Bomb Group, leads six flights of 15th Fighter Group Mustangs over endless miles of ocean. (U.S. Army Air Forces via National Archives)

rotational basis to the fighters on Iwo Jima. They served as navigators to lead the fighters to the target and back.

Once they were in loose formation behind the bombers, the flyers endured hours of boredom while the hot sun beat down on their cockpits. For maximum gas mileage, the pilots maintained high manifold pressure and low RPMs, which was murder on their engines. About once an hour, the Mustangs would speed up and pull ahead of the B-29s, burning away the carbon deposits that developed on their spark plugs. They would then circle around and rejoin the bombers in trail.

The fighters carried two 110-gallon external drop tanks, an internal 85-gallon fuselage tank, and two internal 92-gallon wing tanks. During taxi and takeoff, pilots used fuel from the fuselage tank. Once in the air, the Mustang flyers commonly continued to burn the gasoline in the fuselage tank because the aircraft performed badly when it was full. When 40 or so gallons remained in that tank and the Mustang's center of gravity was more manageable, the flyers switched to their drop tanks. Nearing the target, they jettisoned the external tanks and returned to the fuselage tank.

When the aircraft arrived at their designated rally point, the navigational bombers, and commonly four escort P-51s acting as guards, circled and waited as the Mustangs continued to the target. While over enemy territory, (or in this case, Saipan) when the fuel ran dry in the fuselage tank, it was the signal to return to the orbiting navigational bombers and then back to Agate Base—the radio call sign for Iwo Jima.

Pilots communicated on a number of channels, each with a code name. The A button, "Channel Mike," provided fighter-to-fighter communications. B, or "Channel Nan" was reserved for discussions with the navigator B-29s. "Channel Queen," the C button, was the frequency for air-sea rescue. "Channel Item," the D button, was used for automatic direction finder homing.

On the practice mission, many of the pilots nursing various types of mechanical difficulties radioed they had decided to land at Saipan instead of risking 750 more miles of open sea. All in all, the practice run was a disappointment. A little less than half the Mustangs returned to Iwo Jima without problems.

THE FIRST VLR MISSION

For the most part, the press seemed to avoid Iwo Jima, if they could. But on 7 April, the whole island seemed to be crawling with civilian war correspondents, photographers, and Army reporters from *Yank* and *Brief* magazines. They were hammering out stories with headlines like "First Army Fighters Over Japan," and "Longest Over-water Escort Flight of Record." Some wrote that Iwo Jima's airmen, formerly based in Hawaii, were going north to avenge the surprise attack on Pearl Harbor.

For the flyers, it was a day more about anxiousness and excitement than revenge. As the sun came up, more than 100 Mustangs of the 15th and 21st Fighter Groups were waiting, tuned, waxed for speed, and loaded down with fuel and ammo.

Outside a battered Japanese bunker turned Operations Office, a newsman records the thoughts of a Mustang pilot for the Army's "Interview Hour." Often, the press avoided Iwo Jima—if they could. (U.S. Army Air Forces via National Archives)

Iwo's Mustang flyers pause for a smoke amid preparations for the inaugural VLR (Very Long Range) mission to Japan. On 7 April 1945, the P-51s joined AAF B-29 Superfortress bombers for the first time near Tokyo. (U.S. Army Air Forces via National Archives)

The most experienced pilots—those with 600 to 700 hours in fighters—had been chosen for this first big run to the Empire.

Minutes before 0700, the fighters took off on their historic first mission—a month and a day after the first Mustangs had set down at Iwo Jima's primitive number one airfield. More than 90 fighters massed north of the island and joined in long strings behind three navigational B-29s.

With heavy hearts, some the men were forced to turn back to Agate Base with mechanical problems. Among them was General Ernest "Mickey" Moore, commander of the 7th Fighter Command. He found that he had a malfunctioning gas selector switch. Anxious reserve pilots happily filled the holes in the formation. One spare pilot, Lieutenant Charles Heil of the 15th Fighter Group, raced over the ocean alone, hoping to catch up with the main formations. He located some B-29s near Japan, but the puzzled flyer never saw another American fighter during the entire mission.

Near Tokyo, the main force of Mustangs (with Heil nowhere in sight) rendezvoused with 103 Boeing B-29s of the 73rd Bomb Wing. "During this first mission," recalls the 15th Fighter Group's Major James Tapp, "[the bombers] formed into one large formation, which we never saw again, and headed up the coast."[88] The Mustangs joined up, with the 15th out in front and the 21st covering the flanks. The day was clear and Mount Fuji could be seen off to the left as the Americans made their way northeast into the Tokyo area. After hours of perfect radio silence, one flyer could stand it no more. A single word—"Fujiyama!"—buzzed through everyone's earphones.

At 1045, the Mustangs dropped their external tanks and readied themselves for combat. Soon after, Lieutenant Robert Anderson's 21st Fighter Group Mustang heeled over and dove away, trailing a ribbon of flames and smoke. No one was sure what went wrong—a one-in-a-million anti-aircraft blast, or a catastrophic fuel malfunction. There was nothing the other pilots could do but keep going.

The first enemy plane they spotted was a twin-engine Nick, flying low over Tokyo Bay. The Mustang pilots prudently ignored the single Japanese fighter, figuring it was a ruse to draw the American planes low and separate them from the bombers.

They guessed right. Shortly, a mass of contrails developed high above. Japanese aircraft of almost every variety started down, converging on the lead bombers. The Mustangs pointed their noses up to meet them and the fight was on.

Major Tapp spotted a diving Nick and "poured on the coals" to catch him before the enemy fighter got close to the bombers. His flight of speeding Mustangs gained ground quickly and, "I didn't realize how fast I was going to catch him," said Tapp. "I didn't get as much 'time on target' as I would have liked."[89] As his P-51 roared by, he sprayed the fuselage of the Japanese plane with machine gun fire, switched to the right engine at the last second, and set it ablaze.

As soon as Tapp zoomed into a patch of clear air, he spotted a Tony three miles ahead. Approaching from 20 degrees off his tail, "and slower this time," Tapp figured later that the pilot of the small angular Japanese fighter never saw him coming. When Tapp got close enough, he began to fire. The .50-calibers of the American fighters were loaded with a

Shot from an American aircraft in mid-1945, Mount Fuji stands as a majestic symbol of the Japanese Empire. On a more practical level, American pilots used the 3,776-meter dormant volcano as an unmistakable navigational waypoint. (U.S. Navy via Linda Young)

Major James Tapp, sitting in the cockpit of his Mustang, *Margaret IV.* Tapp learned to fly in the Civilian Pilot Training program and entered cadet school in 1941. He flew nearly every Army fighter in the Pacific—P-36, P-40, P-39, P-47, and P-38—before arriving at Iwo to fly P-51s with the 15th Fighter Group. He told reporters, "A fighter pilot is similar to an athlete. He must continually keep training." He became the Army's first ace over Japan. (Chester Marshall via the 7th Fighter Command Association)

The first time some American pilots encountered a Kawasaki Ki-61 in the air, they reported seeing a German or Italian-designed fighter. But the plane, code-named Tony, was a Japanese creation with a license-built Daimler-Benz engine. The Tony was heavily armed and well armored compared to many Japanese fighters. (U.S. Army Air Forces via National Archives)

mixture of armor piercing, armor piercing incendiary, and incendiary bullets, plus some tracer ammunition. As Tapp's guns blasted away, "I saw incendiary flashes immediately and he burst into flame."[90]

As he passed over the top of the burning Tony, Tapp skewed his Mustang sideways and looked down into the cockpit of the stricken craft. He caught a brief glimpse of the Tony's pilot, "still kind of sitting there in the flames."[91] The number four man in Tapp's flight, trailing somewhat farther back, said that the Tony pilot finally jumped but it was too late. Fire had destroyed his parachute. There was nothing the pilot of the fourth Mustang could do but take a gun camera image of the doomed Japanese flyer as he fell.

Searching for another target, Tapp spotted a Dinah flying head-on toward the B-29s and gave chase. Approaching at nearly 90-degrees, Tapp's charging Mustang inexplicably switched into low blower almost the same second he started firing. It had the effect of putting on speed brakes and the Dinah pulled ahead of him into the formation of bombers.

Major Tapp knew that it was suicide to chase the plane in among the trigger-happy Superfortress formation, so he broke away. Looking downward, Tapp saw a lone B-29 at 17,000 feet, moving away from the group with its number two engine burning. Attacking the bomber was a bare metal Oscar fighter. Tapp spiraled down and curved in behind the Japanese army fighter firing all the way.

The Japanese plane didn't burn, but pieces started flying off in all directions as Tapp hammered away and closed to only a few feet. Later, Tapp's mechanics found large scuffs on his canopy, engine cowl, and a piece of the Oscar's bullet-proof glass wedged in his Mustang's wing root fairing. After the Oscar spun toward the earth, Tapp looked up and saw that the wing had burned off the stricken B-29, and the giant silver bomber was also plunging to the ground.

Scanning the sky, Tapp's eyes settled on six barely discernable specks. In only a few seconds, the specks materialized into four Japanese Zeros and two George fighters coming in fast from head-on. Tapp picked out one of the George fighters and began to fire much earlier than usual because of the high closing speed. It was hard to tell if he was hitting the plane or not. At one point, Tapp said that he saw flashes on the enemy fighter's wing, much farther out than where its guns were located, and figured some of his bullets were hitting home.

The opposing fighters raced past and Tapp turned in his cockpit to keep the Georges in sight. As the Japanese fighter that Tapp had attacked went into a hard left turn, the plane's wing tore completely off, and the fighter dropped from sight.

Tapp's Mustangs were headed back for more when his wingman called to say that his fuselage tank had run dry—the mandatory signal to break off and head to the rally point. After the Mustangs had trickled into the area, a quick head count amazingly revealed only one plane missing (Anderson's). The formation turned toward Iwo Jima.

One flyer knew he would never make it back to Agate Base. Lieutenant Frank Ayres of the 15th Fighter Group only had to look at the sinking needles on his gas gauges to see that returning home was now out of the question. Setting his power for maximum range, an escorting B-29 flew with Ayres until his fuel was virtually gone—still about 200 miles north of the island. Ayres dropped his Mustang through the overcast, hoping to catch a glimpse of a rescue ship in the area, code-named Warcloud, before he bailed out. Warcloud was the destroyer USS *Cassin*.

Pilot Lieutenant Gerhard Rettberg fills out a report on the wing of his Mustang after the first VLR to Japan. Rettberg was a reserve flyer on the mission, returning home after flying about 250 miles from Agate Base on 7 April 1945. (U.S. Army Air Forces via National Archives)

Almost miraculously, Ayres let down through the clouds right on top of the American ship. He climbed back above for additional height and jumped from the cockpit. Some time later, Warcloud radioed Agate Base to say that Ayres was safely plucked from the sea.

Back on Iwo Jima, the Mustangs began arriving after more than seven hours and 30 minutes in the air. Some men who climbed from their cramped cockpits were hardly able to walk. The pilots quickly developed a name for the temporary malady: "butt sprung."

Iwo Jima lost two Mustangs and one pilot. Three B-29s failed to come home. The fighters from Agate Base claimed 21 Japanese fighters destroyed, led by Major Tapp's four confirmed victories. Iwo's fighter pilots also claimed six probable shoot-downs and six others damaged.

Even the lost and lonely Lieutenant Charles Heil came back home. As he climbed down from his wing he fumed, "Where the heck *was* everybody?" He found that he was the only Mustang in the sky because he had stumbled across the wrong group of B-29s near Japan. While Iwo Jima's Mustangs went to Tokyo, Heil made a historic flight to Nagoya—single-handedly flying top cover for another group of 153 bombers! "I thought I would be in for a real calling down," said Heil. "So far nobody has got mad at me!"[92]

IWO MUSTANG MYTHS

The P-51 pilots and their sleek fighters evoked many emotions in the soldiers that populated the Pacific Theater. One B-29 tail gunner recalled encountering the planes on one of his many missions to Japan and wrote, "They were a happy-go-lucky group in their swift steeds, and I envied them."[93]

Sometimes, people's imaginations got the best of them and they generated stories about the flyers that perhaps had little basis in reality. The same B-29 crewman stated that on one occasion, when the fighters pulled near the tail of his B-29, that all of them were wearing different types of hats. "One had on a cowboy hat, another a derby, and another a straw hat."[94]

Is that a Panama hat on the head of the pilot in this 21st Fighter Group Mustang? With the reflection of the sun on the plane's canopy, it's difficult to tell for certain. (330th Bomb Group/Stephen Smisek via the 7th Fighter Command Association)

Another B-29 flyer commented that many of the Mustang pilots carried handwritten signs in their cockpits. A lost P-51 would locate a bomber and gingerly approach, making sure as to give the gunners plenty of time to identify him as a friendly fighter. When the Mustang pilot felt safe, he'd pull in close to the bombers and press his message, pre-written on cardboard, up against the side of his canopy saying, "Please take me to Iwo." The airmen in the heavy bombers often joked that the fighter pilots had a bit of trouble with navigating.

Another Superfortress flyer said that the Mustangs would sometimes fly upside down, perhaps were bored on the long flight home or wanted few moment's relief after hour upon hour sitting in their cramped cockpits. The fighter pilots say this was not true. Staying inverted for longer than a few moments might be disastrous to the health of a Mustang's Merlin engine. Oil starvation was not something to be taken lightly when a flyer was hours from the nearest land.

Perhaps one of the most outrageous stories about the Mustang pilots was told by a member of the Signal Corps based on Iwo Jima. His unit was situated near airfield number one and he often went over to watch movies at the 15th Fighter Group's outdoor theater. Along with the feature, the soldier claimed that the film technician would show some of the fighter pilot's gun camera film from previous missions. More often than not, there was very little air combat. It was mostly images of strafing runs on airfields, trains, buildings, and shipping.

One evening, this soldier claims, a strange bit of footage was shown (and it has never been seen since). As the scene opened, a rural Japanese countryside could be seen. The Mustang fighter taking the footage, slowed, dropped down, and *landed* on a dusty dirt road. Then, the pilot jogged out in front of his airplane, turned, and with Mount Fuji in the background, stood at attention and smartly saluted the camera! The Signal Corps member says that after the film was shown, someone in the back of the packed house sarcastically asked, "Is that all?"

Absolute nonsense, the Mustang pilots say. To have the gun camera rolling, a pilot needed to have his finger on the trigger or, at least toggle the camera independently of the guns. Also, they argue, the P-51 Mustang is a tail-dragger. Any footage taken from a P-51 on the ground would show little more than the sky over Japan.

APRIL'S MISSIONS

The second VLR, on 12 April, was a repeat of the first, but many more problems made themselves known. Some planes wasted too much fuel on the ground, took off late, and had to return. A force of 82 made it to the Tokyo area only to find the B-29s late and in a long, loose formation. The bomber's gunners shot at not only the 80 Japanese planes that closed in to attack them, but also the escorting Mustangs.

A Mitsubishi J2M fighter begins to disintegrate under the gunfire of a 15th Fighter Group Mustang near Atsugi Airfield on 19 April. The Japanese fighter was code-named Jack by the Allies. (U.S. Army Air Forces via National Archives)

Lieutenant William Savidge, Jr. of the 21st Fighter Group shows off his new jacket on airfield number two. Iwo Jima's flyers were proud of being the first Army fighter pilots over Japan, and the design shows a Mustang diving in for the attack near Mount Fuji. (U.S. Army Air Forces via National Archives)

Four flyers failed to return. One was most likely shot down by the American bombers, another crashed due to structural failure during combat, and, most upsetting to Iwo Jima's pilots, two men died during failed bailouts. Others barely made it to Agate Base with a few gallons of fuel to spare.

On the brighter side, 16 planes fell to the Mustang's guns, including a fifth Japanese aircraft, a Tony, for James Tapp. He became the Seventh Air Force's first ace.

The 16 April mission was something new. Instead of flying shotgun for the B-29s, Iwo Jima's Mustangs went down to ground level to sweep Japanese airfields on the southern coast of Kyushu. Mission planners designed the raid to help eliminate the *kamikaze* threat against the American invasion fleet off Okinawa.

To catch the Japanese gunners by surprise and to minimize the risk of casualties, each airfield was attacked by the Mustangs in a line-abreast formation in a single high-speed pass. Pilots said it was a long, long way to travel for a few seconds over the targets and very few enemy aircraft were claimed destroyed. Worse, one plane had disappeared on the way to the target, and another man bailed out of his dying fighter only to plummet into the angry ocean. The fear of jumping from a stricken plane grew among the pilots with every parachute failure or mysterious death at sea.

A 19 April fighter sweep against Atsugi Airfield near Tokyo and Yokohama was much more successful. Completely surprising the Japanese, the Mustangs came barreling through, blasting rows of undispersed aircraft parked on the ground. Other Iwo Jima airmen caught enemy fighters, trainers, biplanes, and cargo planes aloft and completely unaware. The American aircraft zoomed over Honshu at treetop level, clattering bullets into industrial buildings, electrical towers, and locomotives on their high-speed dash back out to sea. The enemy downed two Mustangs over the target. One of the pilots, Lieutenant Arthur Beckington, would spend the rest of the war as a prisoner of war.

A tent in a depression in Iwo Jima's black volcanic sand is the home for five or six pilots. Here, flyers Bill Fisher and Wes Brown make the short climb to the flight line. In the background, bulky external wing tanks are set out for upcoming missions. (U.S. Army Air Forces via National Archives)

BREAKING TIES

The relationship between the Marianas Superfortress groups and Iwo Jima's fighter escorts was always a strange one. The idea of basing fighters within range of Japan was so that they could protect the massed formations of B-29s during daylight precision bombing missions on Japan's industrial targets—similar to the way American bombers and fighters worked together in Europe. But as early as 9 March, the B-29s of the 20th Air Force experimented with a new type of bombing strategy. The bombers went to Tokyo low and at night. Attacking in the darkness using radar, the American planes dropped thousands of tons of firebombs on the general area, causing an immense firestorm in the city.

This new type of bombing mission left the Mustangs of Iwo Jima out in the cold. While still periodically called upon to fly alongside the B-29s by day, much of the time, the P-51 pilots were let loose to fly VLR missions completely on their own. The flyers were ordered to conduct "sweeps" instead of "escort missions."

A sweep was the mission of the day on 22 April, when the fighters from Agate Base hit airfields in the Nagoya area. Two planes and pilots were lost, including another unsuccessful bailout.

The next two missions required the Mustangs to escort the bombers, but both were failures. Terrible weather hounded the Mustangs as they fought to get to Kyushu on 26 April. Six aircraft of the 15th Fighter Group simply disappeared, including an entire flight of four 45th Squadron Mustangs. On 30 April, the schedules of the fighters and bombers were mixed and they never rendezvoused near the Japanese coast.

In the midst of this evolution of roles and string of tragedies, a third P-51 outfit, the 506th Fighter Group, arrived on Iwo Jima. The switch of bomber tactics was even more odd for the 506th because they were assigned to the 20th Air

BEATING BOREDOM

What do young military men do when there is absolutely nothing to do? Free time was rare on Iwo Jima, but it's impossible to work every waking hour. Members of the AAF found all sorts of ways to occupy their time.

Members of Iwo Jima's unofficial "yacht club" work to ready their confiscated Japanese fishing boat for its next voyage in the waters around the island. It is unknown whether the boat was actually launched before men lost interest or fighting in the Pacific came to an end. (U.S. Army Air Forces via National Archives)

Volleyball courts and softball fields sprung up in many places on Iwo Jima's busy 4,850 acres. Here, soldiers temporarily occupy a deserted taxiway for a few quick games of horseshoes. (Arvid Johnson via the 7th Fighter Command Association)

Left: *This rusty, ratty, shrapnel-blasted junker caught the eye of men of the 47th Fighter Squadron. The vehicle was built by Japan's Nippon Nainenki Seizo Company Ltd. and rehabilitated by mechanically minded airmen. Americans everywhere love to cruise—even on Iwo's less than eight square miles. (John Whitcomb via the 7th Fighter Command Association)*

Below: *Pilots enjoy a cold Schlitz beer and hot bath after a long flight over the Japanese Empire. Doctors believed a soak in the galvanized tubs was more than physically beneficial—it was also an emotional relief. One Army news magazine put it another way, saying, "Pilots sleep better and feel better—adding up to more dead Japs." (U.S. Army Air Forces via National Archives)*

Giving out gum, candy, and cigarettes makes this guy one of the most popular on the island. Iwo Jima's PX was getting so much business that it had to be closed much of the time, causing soldiers to grumble. (U.S. Army Air Forces via National Archives)

Below: *Not all downtime is for pleasure. Here, Army Air Force men attend sick call on Iwo Jima with a variety of symptoms. It appears that the medical staff is working out of the back of an ambulance, perhaps left over from the invasion. (U.S. Army Air Forces via National Archives)*

Below: *The first outdoor movie was shown in the 15th Fighter Group's area on the evening of 24 March 1945.* Whistling Dixie *was the feature. It was here that one soldier claims to have seen an amazing bit of gun camera footage that has never been seen again. (U.S. Army Air Forces via National Archives)*

Two homemade scooters were built by the maintenance men at airfield number one. Mechanics used the bikes to shuttle parts along the flight line. Here, a repaired skin panel is delivered to a crew chief working on an ailing Mustang. (U.S. Army Air Forces via National Archives)

Force—they were a fighter unit created to function strictly as bomber escorts. For the most part, their services were unneeded.

Perhaps only a small step above boiled C rations, *Ross and Barton's Slop Chute* was the best option for many AAF men. In the early days, the kitchen and bakery doubled as a movie house from after dinner to sunset. (U.S. Army Air Forces via National Archives)

LIFE ON IWO

As the 506th Fighter Group settled into its dingy, rock-strewn new home, its experiences were much like those of the other two Mustang units. At their new compound near the number three airfield, the flyers were greeted with boiled rations, battlefield wreckage, volcanic rocks, and Japanese bodies. Urged to dig foxholes and slit trenches, they were confident enough in the island's defenses and ground units to ignore the advice.

It seemed that the island of Iwo Jima, called "the foulest hole this side of hell,"[95] was, in fact, gradually changing for the better. After the fighting, engineers concocted hot water showers from the volcanic springs. Pilots were overjoyed to quit bathing and shaving with water they had saved in their canteens and steel-pot helmets.

Food service personnel created a kitchen and bakery, nicknamed the "Slop Chute." Fresh meat, eggs, butter, and vegetables were sometimes added to the regular fare. It hardly mattered, said some, because almost everything tasted like DDT. There was even ice cream—someone had pulled off a literally and figuratively "sweet deal" with the Seabees, most likely for booze. Another illegal trade made an ice machine materialize out of thin air.

In the evenings, the Slop Chute doubled as a theater—open from 1730 until darkness, due to blackout regulations. When the risk of air raids diminished, many outdoor theaters were constructed. At first, the films were "old and not of the best caliber." Later the latest Hollywood releases were shown nightly. Iwo Jima was even the host of live USO shows, which included stars like Gene Autry, Bob Hope, and, most importantly, honest-to-goodness *young women*.

Officers' clubs, day rooms, and I & E (information and education) quarters were built with materials the airmen had stolen in the darkness from the Marines, the Seabees, and one another. A library sprang up with titles supplied by the Special Service Office and the Red Cross. Nearby, the former battlefields of Iwo Jima that were not slated to be forged into the growing web of aircraft taxiways and hardstands slowly became volleyball courts, horseshoe pits, and softball fields.

The first PX, run by the 386th Service Group, opened on 5 March. Some items were free to all comers, including chocolate, cigarettes, and gum. Other hot items were toilet articles, paperback books, and stationery. Cans of warm beer and Coca-Cola were also rationed out to the islanders—usually more beer than Coke. The corporal that ran the establishment found that it was so popular among the GIs that he stayed open only two hours a day to stretch his stock.

A Douglas C-47, rigged to spray DDT, cruises low and slow over Iwo Jima's coastline on 7 April 1945. The "miracle chemical" helped kill the flies and mosquitoes that ran rabid in the island's war-torn landscape. Soldiers said everything they ate and drank tasted like DDT. (U.S. Army Air Forces via National Archives)

A few talented men of the 549th Night Fighter Squadron introduced "The Voice of the Night Fighters—KEDI," a mythical radio station that was broadcast over the squadron's public address system. "There are a 'newscast,' 'sportscast,' 'a jive hour,' 'a concert hour,' and 'a local talent hour'," explained the squadron's history.[96] Later, a *real* but perhaps not as entertaining radio station, MVTX, operated on the island, broadcasting Armed Forces Radio. Though periodically drowned out by "the swarms of buzzing P-51s," the radio signal was touted as the cleanest and clearest in the Pacific, heard over a radius of 50 miles.

Iwo Jima had what one pilot cynically described as "conditions ideal for concentrating on the war"[97] and while leisure time was a rare commodity, the men found a multitude of ways to entertain themselves. Some industrious soldiers sawed the propellers from mangled Japanese aircraft hulks, melted the metal down, and made souvenir paperweights in the shape of the island. Other "rock-happy" souls built strange vehicles for the flight line, including motor scooters and a mini-car with a body made from a discarded drop tank and four junk-pile wheels. They named their glorified go-cart "The Bug." Other airmen commandeered a DUKW ("duck") amphibious truck and tried their hand at deep-sea fishing. They found that the battlefield

Enlisted men of the 15th Fighter Group scavenge the propeller blades from one of the wrecked Japanese fighters that litter the island. Industrious and bored members of the AAF melted down the metal to make souvenir paperweights shaped like Iwo Jima. (U.S. Army Air Forces via National Archives)

Lieutenant Henry Straughn shows off his jaunty felt hat, made on Iwo Jima. Other men preferred wide-brimmed headgear to protect their head and shoulders from the sun. The hats became good luck charms for the flyers who wore them. (Arvid Johnson via the 7th Fighter Command Association)

Built by Corporals Harry Wolski and Robert Baize, "The Bug" had a 110-gallon drop tank body, abandoned trailer wheels, and a chain drive from a wrecked plane. (U.S. Army Air Forces via National Archives)

The remnants of the bitter battle for Iwo Jima were everywhere, and some flyers couldn't help but explore abandoned Japanese bunkers and caves. This photo, shot by a member of the 548th Night Fighter Squadron, shows a typical booby trap. The bottle and package to the right are connected with a fine wire—easy enough to miss in the darkness of the cave. The wartime caption reports, "In that package is enough explosive to send an entire platoon in search of the Pearly Gates." (Air Force Historical Research Agency)

Outside *Ye Olde Iwo Jima Spa*, fighter pilots speak the way they always do—with their hands. In this photo, a Mustang flyer reenacts a recent aerial maneuver for his buddies. (U.S. Army Air Forces via National Archives)

Corporals Roy Ginstrom and Robert Yeager pause to look over Iwo Jima University's "course catalog." Informal classes were open to all of the island's officers and enlisted men. (U.S. Army Air Forces via National Archives)

waters surrounding Iwo Jima were almost devoid of fish due to months of explosions.

A fad of creating various styles of hats cropped up among the flyers. "With names, insignia, and the association of previous campaigns, these good-luck charms have become the mascots of the men who wear them," explained one reporter. The same article stated that, "The Mustang flyers wear their helmets, of course, over the target. But during the long, dull mission hours, they sport their favorite headgear."[98] This statement gives credence to the tale told by a B-29 crewman who swore he saw Mustang pilots sporting all varieties of hats while airborne.

Perhaps the most dangerous and frowned-upon pastime of these young men was exploring the island's numerous battlefields and caves. The driving force to locate a souvenir wristwatch, pistol, or sword among the dead Japanese that were everywhere often clouded their common sense. Rumors abounded of booby-trapped bottles of sake, wrecked enemy airplanes packed with explosives, and, worst of all, hideouts that were still populated by angry, starving, and very much still alive Japanese troops.

Another addition to the growing Iwo Jima airbase complex was "Ye Olde Iwo Jima Spa." Built as a method to fight "sprung butt" and other maladies created by seven or eight hours stuffed into the tiny cockpit of a fighter, the spa offered hot baths, cold beer, and a rubdown for the returning Mustang pilots after their debriefings.

The airmen even established the Iwo Jima University, "the nearest American college to Japan, boasting the worst campus of any institute of learning in the world," wrote one soldier. Former schoolteachers and college professors taught informal classes that were very popular among the GIs. Classes offered included Russian, Spanish, physics, geometry, calculus, and psychology. "The entrance requirements are simple," explained a reporter. "Just get yourself shipped to Iwo Jima."[99]

CHAPTER 8

WOE IS IWO

Lieutenant Phillip Altson's 506th Fighter Group Mustang was fully loaded with fuel and ammunition for a mission over Japan on 28 May. But his plane never made it off Iwo Jima. Caught in the propwash of another aircraft during takeoff, his P-51 slid into the island's rocky landscape, shedding its fuel-filled wings and external tanks. As fire consumed much of the plane, Alston was trapped inside. Finally, help arrived and wrenched open the canopy, freeing the shook-up but unharmed young pilot. (U.S. Army Air Forces via National Archives)

April turned into May as the VLR missions continued. The long-range flights included two escort and five strike missions for the month among the three fighter groups. Two VLRs were turned back due to weather conditions.

The 506th Fighter Group flew to Japan for the first time late in May. As if part of an initiation, the new pilots gained acceptance flying boring and endless combat air patrols around Iwo Jima and thanklessly hauling bombs up to Chichi Jima. They were anxious to fly to Japan and engage real fighting.

THE BIG TIME

On the morning of 28 May 1945, 53 flyers of the 506th got their first shot at the big time. Over Kasumigaura Airfield, northeast of Tokyo, eight Mustangs came screaming down from 10,000 feet in 60-degree dives, spraying anti-aircraft emplacements.

With the attention of the Japanese drawn skyward, 14 American fighters raced in at treetop level, machine-gunning parked aircraft and buildings. They pulled the trick twice, with another group of eight P-51s coming in high and 16 more emerging "from the weeds" at the last moment.

The 506th planes then roamed over airfields in the neighborhood, looking for appealing targets. One flyer, a veteran of the African campaign, made a head-on pass at a parked plane in a revetment and never pulled up—a classic case of target fixation. His Mustang exploded in a ball of fire.

That evening at Agate Base, the excited flyers took stock. They had completed the deepest penetration of the Empire by AAF fighter aircraft so far, destroyed at least one aircraft in the air, and hit dozens more on the ground.

But there were also lessons to be learned. Many men were disappointed when they viewed their gun camera images. Naturally, many newer pilots were moving fast

A Mustang pilot duels with the Japanese gunners protecting the area near Kanoya East Airfield. The two dark blasts in front of the hangars are thought to be buried mines, triggered by ground troops in hopes of bringing down a low-flying P-51. (U.S. Army Air Forces via National Archives)

The Japanese often used dummy aircraft to lure an American fighter pilot down low and into the teeth of enemy anti-aircraft guns. This fake fighter, complete with national insignia, looked incredibly real when seen from the cockpit of a speeding Mustang. (U.S. Army Air Forces via National Archives)

and spraying bullets all over the countryside. Lieutenant William Willis' gun camera film showed something different. Another transplanted fighter pilot from the battles in Africa and the Mediterranean, Willis had the practiced skill and calm demeanor of an 80-mission veteran. During the attack, he had moved his focus from parked plane to hangar to fuel truck, methodically executing each with a dead-on stream of hundreds of bullets.

The pilots also noted they needed to work on sticking together. After the initial attacks, "the 506th planes were spread all over the map, 'from Hell to breakfast,' as one of the participants phrased it. They would have been duck soup for aggressive Jap interception," a report stated.[100]

On the following day, 29 May, the 15th and 21st Fighter Groups flew an escort mission with 450 B-29s to the Yokohama area. The pilots encountered a large group of aggressive Japanese fighters and a wild dogfight ensued with Mustangs dueling Oscars, Zeros, Jacks, Tojos, and Georges. The most enemy aircraft yet were destroyed in the air—26 confirmed, nine probable, and 23 damaged. One Mustang was shot down and its pilot lost. Others had to bail out and were

On a good day, Iwo Jima didn't look all bad. Here, 21st Fighter Group P-51s are parked on the edge of airfield number two. Behind them, the main runway of airfield number one can be seen. In the distance, Mount Suribachi at the south end of the island. The island certainly could use a few shady palm trees though. (U.S. Army Air Forces via National Archives)

rescued. One flyer, pulled aboard a destroyer escort, promptly lost all of his money while playing cards with his rescuers. The sailors encouraged him to tell his fellow pilots to carry more cash. "It hardly pays to fish you guys out at only 10 bucks a head," one told him.[101]

THE WEATHER MISSION

On 1 June, all three Iwo Jima Mustang groups flew together for the first time on an escort mission to Osaka. The failed VLR would become universally known among the pilots as "the weather mission."

Led by several navigator B-29s, the formations of more than 150 Mustangs approached a massive front of storm clouds around 400 miles north of Agate Base. In the electrically charged air near the weather, a frantic, sometimes broken and unintelligible radio conversation took place. They needed to climb. They needed to find a clear spot. Going into the storm front could be a disaster.

The Mustang pilots had found, on earlier missions, that B-29 crews had a different idea of what types of weather were penetrable, flying in their heavy four-engine behemoths. The crew of a Superfortress would often underestimate the impact of a storm front on the much lighter and smaller P-51s they had in tow. Sometimes, most frustrating for Iwo Jima's flyers, their navigation ship would dive into a wall of clouds, casually telling the flock of fighters, "We'll pick you up on the other side." As a result, fighter command officers regularly rode aboard the bombers, to advise the pilots on exactly what type of flying would bring the P-51s through in one piece.

But on this day, things were rapidly slipping away from everyone involved. As the bombers led their trailing P-51s in a gentle circle, more conflicting radio reports crackled over the broken airwaves. "It is clear at our angels plus one," someone said, meaning one flight saw an opening at a slightly higher altitude. Another said, "It's clear underneath." "The oranges are sour," another pilot reported on the weather frequency—meaning, in radio code, that the weather was bad for miles ahead of the flight.

The B-29s completed a 360-degree circuit and climbed only slightly as they attempted to guide the mass of aircraft through a saddle between angry, towering storms. Within a few moments, the hole shrank considerably and the formation of aircraft became compressed together. Then the hole simply disappeared. As the entire world turned to gray, the pilots tried to tighten up their formations and stick together.

The storm's interior carried some of the most violent turbulence any of the pilots can recall. The fighters were bounced all over the sky. In the jostling whiteout, many flyers experienced severe bouts of vertigo. The wingtips of two 15th aircraft crunched together in the murk with a sickening thud. A propeller from one 506th Mustang sawed into the tail of another. Others instinctively dodged away from the disintegrating P-51s in the snow-filled clouds and were left alone and lost.

"Inside the front," the 506th report said, "aircraft were observed in every position of flight, inverted, spinning, diving, climbing in steep banks, and headed in all directions." The B-29 leading the remaining portions of the 506th attempted to turn around, directing the straggling planes straight into the 15th's formation.

Lieutenant Gordon Scott of the 15th Fighter Group recalled seeing two 506th Mustangs skidding out of the clouds, heading at a right angle to their own line of flight. The pair rocketed through their line of Mustangs, smashing into the number two and number four men in the flight ahead of his. The jumbled pieces of crushed aircraft disappeared into the haze almost as quickly as they had come.

Cruising above an overcast sky, Mustang fighters of the 15th Fighter Group fly toward Japan, drawing fuel from their 110-gallon external tanks. (The 7th Fighter Command Association)

As dust from a recent takeoff obscures the runway at airfield number three, a 506th Fighter Group, 458th Fighter Squadron Mustang is readied for flight. During the tragic "Weather Mission," Lieutenant Gordon Scott recalls seeing a pair of these zebra-striped P-51s crash into the Mustangs flying immediately ahead of his own aircraft. (U.S. Army Air Forces via National Archives)

A 506th Mustang is pushed from the dispersal area on Pierced Steel Planking (PSP). Behind the canopy, the dual antenna of the "Uncle Dog" homing system used on Iwo Jima's fighters can be seen. The photo was taken in July 1945. (U.S. Army Air Forces via National Archives)

Two other 506th aircraft appeared and carefully turned in to join Scott's flight. Together, they dove down to 5,000 feet to get away from the chaos. Pilots everywhere were on the radio, calling for help, barking directions, hopelessly lost, or bailing out. There was so much going on all at once that the emergency calls were canceling each other out.

The radio reports that could be heard were discouraging. A 506th historian wrote, "Fragments of conversation overheard on the radio indicated that some of the pilots would return from the mission, if they returned at all, on the deck of a destroyer or inside a sub."[102]

Back on Iwo Jima, Captain Hamlin Williston of the 302nd Fighter Control Squadron placed 50 Mayday calls on the plotting table at one time. Agate Base gave the lost aircraft a single vector to get them back to within sight of Mount Suribachi. The distinct land mass at the south end of Iwo Jima was called "Hotrocks" by the flyers when discussed on the radio.

Other pilots relied on their DU homing devices, an automatic direction finder nicknamed "Uncle Dog." A radio station on Iwo Jima (or another location or even another aircraft) could send out a radio signal and Iwo Jima's Mustangs, with the help of two VHF antennas on the rear fuselage, could receive the signal. If a pilot was to the left of the radio beam, he would hear a Morse Code "U" (dit-dit-dah) in his headphones and would correct by changing course to the right. Receiving a "D" (dah-dit-dit) meant the opposite applied. The pilots could follow the beam from Iwo Jima's homing station, code-named Brother Agate, home to roost without the help of navigator B-29s.

On this day, aircraft came back to Agate Base alone or in small groups for hours afterward. A mixed group of 27 Mustangs bore through the storm and didn't hear the radio calls canceling the mission. They proceeded to Osaka and latched on to returning bombers, convincing them to divert over Iwo Jima in their way home to bases in the Marianas.

When all of Iwo Jima's fighters were accounted for, 26 planes and pilots remained missing in the storm-tossed ocean. One man, Lieutenant Thomas Harrigan of the 506th Fighter Group, was rescued in his raft by a destroyer on 3 June. Another, Lieutenant Arthur Burry of the 15th Fighter Group was miraculously located purely by accident by the alert crew of the submarine USS *Trutta* on 7 June. Burry was delirious and exhausted after six days in rough seas aboard his tiny yellow raft.

This little beast isn't a guided bomb. It is an "Uncle Dog" trainer set up so pilots could practice navigating with the homing system. Many squadrons had similar devices. This one carried the distinctive stripes of the 458th Fighter Squadron. (Air Force Historical Research Agency)

JUNE FLIGHTS

Five of the VLR missions scheduled for June turned back due to bad weather while six more netted satisfactory results. The highlight of the month came on 10 June during an escort mission to the Tokyo area. More than 100 Japanese army and navy fighters came in to attack the bombers, and the Mustangs of the 15th and 506th were there to fend them off.

Pilots of the 506th Fighter Group had never before seen so many enemy planes in the air. They piled in, anxious to make the most of their decreasing opportunities. "The 506th pilots, it was agreed, were eager to close and come to grips with the enemy," the group history stated. "So much so in fact that they very nearly ran one another down in the mad scramble to tap the few Nips sighted. As Lieutenant [Chauncey] Newcomb of the 457th [Fighter Squadron] put it, 'It's getting so we've almost got to fight the other boys off to get to take a solo shot at a Jap plane'."[103]

When it was over, no Mustangs or bombers were missing. But Iwo Jima's pilots claimed 26 enemy aircraft shot down, six probably destroyed, and 11 more damaged.

On 23 June, the duo of the 15th and 506th located a mass of Japanese planes in the air while on a sweep mission to the Kasumigaura and Hyakurigahara area. The P-51s jumped numerous flights of Japanese aircraft, sending Oscars, Tojos, Zekes, and Jacks crashing to the ground in flames. The 506th reported, "The repertoire of evasive tactics employed by the 20 or so Nips engaged was extremely limited, consisting mostly of half rolls and split S's. Incidents of this type contributed to the somewhat unflattering opinion many of the flyers were beginning to form of the combat effectiveness of the Nips."[104]

STRANGE ENCOUNTERS

Flyers couldn't help but talk about their experiences with their fellow pilots. Over a warm beer in Iwo Jima's Quonset hut clubs, airmen discussed their sweethearts back home, their miserable living conditions, or the war's latest news. But the

After shooting two Japanese fighters from the skies on a mission near Yokohama, Captain Peter Norwick recounts the action to his crew chief, Staff Sergeant John Stanfield on 10 June 1945. Both men are from the 506th Fighter Group. (U.S. Army Air Forces via National Archives)

Inset: There were a few long-running gags among Iwo Jima's bored AAF men. One was the modified hotfoot—a lit cigarette slipped into the back pocket of an unsuspecting victim. Here, the man about to get an unpleasant surprise is Flight Surgeon Doctor Jack Lapides of the 15th Fighter Group. (John Fitzgerald via the 7th Fighter Command Association)

A 21st Fighter Group pilot uses some of his down time to carve faces inspired by Japanese artwork he found on Iwo Jima. His pet chicken, always the art critic, looks on from the flyer's shoulder. (U.S. Army Air Forces via National Archives)

conversations inevitably turned to flying. They spoke of life and death as casually as they discussed the latest baseball box scores. They wondered why some men never came back while they were miraculously saved.

They puzzled about the day in May when the fog closed in on Iwo Jima while they were north, harassing the Empire's airfields. By the time they made it back near Agate Base, the ceiling and visibility were zero-zero. Preparations were made for wholesale bailouts over the island.

When the planes were 70 miles out, the runways were still described as "pea soup" according to those on the ground. "Then, miraculously it seemed, the low clouds began to disperse," said the 21st's historian. "The clear spot over Iwo held until all returning pilots were down safely and then the fog closed in again. No one could explain it."[105]

The pilots didn't fear air combat. In fact, they eagerly sought out enemy aircraft to tangle with in the skies over Japan. Much scarier, in their minds, was the chance they'd die from the weather or a senseless equipment failure so far from home. They endlessly theorized about what to do should their engine conk out, or if they looked down to discover their fuel state in the red. One piece of equipment that drew special attention was their bigger 165-gallon fuel tanks. The flyers discovered the tanks had the alarming habit of smashing into their planes' flaps and tail when released over Japan. After one "bull session" on the island, pilots perfected a plan to slosh the remaining fuel to the rear of the tank with a sharp pull up and then release the tank.

Lieutenant Frank Albrecht of the 506th Fighter Group had a tank that held on stubbornly on 10 June. The hung tank caused drag, increased gas consumption, and made for the very real possibility that the problem would land him in the drink. Lieutenant Henry Fletcher came to the rescue, pulling his own Mustang dangerously close and tapping the tank loose with his wingtip.

On the 26 June, Lieutenant William Hutchinson's Mustang began to fall behind the formation. Over the radio,

With the help of his crew chief, pilot Bill Ebersole readies himself for a VLR mission in July 1945. (U.S. Army Air Forces via National Archives)

the flyer reported that the supercharger wouldn't engage except when used manually. After several minutes of jury-rigging, Hutchinson managed to tie the supercharger switch in place with a piece of parachute string that he was using to secure his pocket knife to his person. He made it back to Agate Base worried, but unharmed.

Other pilots shared stories, looking for answers to encounters they found simply puzzling. Several flyers of the 506th reported a strange array of objects in the air with them while they were attacking Yachimata Airfield. They were bright red kites, perhaps two feet by four feet, flying at 150 to 200 feet. There must have been 25 to 30 of them. The pilots swerved their Mustangs to avoid them the best they could. "Who knows what kind of damage they might do?" they later stated.

But injury from lowly kites were the least of their concerns. Flyers returned to Agate Base with conventional wartime wounds to their planes—crushed tail surfaces, slowly disintegrating engines, or their canopies smashed open. While they felt they could handle Japanese fighters, ground fire was more like Russian roulette. There were huge, gaping holes

A hole in the hide of Lieutenant Quentin McCorkle's Mustang was created, not by a Japanese fighter, but a B-29 bomber gunner who was not too discerning when it came to aircraft identification. McCorkle glumly wonders what would have happened if this rogue shooter had slightly better aim. (U.S. Army Air Forces via the 7th Fighter Command Association)

Posing with the blasted tail of his P-51 Mustang, 21st pilot Lieutenant Irving Skansen (on the left) is lucky to be alive, intact, and ready to fly another day. His plane was hit by 20-mm fire over Japan on 16 July 1945. (John Wilson via the 7th Fighter Command Association)

from 40-mm anti-aircraft blasts and neat, clean punctures created by Japanese machine gunners on the ground. More than one plane returned with holes that, upon closer examination, appeared to come from American .50-calibers.

On 16 July, Captain Abner Aust of the 506th landed on Iwo Jima after claiming three Franks destroyed and another damaged. Upon inspection of his Mustang, his crew chief noted that Aust had collected two mysterious armor-piercing .50-caliber slugs on the trip. No pilot in his flight would fess up to depositing them in Aust's hide.

They spoke of amazing victories and heart-breaking losses. Gutsy Lieutenant Robert Anderstrom was the talk of his squadron at the officer's club when he ventured into downtown Osaka and sieved a trolley car clattering down a main street in front of the startled locals.

But on another day, Captain E. K. Neff was blasting fishing boats near Atsugi when he banked his Mustang into a hard turn right down on the deck. His wingtip touched the water and, in a fraction of a second, Neff's plane was reduced to a ball of flames on the surface of the ocean. The tragedy could have been avoided. It all seemed so senseless. And, more than anything, most flyers came to the realization, "That could have been me."

On one VLR mission, Captain Edward Mikes bailed out near Tokyo and landed in the water. A "Dutchman" rescue B-17 raced in and dropped its motor boat. As he was quickly cruising out to sea, Mikes was thrilled to be joined by a pair of Navy Privateer patrol bombers. Trying to show him the way to a rescue submarine, the American planes headed toward the horizon in the direction of the approaching vessel.

Fighters appeared soon after the patrol bombers left. At first, Mikes figured they were Mustangs standing guard over the sub. But when they got closer, he was horrified to find they were Japanese aircraft. As the planes blasted his boat, Mikes lay in the bottom, one hand reaching up, still guiding the rudder.

The Navy Privateers returned and chased the fighters away as Mikes' boat raced toward the surfaced submarine, which was, in turn, running toward him, spewing a black cloud of diesel smoke. As the pair converged, a Japanese Pete observation biplane dove

Mitsubishi F1M observation aircraft twice foiled Captain Edward Mikes' escape in the waters near Tokyo. This image was used by Army flyers for identification and actually shows a model of the floatplane, code-named Pete by the Allies. (U.S. Army Air Forces via National Archives)

Lieutenant Leon Sher of the 15th Fighter Group made a diving run on a Japanese ship in Outer Osaka Bay on 10 July 1945. As he got closer, he realized it was a warship. It was too late to turn away and Sher had no choice but to blast the destroyer escort with his .50-calibers as sheets of anti-aircraft fire rose up to meet him. His bullets touched off a magazine near the ship's front turret and it exploded violently. Sher didn't stick around to observe the final results of his attack. Reports indicate the sinking ship was intentionally grounded after the fighter attack. (Leon Sher via the 7th Fighter Command Association)

into the mix. The Navy patrol planes and the sub's own 20-mm cannon tried desperately to catch up with the Pete as it broke through.

Mikes' hopes were dashed as the Japanese plane dropped two bombs 75 feet away from the crash-diving sub. But the two Navy patrol plane pilots, wrenching their big blue monsters around the sky like they were fighter planes, chased the Pete down and sent it flaming into the sea.

The submarine resurfaced and Mikes was motoring toward it at full speed when another Pete came barreling into the rescue scene. Again the sub disappeared as bombs came crashing down. And again, the Privateer flyers hunted the offender down and blasted him from the skies.

"When the sub went down a second time, I was ready to cash in my chips," Mikes later said. "I felt sure they would never come back, and I wouldn't have blamed them."[106] Luckily for the beleaguered pilot, this late in the war the military men of the United States considered the Pacific Ocean—every drop up to Japan's shores—*their* territory. The sub's periscope soon poked above the waves and then surfaced. The submarine's crewmen dragged Mikes aboard and stuffed him down through a hatch seconds before it disappeared under the surface.

The pilots found that living and dying was often measured in inches or fractions of a second. Sometimes a

With the help of Iwo Jima's airfields, Consolidated PB4Y-2 patrol bombers could loiter near the coast of mainland Japan, causing trouble. When Mustang pilot Captain Edward Mikes was shot down near Tokyo, a pair of the Privateers appeared to help. Flying the huge planes like fighters, the Navy bombers chased down and destroyed Japanese scout planes attempting to ruin Mikes' rescue. (Naval Aviation Museum)

quick-reacting flyer could yank himself back from the precipice of disaster with what they called a "JC maneuver." The violent burst of input on the stick was usually done at seemingly the last second to avoid the ground, an airplane, or some other object. It earned its name because the action was commonly paired with a particular exclamation blurted by the pilot—"Jesus Christ!"

On 23 June, Lieutenant Wilhelm Peterson reacted moments too late. As his flight leader machine-gunned an enemy plane, Peterson followed, and watched the Japanese pilot bail out. The falling flyer's parachute blossomed right in front of the nose of his onrushing Mustang as he tried to dodge out of the way. The group's report snidely stated, "Obviously 'Watanabe' had quite a letdown."[107]

Lieutenant Gordon Scott had a similar experience. On his first mission to Japan, he too encountered a falling enemy airman, missing him by mere feet. That evening, after telling his fellow airmen about the chance encounter, he didn't think too much more about it.

Years later, while conducting transition training for Korean pilots, one of his students mentioned that he had been an airline pilot in Korea before the Japanese forced him to fly fighters over the Empire. Unbelievably, he told Scott about the day he jumped and was almost run down by one of Iwo Jima's Mustangs. After comparing the date and the Korean pilot's description of Scott's plane, *Sparkin Eyes*, the pair determined that they had, indeed, *almost* met years before.

PRISONER OF WAR

Spread in a long line, 16 speeding Mustangs of the 15th Fighter Group approached the Kasumigaura aircraft assembly plant in a 20-degree dive. All at once, the fighters let loose with 96 five-inch rockets. It was, after all, the Fourth of July, 1945. Moments after the projectiles went crashing through the side of the long metal building and exploded, the Mustangs raced by.

One of the planes was flown by Lieutenant Scott. Beyond the factory, he spied a new radial engine fighter parked in a revetment. Quickly switching to guns, he fired at the aircraft. As his stream of bullets threw up dust around the Japanese plane, Scott noticed some of his gunfire ricocheting into the building beyond.

As his Mustang passed over the top, the building blew up in a tremendous explosion. It lifted his plane skyward, into the overcast clouds. When he regained control of the fighter, Scott dove out of the clouds over Lake Kasumigaura. Directly in front of him was a seaplane hanger and two amphibious biplanes in the middle of their takeoff runs.

As the closest enemy plane's tail gunner began to shoot at the rapidly closing Mustang, Scott moved the pipper of his gun sight on the plane's fuselage and fired. From 50 feet, the biplane nosed over, hit the water, and exploded.

The second biplane was farther along, up to about 200 feet when Scott's P-51 ran right up behind him. This plane

Flyer Lieutenant Gordon Scott shot down two Japanese aircraft on the 4 July mission to Kasumigaura aircraft assembly plant, but he never got credit for either. His gun camera film, along with his Mustang, sank to the bottom of a nearby lake a few moments later. After he swam ashore, Scott became a prisoner of war. (Jim Vande Hey via the 7th Fighter Command Association)

exploded in mid-air, causing Scott to rake his plane into a hard right turn to avoid the debris.

In the turn, Scott noted that his engine was running rough. White smoke was coughing from all 12 engine-exhaust-stacks. Glancing down at the coolant temperature gauge, Scott found his worst fears had become reality. The temperature needle was pegged to as hot as it would go. Reducing power didn't help as he skimmed over the lake.

About that time, Scott got what pilots joked about as "The Big X"—his propeller simply froze. Looking out his oil-covered windshield, Scott could see that he was only about 100 feet off the water. He jettisoned his canopy and lowered his flaps.

At the last second, Scott let go of the stick and put both hands on the gunsight. "Thinking back," he later wrote, "it seems weird in that predicament—90 miles per hour, about to hit the water which would be like hitting a brick wall, in a country not known for kindness to prisoners, and thousands of miles from home—I took the time to protect my face!"[108]

The oil radiator belly scoop dug into the water and flopped the Mustang over nose first. Just before going under, Scott took a deep breath. As his plane sank, Scott struggled to push free from his seat, with a parachute, seat pack, and uninflated raft weighing him down.

He broke the surface and gulped another breath before his load of survival equipment dragged him back under the water. He unbuckled his chest and leg straps, shed his parachute, and yanked the lanyard to inflate one chamber of his Mae West lifejacket. Scott was able to get another breath before his life raft and seat pack, still connected to his soaked parachute at the other end, pulled the flailing pilot under again.

He needed that raft. But it was dangling at the end of a 25-foot lanyard along with his chute and survival equipment. Scott made two tries to get it, nearly drowning during each attempt. Finally, completely spent, he unclipped the lanyard and let the whole soaking mass sink to the bottom.

Looking around, he found he was in the middle of the huge lake, miles from shore. The airfield to the west was a chaotic scene. Black smoke rose thousands of feet in the air. Closer were the two smaller smoke columns from the two

Lieutenant Gordon Scott prepares to take off in his Mustang, *Sparkin Eyes*, from Iwo Jima. The fighter was a replacement aircraft, yet to be fully adorned with the colors of the 15th Fighter Group, 78th Fighter Squadron. (The 7th Fighter Command Association)

biplanes Scott had blasted. He decided there was no good reason to swim back in *that* direction.

He was going to go east, toward the opposite shore. Perhaps, he thought, he could even make it overland to the Pacific. There were American submarines offshore. It was the longest of long shots, but there wasn't really any other choice.

After an hour of breaststroking, Scott noticed swarms of Japanese fighters arriving from the north. Clearly, the Americans' arrival had been known by the Japanese ahead of time and almost every new fighter that could be flown away to safety had escaped before the marauding Mustangs had arrived on the scene.

As Scott slowly moved closer to shore, he began encountering boat traffic. When a boat neared, Scott would deflate his life jacket and pause, with only his eyes and nose above the water. Finally, he made his way into the reeds about 50 yards offshore, near a small village.

Just before dark, an old man and a group of children came near, poling through the shallows in a flat-bottomed boat. Scott went under water when the boat came within about 30 yards. When he could hold his breath no longer, he came to the surface.

One of the small children, looking back, spotted him. "The boy started screaming to the old man, who turned the boat around to see what the kid was yelling about, and he saw me."[109] When the boat touched the shore, all five children went screaming up the slope and into the village.

In just a few minutes, the locals came down to get him with rice knives, bamboo poles, pitchforks, and a few antique guns. "A thought flashed through my mind: This is a terrible way to celebrate the Fourth of July."[110]

The rag-tag band of farmers tied Scott's elbows behind his back then pushed and dragged him to a schoolhouse a few hundred yards away. Inside waited a short, bald Japanese man in his 60s—most likely the village prefect or magistrate.

"I was probably a sorry looking representative of the United States Army Air Corps," Scott wrote later. "My flying suit was still sopping wet, and muddy and dirty from falls on the bank of the lake and on the trek to the schoolhouse."[111] It hardly mattered. The angry man quickly served up a death sentence for Scott. He was to be shot before the sun came up.

As the crowd jostled him away, Scott was hit with sticks, punched, kicked, spit on, and most painful of all, slashed with rice knives. They moved him to a cherry tree in the courtyard and tied him in place. Before they pulled a rice sack over his head, Scott saw local militia men lining up with their rusty rifles.

Over the "*banzai*" shouts of the crowd, Scott heard another sound—a strange chugging. A group of men pulled up in their dented old jalopy. "Someone had apparently notified the army, and these strangers were Japanese soldiers," Scott recalled. "Bless them. They saved my life!"[112]

The locals were unhappy about Scott's change of fortune. One or more of the would-be executioners stepped forward and smashed their gun butts into his ribs and face. One blow broke Scott's jaw. He lost consciousness.

When Scott awoke, he had been lifted into the car and placed on a plank spanning the rear seat. He rode high, sitting in the roofless car, with his feet resting on the seat. The smell of burning wood perforated the bag still over his head. Scott finally realized that the auto had been converted to run with wood as fuel. "A rather remarkable invention I thought, and I wish I could have been able to see how they did it."[113]

At every hamlet and village, angry Japanese would punch him and throw rocks at him. When the group arrived at a larger town with a rail junction, there was another trial, but the outcome was the same—Scott was to be put to death.

His train reached Tokyo around midnight. Scott was taken to the Emperor's prison, Kempi Tai. He was only a few blocks from the Emperor's palace. They shoved him into a cage among a group of other men. In the light of a small 25-watt bulb, Scott saw two other Americans. They were bearded and were wearing old-style flight suits. The sight of fellow flyers, who had obviously been locked up for a long while, was comforting to the bedraggled fighter pilot seemingly on death row. "I thought, my God, I've got it made, I'm not going to die tomorrow morning!"[114]

The two Americans in his cell were B-29 airmen. There were also five Japanese—two Osaka industrialists who were at odds with the Emperor, a pair of professors objecting to the war, and, says Scott, "an epileptic *kamikaze* pilot who wouldn't *kamikaze*."

It was strange company, to be sure. He wished he was able to talk freely with all of them, but the guards prevented anyone from uttering a word. Lieutenant Scott slid into the corner and stared straight ahead. He had never thought that he would long for his days on the dusty island of Iwo Jima.

Working Around the Clock

It was the mechanics that kept everything on Iwo Jima up and running. No pilot could make it into the air without a small army of AAF men—crew chiefs, wrench-turners, armorers, radio experts, and other specialists. Often, the only down time these men had was when their aircraft were flying to Japan.

Iwo Jima's dusty environs and primitive conditions made caring for these complex fighters a difficult task. And there was no room for error—when one of fighters took off, it was usually to go over 1,400 miles non-stop. From Iwo to Iwo in seven or eight hours, there was nothing but ocean and the enemy's homeland in between.

Mechanics swarm over a 15th Fighter Group Mustang that ran into trouble. Parts are removed as they work to put the plane back on its gear. When the propeller of a fighter struck the ground, it usually destroyed the engine. This aircraft will require many hours of hard work to get it back into the air. (U.S. Army Air Forces via National Archives)

Looking slightly "rock happy," a busy mechanic pauses work on the flight line just long enough to dig into his K ration dinner. (U.S. Army Air Forces via National Archives)

Even on Iwo Jima, Army Air Forces men couldn't escape mountains of paperwork. Here, a mechanic fills out a report on the wing of a 15th Fighter Group P-51 Mustang. (U.S. Army Air Forces via National Archives)

Ground crews on Iwo Jima were often the front line during emergencies. Here, they smother the 15th Fighter group aircraft, Foxy, *with fire-fighting foam. The plane burned after being struck by another Mustang on Iwo's number one airfield on 10 March 1945. (U.S. Army Air Forces via National Archives)*

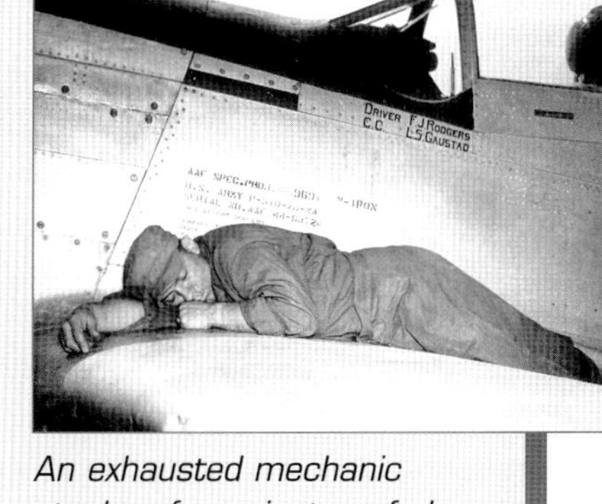

An exhausted mechanic steals a few minutes of sleep on the wing of a 21st Fighter Group Mustang. The fighter belonged to Lieutenant Frank Rodgers, one of the flyers injured during the 26 March banzai attack. (U.S. Army Air Forces via National Archives)

Right: *Jim Tapp's crew chief, Sergeant Ricardo Blanco, was from Havana, Cuba. While based in Hawaii, Tapp took off with a dust cover installed over the oil cooler air scoop on his P-47 Thunderbolt. After Tapp landed the overheating fighter safely, Blanco was so mortified by his mistake that he insisted Tapp shoot him with his service pistol. Of course, Tapp declined and the pair later served on Iwo Jima. (Arvid Johnson via the 7th Fighter Command Association)*

CHAPTER 9

SAFE HAVEN

The bomber crewmen were almost unanimously grateful for the Marines who fought and died for Iwo Jima. Men of the 9th Bomb Group were inspired to change the nose art on one of their bombers to honor Iwo's Marines. After the war, many B-29ers said they wished they could have done more for the men who made the island available to them—at such a terrible cost. (U.S. Army Air Forces via National Archives)

Gunner Sergeant James De Gregonio drops to his knees and gives thanks to the heavens for this rocky outpost in the middle of the Pacific. Over Japan, a collision sawed off 10 feet of the bomber's vertical stabilizer. The Saipan-based B-29 made it to Iwo with two engines out, and 11 crewmen survived, unharmed. (Arvid Johnson via the 7th Fighter Command Association)

After the war, an official Army Air Forces publication explained the island of Iwo Jima like this: "To every B-29 crew who flew to Japan after March 1945, (after Iwo Jima had been captured) the fact that Iwo had become a U.S. base was a cause for thanksgiving. If you had engine trouble, you held out for Iwo. If the weather was too rough, you held out for Iwo. Formations assembled over Iwo and gassed up at Iwo for extra long missions. If you needed fighter escort, it usually came from Iwo. If you had to ditch or bail out, you knew that air-sea rescue units were sent from Iwo. Even if you never used Iwo as an emergency base, it was a psychological benefit. It was there to fall back on."[115]

In the last six months of fighting, the tiny island in the middle of the Pacific became a safe haven for more than 2,400 needy B-29 bombers—an amazing number, considering that only 3,965 were built. If not for Iwo Jima, a significant portion of these aircraft would have been lost at sea. More importantly, many of the aircrews would have been lost—typically 11 airmen per bomber. It is safe to say that, without the option of Iwo Jima, the United States' bombing campaign against Japan would have been much more costly, and the Pacific war might have lasted months longer.

Not only was Iwo Jima an emergency field for bombers, it also increased their productivity. With the option of Iwo Jima, bomber crews flew with less gasoline in reserve. Carrying less fuel meant the planes could carry larger bombloads. Other B-29 units used the island as a forward base, extending their bombers' range to accomplish aerial mining missions over many of Japan's most critical shipping lanes.

The Boeing B-29 Superfortress was large and fast—and one of the most modern aircraft flying in the Pacific. Here, *Padre and His Angels* of the 505th Bomb Group cruises toward Japan. (Harry Hadlock and Loren Cockrell)

Aboard a B-29, the pilot and his flight engineer sweat out their fuel situation on the flight back to the Mariana Islands. With Iwo Jima in American hands, the bombers could carry less fuel in reserve and bring more bombs to their targets. (U.S. Army Air Forces via National Archives)

PACIFIC REPAIR SHOP

When *Dinah Might* landed on 4 March, Iwo Jima was far from a functional repair depot. Iwo's workers promised Malo and his crew that there would be changes—and quick. Over time, they began to make good on their promise to improve the island's facilities for the hundreds of needy B-29s. On 7 March, Seabees began work on airfield number two, which would also be called the "Central Field." By early April, Army engineers and Navy Seabees had made the main runway of airfield number one, the "South Field," 6,400 feet long. The home for P-51 Mustang day fighters and P-61 Black Widow night fighters and their supporting service groups, the southernmost field often had visits from stricken Superfortress bombers before airfield number two was ready.

The 386th Air Service Group, sent to Iwo Jima to look after the fighter planes, often found itself in the business of fixing the "big birds" that came to roost in their nest. They did the best they could, looking after the Boeing bombers with a little help from a few specialists sent from the bomb groups in the Marianas.

One 386th member recalls a B-29 that came into the number one airfield with damaged nose gear which collapsed on landing, battering the propeller tips into Iwo Jima's ashen soil. They took a long steel bar and jammed it horizontally through the skin of the bomber near the nose, hoisted the plane up, fixed the nose wheel, and then began to consider what they could do about the battered props. When the repair crews ran up the engines, it was found that all the propeller blades were bent uniformly and caused no discernable vibration—good enough to get the plane back to the Marianas and, most importantly, off their busy airfield. The Superfortress took off in less than four hours.

On 24 April, a 504th Bomb Group B-29 plowed into nine 15th Fighter Group Mustangs parked at airfield number one. Two of the bomber's crew were seriously burned. One flyer wrote, disapprovingly, that the flames didn't keep some of Iwo Jima's ground crewmen from climbing into the burning wreck, looking for .45-caliber service pistols left behind by the escaping bomber flyers. (R.J. Cameron via the 7th Fighter Command Association)

On 24 April, a stricken 504th Bomb Group B-29 slid into a line of nine parked Mustangs and burst into flames while attempting a landing at the number one airfield. Clearly the area was overcrowded and hampering the work of the fighters based there. The number two airfield, destined to become the main hub of large aircraft activity, was paramount to the success of Iwo Jima's "safe haven."

By April, three million yards of earth had been moved, making the main runway on airfield number two 10,000 feet long—the longest in the Pacific. Central Field was to become famous among Superfortress airmen as "Rocky's Wayside Service Station." Iwo Jima's B-29 maintenance chief, Major Charles "Rocky" Stone, was an ex-navigator who had been a trucker in California before the war. Rumor had it that Stone got his job at Iwo Jima by telling a stateside colonel, "Sir, I think your maintenance sections stinks."

Most would think exile to Sulphur Island was punishment, but perhaps the colonel recognized the difficult conditions on Iwo Jima required a tough man to lead the vital repairs. Rocky looked the part of a shop foreman in his dirty khakis and ratty, sweat-stained baseball cap as he directed the almost continual flow of bombers into his repair facility.

He was usually up at 0330 following a night raid, standing in his jeep near the airfield with a plug of tobacco in his jaw. He waited for the first planes to appear out of the darkness. Rocky would diagnose the problems of the B-29s while they were on final approach, planning where each ship should be

Major Charles "Rocky" Stone (in the grease-smeared hat) was Iwo Jima's Superfortress maintenance chief. Some said he got the job on dirty Sulphur Island as punishment for being a bit too honest with a stateside superior officer. But regardless of how he got there, Stone did such an excellent job at managing the sprawling, busy base that B-29 flyers came to call "Rocky's Wayside Service Station." (U.S. Army Air Forces via National Archives)

Rows of dead engines are retained for parts at airfield number two. In the background lies a 6th Bomb Group aircraft, *Forever Amber*. The plane received a direct anti-aircraft hit over Kobe that tore out much of the left side near the rear bomb bay. After the pilot landed the ravaged plane on Iwo Jima, it was judged too damaged to ever fly again. It, like the engines, would be picked over for useful parts. (U.S. Army Air Forces via National Archives)

Iwo Jima's Mustangs return from a mission as a crash crew truck hauls away pieces of a completely washed out 6th Bomb Group Superfortress. This photo was taken in July 1945. (U.S. Army Air Forces via National Archives)

parked and what the repairmen would need to do to get the plane back in the air. On the first arrival of the day, he began his commentary: "The engines are okay. Refuel job." The next plane appeared with a mangled wing and one engine crushed. "We'll put her over on the maintenance mat."[116] Aircraft came in and were immediately set upon the minute they were parked. Rocky's crews were a whirling dust cloud of ambulances, flatbeds, cranes, jeeps, and fuel trucks.

Soon, "Rocky's Wayside Service Station" had bomber repair down to a well-practiced science. After radar operator Lieutenant Harry Hadlock's 40th Bomb Group B-29 bombed Fukuyama, the pilot coaxed the bomber back to Iwo Jima with two dead engines. After landing, Hadlock recalls watching from the flight deck as their aircraft, nick-named *Cross Country*, taxied past Iwo's forest of directional signs. "Medical aid over here. Engine repairs, turn here. Fuel, this way," recalls Hadlock. "It was all very organized. It was just like going into a gas station."[117]

One day, a B-29 crew almost wrecked Rocky's highly organized air depot. A burning Superfortress slammed down on the runway and the airmen tumbled out of the flaming craft

A slightly used vertical tail, cannibalized from a 500th Bomb Group wreck, is readied for installation on another damaged Superfortress on Iwo Jima. Mechanics on Iwo became experts on major aircraft surgery—anything to keep the almost continual flow of damaged aircraft on their way back to the Mariana Islands. (U.S. Army Air Forces via National Archives)

After a night mission, the maintenance mat at Iwo Jima's airfield number two was often filled with B-29s. A portion of the original Japanese runway was turned into a large, long parking apron for the aircraft. On Iwo's busiest days, the planes were often packed in two or three aircraft deep. (U.S. Army Air Forces via National Archives)

Lieutenant Harry Hadlock, on the far left, top row, poses with the crew of the 40th Bomb Group Superfortress *Cross Country*. The plane made it to Iwo Jima on two engines in July 1945. (Harry Hadlock and Loren Cockrell)

while it was still rolling. Rocky drove alongside in his jeep, signaling the pilot to stop. But there was no pilot—he had abandoned the burning ship with his men. And the unmanned behemoth was headed for a line of Rocky's parked aircraft. Rocky, cussing up a storm, jumped from the jeep while it was still moving, climbed into the Superfortress, made his way to the flight deck, and jammed on the brakes, stopping it just feet from his row of parked aircraft.

The men at "Rocky's Wayside Service Station" had some amazingly busy days. On 1 June, the day the weather was so terrible, Iwo Jima took in 81 B-29s. On 24 July, Iwo played host to an astounding 197 Superforts; 2 August brought 112 more, and on 6 August, a total of 76 bombers found their way to airfield number two.

This 504th Bomb Group aircraft skidded off the runway at airfield number two and slid over the embankment. Crash crewmen now have to figure out how to pull the 37-ton bomber back to solid ground. It is doubtful the plane ever saw service again. (Arvid Johnson via the 7th Fighter Command Association)

The whole scene looked like chaos to most watching on the ground. Swarms of B-29s packed into the landing pattern, all hoping to be in position when the tower gave the green light for an aircraft to land. The bombers were dispersed to parking spots as quickly as possible, but often there were backups and those still flying had to wait. If a plane was unable to move off the runway under its own power, it was towed, or in extreme cases even bulldozed to the side.

Those unable to land circled over Iwo Jima while the crews bailed out. One soldier, Technician Fourth Grade Frank Saffarrans, Jr., recalls watching the action one day. "I watched the crews of 12 B-29s bail out over the island. People were literally raining out of the sky. The airplanes then crashed just off the west beach of the island. One B-29 cartwheeled across the water, making three complete rotations with only the wing tips making contact with the water. All of the crashes happened in less than 15 minutes."[118]

Iwo Jima was so popular, so well used, that on occasion it almost became "full." A pilot of the 40th Bomb Group, Flight Officer Dick Veach, describes returning from Tokyo with engine trouble. "We called ahead to Iwo and told them we were coming in on three engines. When we got there, we found that two planes were crashed on the runway, and three or four more damaged planes were waiting to land after the runway was cleared." Despite warnings from Iwo Jima's tower not to try it, Veach decided to keep going. During the lonely hours between Iwo and Tinian, his home base would periodically call and ask, "Are you still up?" "Yes," he would tell them, "Hold dinner."[119]

RED ERWIN

Staff Sergeant Henry "Red" Erwin was the radio operator of the 29th Bomb Group's lead bomber on a mission to Koriyama, Japan on 12 April. At the assembly point, Red's bomber, *The City of Los Angeles*, was tasked with launching flares and a white phosphorous bomb to aid in the formation of aircraft behind the leader. When Red dropped the bomb through the B-29's launching chute, it ignited early, springing up into his face and tumbling onto the floor of the bomber. The 1,300-degree bomb obliterated Red's nose, right ear, and blinded the young flyer. Though in shock, he knew that in a matter of moments the hissing canister could explode the three tons of incendiary bombs stored just a few feet away in the plane's bomb bay—killing everyone on board. Thick white smoke and terrible heat began to fill the plane.

Red blindly found the burning bomb by touch, scooped it up, and moved toward the flight deck, hoping to make it to the copilot's window. The white-hot canister seared his bare skin, ignited his clothes, and burned him to the bone as he maneuvered around the gun turret assembly and crashed into the navigator's folding table. Stuffing the glowing 20-pound bomb between his forearm and body, Red unlatched the table and forced himself

Staff Sergeant Henry "Red" Erwin was terribly burned when he sacrificed himself to save the lives of his buddies aboard the B-29 *City of Los Angeles.* After receiving emergency medical attention at Iwo Jima, his superiors rushed to award him the Medal of Honor while he was still clinging to life. (U.S. Army Air Forces via National Archives)

Struggling to Safety

It was hardly ever dull when the B-29s came to roost. Iwo Jima became a hive of activity as medical and crash personnel shifted into high gear. Others simply gathered to watch, silently hoping that each bomber would make it down in one piece.

Too often, the flights of B-29s came packed fairly close, with the first aircraft touching down as followers stretched into the distance far over the northern horizon. The radio waves were soon overloaded, as were Iwo Jima's runways and taxiways. Mangled planes gingerly jockeyed for position as others, slightly farther away, disgorged men under brilliant white parachutes.

One Superfortress soars into the skies as another awaits a recovery crew to drag its battered carcass back onto the runway. The plane overhead is a photo-reconnaissance ship, most likely headed for Japan. Both aircraft made fairly early stops at airfield number one on Iwo—the photo was taken on or around 11 March 1945. (Author's Collection)

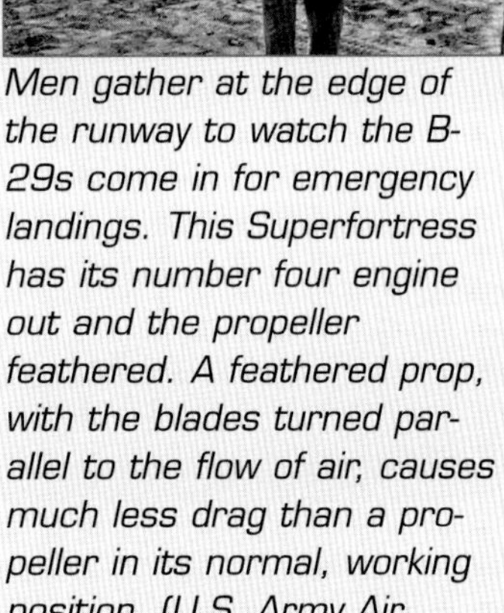

Men gather at the edge of the runway to watch the B-29s come in for emergency landings. This Superfortress has its number four engine out and the propeller feathered. A feathered prop, with the blades turned parallel to the flow of air, causes much less drag than a propeller in its normal, working position. (U.S. Army Air Forces via National Archives)

When fog separated the crew of this 6th Bomb Group B-29 from Iwo Jima's runways on 26 May 1945, they chose to ditch at sea. The torn-apart bomber was towed near shore. When a cable snapped on the bulldozer being used to recover the water-filled aircraft, the project was abandoned. Days later, the soldiers on Iwo woke up to find the sea had pulled the Superfortress completely out of view. (U.S. Army Air Forces via National Archives)

Like a scene from a flyer's nightmare, the damaged propeller of this 505th Bomb Group aircraft sheared off, gashed into the fuselage of the plane, and then bounded into the running blades of the adjoining engine. The pilot brought the mangled Superfortress into Iwo Jima with only the two remaining left side engines. (U.S. Army Air Forces via National Archives)

If it wasn't for Iwo Jima, there is little doubt that more B-29 Superfortress bombers would have ended their combat careers like this—lost at sea. Amazingly, this 499th Bomb Group aircraft, with all its fuel burned away, floated for over 17 hours. After the crew was rescued, the plane was sunk by gunfire from a destroyer on 14 December 1944. (U.S. Army Air Forces via National Archives)

Right: *This 505th Bomb Group B-29 came into Iwo Jima with a gash in the radio compartment and two engines running, and one of which was on fire. Considering the circumstances, the skillful pilot made a good landing. The plane came to rest after hitting a stranded 497th Bomb Group aircraft. The only injury was the bombardier, who sprained his ankle. (U.S. Army Air Forces via National Archives)*

past, finally cramming the phosphorous canister out the window.

Red fell to the floor in agony as the smoke on the flight deck cleared and the pilot regained controlled flight of the aircraft just 300 feet above the water. Fire extinguishers were turned on Red's flaming body as the aircrew automatically turned the Superfortress toward Iwo Jima—the closest place for medical aid. They gave Red morphine and tried to stabilize him. Amazingly, the severely burned radio operator stayed conscious on the lonely flight to Iwo Jima and asked about the safety of his companions.

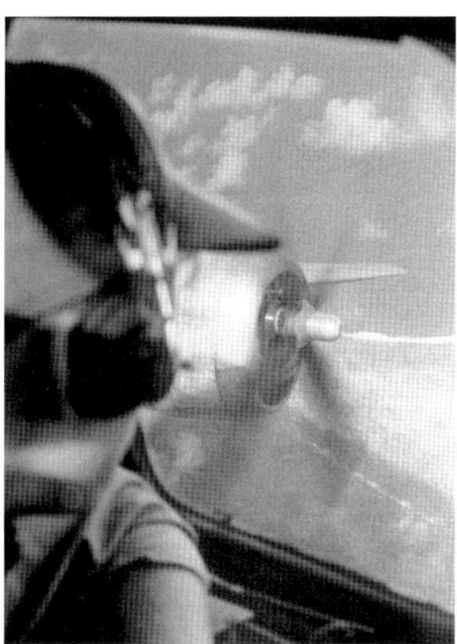

Above left: **A B-29 flyer nervously watches over a rough-running engine on his B-29 during a return flight from Japan. (Harry Hadlock and Loren Cockrell)**

Above right: **An injured 29th Bomb Group Superfortress sticks close to a buddy as the bombers near Iwo Jima. With one engine out, the plane pictured will most likely land on the island for repairs before returning to Guam. (U.S. Army Air Forces via National Archives)**

No one aboard the B-29 figured Red would survive. At Iwo Jima, the Superfortress came straight in for landing and medics were on the scene as the bomber braked to a stop. Red was loaded on a stretcher carried away for skin grafts, transfusions, and urgent surgery. As soon as Erwin was stable enough, he was flown to the medical facilities on Guam for additional attention. Despite the heroic efforts of the Army doctors, they too, were sure Red would die.

Officers quickly cut through red tape in an effort to present the young airman, who had saved his crew from death by sacrificing himself, the Medal of Honor while he was still clinging to life. Red's brother, a Marine, was flown in to visit the burned flyer who was wrapped head-to-toe in bandages. General Curtiss LeMay gave the Medal of Honor to Red in a Guam hospital, telling him, "Your effort to save the lives of your fellow airmen is the most extraordinary kind of heroism I know." Erwin weakly replied. "Thank you, sir."

Amazingly, this true hero did survive. After 41 surgeries in 30 months, Red regained his eyesight and the use of one of his arms, and returned to his home state of Alabama. He passed away on 16 January 2002, more than 55 years after the war.

IWO'S ACCOMMODATIONS

The aircraft based on Iwo Jima often searched for the crews of downed bombers or helped locate and bring in damaged or lost B-29s. The radar-equipped Northrop P-61 aircraft of the island's two night fighter squadrons were particularly useful for the latter.

On 19 May, a B-29 of the 40th Bomb Group struggled toward Iwo Jima with a faulty number two engine. When an oil leak forced the crew to shut the engine down, the propeller refused to feather entirely. It continued to rotate and vibrate as more and more oil gurgled out and was swept away.

The radio operator and navigator, stationed in the fuselage near the dying engine, watched as the prop shaft went from glowing red to white hot as it continued to windmill. When the pilot called for them to move forward, they wasted little time.

North of Iwo Jima, three P-61s found the injured Superfortress. A Superdumbo B-29 rescue plane also patrolled nearby. Central fire control gunner Staff Sergeant Roland Geisler recalls that the P-61s briefly flew a tight formation around the damaged bomber. "They were close enough that we could see their faces, and they would wave at us," he wrote. "When the prop came off, it just missed one of them. After that, they were just little specks way out in the sky."

At that same moment, navigator Lieutenant Vince Ford, recalls the nearest P-61 was telling Agate Base over the radio, "I don't see anything wrong with this plane except an oil leak on the number two engine." Just then, the 16-foot prop sprang loose, bounced off the side of the fuselage, and spun into the air. The Black Widow violently dodged out of the way as it tumbled by.

The Superfortress made it to Iwo Jima, and due to damage caused by the runaway prop, the crew elected to jump. All 11 men bailed out in two passes over the island. Each one landed on the island's craggy landscape. Six men sustained injuries, but all considered themselves lucky to be back on solid ground.

On average, a damaged B-29 stranded on Iwo Jima took four days to repair. Many of the aircraft were fixed in a matter of hours, but some extensively damaged planes took several weeks—skewing the typical time span upward significantly. If the repairs were minor, crewmen relaxed, wandered, or waited. When the damage was massive, flyers usually had little trouble hitchhiking back to the Marianas on a newly repaired bomber.

The men in limbo were those in the middle. After a major strike, the average number of transient crewmen on the island was 400. Upwards of 650 men could be quartered and fed at the busiest times. Many of the squad tents for the guests were on a hillside near the airfield. Flyers noted that, when it rained, water cascaded across the black ash floors during its rush down the hill. It could be worse, they said; at least it didn't gather in puddles in the tent.

Lieutenant Hadlock of the 40th Bomb Group recalls being billeted on Iwo Jima while he was awaiting repairs to the engines on his B-29. His tent was located yards from the end of the runway. Heavily loaded Mustangs seemed to be constantly thundering into the air just a few feet over the tent poles.

With the idea of taking a peaceful nap pretty much out of the question, many flyers passed their time doing something they shouldn't have—exploring Iwo Jima's caves and looking for souvenirs.

Lieutenant Phil Boguch of the 504th Bomb Group remembered that the young tail gunner from his aircraft only went a short distance from the flight line to get into trouble. While Boguch and the other airmen stood in a circle conversing about their plane and upcoming mission, the young man sauntered off and found the body of a Japanese soldier that had been pressed into an embankment by a Seabee bulldozer. After rifling through the dead man's pockets, he came back to the group with a strange, dirty object that looked like a Sterno can, and held it out, asking, "What do you suppose *this* is?" The flyers stared. "Uh, *that* is a Jap grenade," someone stated. "Get that thing out of here!" The gunner stiffly and slowly walked back to the body and returned the grenade to the dead man's pocket.

Tail gunner Staff Sergeant Joe Majeski of the 6th Bomb Group remembers having the urge to take home a souvenir from Iwo Jima as well. While waiting for fuel, perhaps he could find a Samurai sword for his mantle back home. His attention turned to an abandoned Japanese tank in the distance. Majeski carefully made his way through the snarled battlefield, being extra sure to avoid the live grenades lying around.

When he reached the tank, he climbed up and peeked inside. It was a mistake. There was no Samurai sword, just the decomposing body—or rather *half* of a decomposing body—of the tank's operator. "That was the end of my investigating Japanese tanks," Majeski later wrote.[120]

The crushed and battered B-29s littering the areas around Iwo Jima's runways had a similar effect on those who had never seen the inside of the giant bomber. While the visiting B-29 airmen couldn't have cared less, soldiers based on Iwo often ignored the rules and explored the aircraft.

Technician Frank Saffarrans, Jr. recalls looking inside one battered Superfortress than had been pushed off the runway. "I ducked into the bomb bay and was marveling at how the airplane made it back as everything in front of the windshield had been blasted away." Looking around, he felt a drop of liquid on his face. He knew right away it was aviation gas. Looking down, he found that he was standing in a small pool of the volatile substance. "I had a lit cigarette in my mouth at the time," Saffarrans wrote. "I quickly took the cigarette, put the lit end in my mouth, and immediately got the hell out of there."

Derelict Japanese tanks, like this one, were often too much to resist for souvenir-hungry explorers on Iwo Jima, though peeking inside might bring unpleasant surprises. Many of the tanks on the island were buried before the invasion to function as immobile pillboxes for Japanese defenders. (The 7th Fighter Command Association)

Ramblin' Roscoe **of the 500th Bomb Group arrived over Iwo Jima on 15 April 1945 with landing gear and engine damage. The landing went bad—*Roscoe* smashed into a truck, killed a Seabee, and plowed over a tent, injuring two soldiers. The bomber came to rest on an embankment and would never fly again. (U.S. Army Air Forces via National Archives)**

MISSING MEN

One crew of a B-29 from the 6th Bomb Group, or rather *part* of the crew, made the long flight to safety at Iwo Jima on the morning of 24 May. It started the night before, on a bombing run over Tokyo. Just after the bombs tumbled into the darkness over the target, anti-aircraft shells smashed into the bomber's port wing, setting it afire.

The burning plane plummeted into the blackness, diving from 7,000 feet down to 2,000. Over the interphone, pilot

When crewmen examined the damage to this 6th Bomb Group B-29, they couldn't believe it made it to Iwo Jima. The night before, as the flak-blasted airplane plunged over 10,000 feet in the darkness over Japan, some of the crew didn't think the bomber would make it either—six men bailed out. The remaining crew struggled to keep the Superfortress aloft and landed safely. (U.S. Army Air Forces via National Archives)

Lieutenant Jay Anderson gave the order, "Stand by to bail out." Searchlights caught the B-29 and more flak exploded nearby. Anderson wanted to stick with the plane, see if the fire in the wing would go out, and get out over the sea before he ordered his men to jump. After escaping the Japanese coast, the prospects of survival began to look better. Anderson asked the navigator to give him a course to Iwo Jima. It was then he discovered the navigator was gone.

In the chaos over the target, the order to "*stand by* to bail out" may have been misunderstood or only partially registered through the bomber's interphone. When Anderson took stock, he found that six of his men had hastily escaped from the falling plane over the burning target.

The bombardier looked at the missing navigator's log, computed the winds recorded on the way into the Tokyo area, and shrugged slightly as he gave Anderson a rough heading to Iwo Jima. Over the next few hours, the fire in the wing faded and died as the remaining flyers tried coaxing the radios to function despite the bomber's damaged antennas. When they finally raised a Dumbo rescue plane, they were just 200 miles from Iwo Jima.

But there was another problem. As the rescue aircraft and the battered B-29 flew into the early morning light, they discovered the island was socked in with fog. Minutes later, Agate Base called to say the haze was clearing and they would be up and operational within five minutes.

Despite a torn-apart left main tire, the Superfortress—with five thankful airmen—touched down safely. Inspection of the B-29's ravaged port wing was sobering. The number one engine was a shambles and no one could figure out why the number two engine was still functioning. As for the crew that had disappeared over Tokyo, after the war it was discovered that they had all safely parachuted to earth, were captured, and interned as prisoners of war.

BACK FROM THE DEAD

Arnie Bader was a young Staff Sergeant, the central fire control gunner on the *City of Maywood*, a B-29 from the 19th Bomb Group, based on Guam. He was on his "lucky thirteenth mission," 15 June 1945. The target for the day was Osaka, but Arnie's bomber never made it. Off the Japanese coast, Bader's plane wandered through the tall cumulus clouds at 22,000 feet, looking to locate their squadron mates and join in formation. They found a Japanese Kawasaki Ki-45 fighter instead. "This twin-engine Nick popped out of a cloud right smack in front of us." Bader said. "Before the bombardier or anybody up front even had a chance to hit the interphone or say a word, this guy hit us with his 20-mm cannon."[121]

One cannon shell buried itself in the tail while another blasted the supercharger on the B-29's number three engine. A third projectile, strangely enough, smashed into the lower front gun turret, fracturing all the anchor bolts. "That entire turret fell out of the plane. It went, I don't know, 8,000 feet under the ocean."[122]

Another shell crashed through the Plexiglas nose of the Superfortress just above the bombsight. The bombardier, Lieutenant Dave Baird, had seen the Nick coming and reached for his optical gunsight. "That 20-mm came through the nose, and it hit the swing arm on the gunsight and exploded."[123] From neck to feet, Baird was sprayed with fragments of Plexiglas and metal.

Bader recalled the conversation on the interphone as wild and hectic as the Superfortress depressurized, and the pilot shoved the nose forward and banked into a cloud. After feathering the propeller on the number three engine, the flight engineer pushed his way forward and grabbed Baird by the collar, dragging him over his seat and aft to behind the pilot's and copilot's stations. They administered morphine and doused the injured flyer's wounds with sulpha powder and began to bandage most of his body.

The flyers pushed a pack parachute against the hole and repressurized the ship. It was obvious where they were headed. They raced to get Baird to Iwo Jima, about five hours away, on three engines.

They made it to Agate Base. Bader took care of stowing the equipment in his station and walked up the B-29's nose just as they were taking Baird away in an ambulance. "I walked over to our flight engineer, [Tech Sergeant] Joe Miller, and looked at him and asked, 'How's he doing?' And Joe just shook his head."[124] The flyers sat forlornly around the nose wheel of their aircraft as it was repaired.

The men never saw Dave again and, for 55 years, the crew figured he was dead. Recently, Arnie Bader got a telephone call. It was his "long gone" bombardier, Dave Baird—one of the thousands of bomber crewmen saved by Iwo Jima's dusty runways and medical facilities.

CHAPTER 10

Flying from Sulphur Island

Marine bomber pilots become mechanics on Iwo Jima's airfield number one. In some off time, they are working to repair a Navy fighter that made a forced landing during the invasion. In the background lies an almost completely picked-over Privateer patrol bomber. (U.S. Marine Corps via National Archives)

While the sleek P-51 Mustangs and their pilots seemed to attract the attention of the press, there were additional elements to Iwo Jima's air operations that were important. The Mustangs were the island's offensive punch and could protect Agate Base from attack in the daylight hours. However, there were many other critical jobs. Iwo's airfields had to be guarded at night. The ships near the island needed protection from attack by Japanese surface vessels and submarines. And the island was the perfect springboard for extending the range of Navy patrol activities.

ANTI-SUB/ANTI-SHIP

Though the Marine Corps fought hard to capture Iwo Jima, few Marine pilots flew from the island. There were a few exceptions. The first Marine aviators to make Iwo Jima their home were elements of Marine Torpedo Squadron 242, sent north from Tinian. Commanded by Major William Dean, the General Motors TBM Avengers of VMTB-242 arrived at Iwo's airfield number one on 8-9 March 1945.

The first days were rough. The aviators held their first flight briefings in a large crater as Marine artillery boomed nearby. Almost immediately, the Avengers began flying air defense missions around Iwo Jima in the daytime and during the night. The squadron also relieved the Navy's carrier aircraft from anti-submarine duty. After 23 days of flying from the war-torn island, VMTB-242 departed.

In early April, the North American PBJ medium bombers of Marine Bombing Squadron 612 flew from Saipan to Iwo Jima's airfield number one. The PBJ was a Marine version of the Army's twin-engine B-25 Mitchell. Flying from Iwo Jima at night, the PBJ crews would prowl for shipping up to the Japanese coast. During VMB-612's operations from Iwo, they claimed 53 Japanese vessels

The first briefing for Marine anti-submarine pilots took place in a shell hole near their primitive quarters adjoining airfield number one. At the time, Japanese forces still controlled the northern end of Iwo Jima and fighting still raged. (U.S. Marine Corps via National Archives)

Marine ground crewmen work to load a depth charge into the belly of a TBM Avenger. After the Navy carriers departed, anti-submarine patrols were launched from Iwo's airfield number one. (U.S. Marine Corps via National Archives)

With 55-gallon drums in the place of real maintenance stands, mechanics work to maintain a line of Marine Corps TBMs for patrols near Iwo Jima. In order to occupy less space on the island's recently re-opened and busy airfield number one, all the aircraft are parked with their wings folded. (U.S. Marine Corps via National Archives)

The Marine PBJ medium bombers based on Iwo Jima with VMB-612 were painted all black for night missions. The planes located enemy vessels with a nose-mounted radar system. Here, two Tiny Tim anti-shipping rockets are affixed to the belly of the plane with homemade mounts. (U.S. Marine Corps via National Archives)

With Mount Suribachi in the background, a VMB-612 aircraft begins its takeoff run. When night missions around Iwo Jima weren't as profitable as they had hoped, the Marine aviators began to travel north, toward Japan, to search for targets in the daylight hours. (U.S. Marine Corps via National Archives)

Tiny Tim rockets weren't so tiny—they were over 10 feet long and 1,200 pounds. Delivered by Iwo Jima's Marine bombers, the projectile was designed to punch through shipborne armor and explode. In this image, a Tiny Tim (with its fins yet to be installed) is displayed on a modified bomb-loading cart. (U.S. Marine Corps via National Archives)

When not experimenting with the new Tiny Tim rockets, the PBJs of VMB-612 launched from Iwo Jima with more conventional weaponry. A load of five-inch rockets and bombs are the complement for this aircraft before takeoff. (U.S. Marine Corps via National Archives)

damaged and five probably sunk. In addition, the PBJs attacked and destroyed many smaller targets never listed in Japanese postwar records.

Commonly, the PBJs carried .50-caliber machine guns, 5-inch rockets, and conventional bombs, but while on Iwo Jima, the squadron began experimenting with the Tiny Tim anti-shipping rocket. The Tiny Tims weren't so tiny—more than 10 feet long and almost 12 inches in diameter. Each weighed over 1,200 pounds and carried a 150-pound warhead.

Soon, the PBJs were not only flying at night but conducted daylight attacks as far north as Kyushu and Honshu. VMB-612 flew 251 sorties from Iwo Jima, losing seven aircraft. Three losses were combat related. One of the bombers was shot down over Japan by Navy Corsairs in a case of mistaken identity. On 28 July, the aircraft departed, bound for a new home on the island of Okinawa.

THE NIGHT SHIFT

The Northrop P-61 Black Widows of the 548th Night Fighter Squadron touched down on Iwo Jima on 6 March, the same day as the first Mustangs. The strange, glossy-black twin-engine machines drew a large crowd of Marines.

The Black Widow was, indeed, an odd bird. The largest and heaviest fighter of the entire war, the P-61 was armed with four .50-caliber machine guns and four 20-mm cannons. The fighter carried a crew of three—pilot, gunner, and radar observer.

Radar was the key to the Black Widow's operations. The radar set allowed the P-61 to be used as a nighttime counterpoint to the Mustang, flying combat air patrol and conducting semi-local attacks on "the Jimas" in darkness. Basically, the P-51 groups were responsible for protecting Iwo Jima from aerial attackers by day, "our responsibility was to maintain a two-ship night patrol from 6:15 pm to 6:30 am," wrote the 548th Night Fighter Squadron's historian.[125]

Less than 30 hours after reaching the island, the first Black Widows lifted off from Iwo Jima's airfield number one in the gathering dusk. While the night of 7 March was quiet, the following night brought a little more action.

Two unidentified aircraft were detected and a pair of P-61s gave chase. The pilots later speculated that the mystery planes released "window"—reflective metal strips that interfered with radar. "It was really the weather which determined the outcome. Bad atmospheric conditions finally obscured the targets to the extent that no visual observations were possible."[126] The enemy planes, slipping away into the darkness, were unable to find their way to bomb Iwo Jima or the surrounding ships.

The P-61s of the 549th Night Fighter Squadron arrived on Iwo Jima on 20 March. Two days later, on the evening of 22 March, the two squadrons began to share combat air patrol duties over the island.

The first Northrop P-61 Black Widows arrived on Iwo Jima on 6 March 1945. In hours of darkness, the night fighter crews were responsible for keeping the island safe from air attack. This plane is *Midnite Madness* of the 548th Night Fighter Squadron. (U.S. Army Air Forces via National Archives)

On the night of 25 March the 548th Black Widows were on patrol, cruising the cold skies over Iwo Jima. In actuality, the aircraft and crews were from the 6th Night Fighter Squadron, reassigned to the 548th. These combat-experienced "night watchmen" had been transferred before the unit moved to Agate Base.

At 2100, Iwo Jima's radar spotted seven unidentified aircraft and vectored P-61s in to intercept. It proved to be a difficult job. The fast-moving P-61s raced to catch their quarry, using their semi-reliable radar sets in the blackness.

Captain Ernest Thomas and his crew, flying *Sleepy Time Gal*, finally spotted a Betty in the night sky south of Iwo Jima. Their target, too, seemed to have difficulty traveling in the inky darkness and had missed the island on its way in. Thomas overshot and then turned back again and again as the Betty flew, unaware, away from the island.

Finally, the crew of the Betty either spotted the night fighter or came to the realization that they had missed Iwo Jima. They began a turn to the left as Thomas gave the Japanese bomber a quick blast with all the P-61's guns. The intruder burst into flames and almost collided with the Black Widow as they passed. The Betty exploded into pieces seconds later and dropped into the clouds, which lit up brightly from the flaming debris.

Nearby, Lieutenant Myrle McCumber and his crew, flying *Midnight Mickey*, spotted another Betty and sent two short bursts crashing through the bomber. It coughed a bright flame as pieces of the craft fell away. As the plane dove into the ocean, McCumber began stalking his next victim. He later said, "We knocked an engine off and it started to come apart but we didn't see it hit the water, so we only got a probable on that one."[127]

The air raid had an unforeseen consequence for the members of Iwo Jima's other night fighter squadron, the 549th. Their living area was located near the 21st Fighter Group, northwest of airfield number two. In the darkness, necessitated by the air raids, groups of Japanese soldiers moved in.

Six enlisted men of the 549th died in the 26 March "banzai charge" and four were seriously wounded. While the 21st Group area took the brunt of the attack, it is estimated that 50 to 75 of the 300 Japanese soldiers focused on tents manned by the night fighter outfit. "This was a Baptism of Fire that will never be forgotten by any member of this unit," wrote the 549th's historian.[128]

In the cockpit of the P-61 named *Sleepy Time Gal*, Captain Ernest Thomas and his crew stalked and destroyed a Betty bomber. Hunting for Iwo Jima in the darkness on 25 March 1945, the Japanese aircraft overshot the island. Following closely, Thomas gave the Betty a short blast from all of the Black Widow's .50-caliber guns and 20-mm cannon. (Ernest Thomas via the 7th Fighter Command Association)

The assistant crew chief from the 548th Night Fighter Squadron paints a Japanese flag victory symbol on the side of his Black Widow aircraft. The P-61 shot down a Japanese Betty bomber trying to slip in and attack Iwo Jima in the darkness. (Jimmy Alford via the 7th Fighter Command Association)

The following night, the crew of a 549th Black Widow viewed "the lights of an airborne object," following them through a number of turns. As they circled north of Iwo Jima, the lights turned away. There was slight contact made on the airborne radar set, but the object moved out of the area quickly. The unexplained occurrence happened again the following night with a different P-61 crew.

The night fighter crews were anxious to fly missions beyond the cold, boring, and seemingly endless combat air patrols. On 29 March members of the 549th got their first chance. The idea of the "intruder missions" was simple—keep the Japanese inhabitants of the other "Jimas" awake and nervous. Also, there was a good chance the Black Widows might locate enemy shipping moving about at night.

As the sun sets over Iwo Jima, ground crewmen prepare 549th Night Fighter Squadron Black Widows for another cold and lonely night patrol near their Pacific outpost. (Air Force Historical Research Agency)

Keeping an aircraft and all of its intricate components in top shape was a tough job in the humid, salty, and dusty conditions of the Pacific theater. Here, an AAF man cleans the 20-mm cannons installed in the belly of a Black Widow. (Arvid Johnson via the 7th Fighter Command Association)

Major Joseph Payne and his crew flew the first such mission to Chichi Jima. Just out of anti-aircraft range, the P-61 cruised for 30 minutes, looking for shipping and keeping Chichi Jima's population of soldiers out of bed and annoyed. When it was time to depart, Payne power-dived from 10,000 feet to 6,000, firing his 20-mm guns and dropping 1,000 pounds of bombs into the darkened landscape. Two other Black Widows went to Haha Jima and one to Ani Jima the same night.

From then on, Iwo Jima's two night fighter groups, with their valuable radar sets, flew a mixture of combat air patrols, intruder missions, searches, rescue, and weather missions. Ground control approach radar, code-named "Darkie," helped with night landings. The system was not only used for the P-61s, but was also available to crippled B-29s, groping for Iwo Jima's airfield number two in the darkness.

When Darkie was on the fritz, the night flyers had trouble. On 20 April, a 549th P-61 piloted by Lieutenant Blois Merriam was returning from an intruder mission over Haha Jima. Over Iwo Jima, Merriam attempted three landings using Darkie but was unsuccessful. Finally, their fuel getting low, Merriam and his crew were forced to jump. They were rescued in the water soon afterward. A group of Marine PBJs returned to the island next. One of the bombers crashed short of the runway and two others were forced to ditch at sea.

Later that morning, when the sun came up, things were no better for the P-61 airmen. Four aircraft of the 548th moved in to land and found that Iwo Jima was under a solid blanket of fog. It was so thick, soldiers on the ground knocked off their patrols because they couldn't see where they were going. As with Merriam, the fuel situation in the four orbiting aircraft was becoming critical.

Midnite Madness, flown by Captain James Bradford, braved the solid carpet of haze first. His landing was as good as could be expected in zero visibility, but rough enough to burst a tire. *The Spook*, piloted by Lieutenant Melvin Bode, came next. "We were coached to within 100 feet of the ground over the runway approach," Bode later said.

"I could see two blurred lights but I couldn't tell whether they were right or left of the landing strip," Bode said. "I choked the throttles and started to land, and was only about 25

Above and Below: Over fog-covered Iwo Jima on the morning of 20 April 1945, a group of P-61 flyers considered their options. They could bail out, ditch at sea, or try to feel their way through the mist for a white-knuckle landing. *Midnite Madness* (above) came first, making it down with only a burst tire. *The Spook* (below) was next, and collided with *Madness*, still parked on the edge of the runway. The collision left only a few bumps and bruises on the lucky flyers, but destroyed both aircraft. (U.S. Army Air Forces via National Archives)

feet off the runway when I realized that we had drifted sharply to the right. I banked and tried to slip her in, but the left wing tip dug into the ground and I lost control of the ship."[129] *The Spook* hit the parked *Midnite Madness* and bounced into the air before coming down on its belly.

As *The Spook* skidded over the ash and dirt near the runway, the 20-mm guns in the plane's belly began to blast away. They didn't stop until they were torn free from the fuselage. Bode and his crew, with only a few scratches, stepped from their mangled airplane, amazed to be alive.

Lieutenant Harry Burney, flying the third P-61, was listening to the carnage down below and decided it might be safer to jump. Tech Sergeant James Collins awaited the signal to bail out while thinking about a friend of his, a parachute rigger, who had packed his chute. "I was wondering whether it would open," he later said, "and pondering that stale old gag about how I would sure beat hell out of him if it didn't."[130]

All the men made it out of the plane, nicknamed *Late Date*, and safely parachuted through the thick fog. Only a split second after emerging from the fog, each man hit the ground. All three landed on Iwo Jima's volcanic landscape and took several minutes to stumble through the white void and locate "civilization."

Captain William Dames, flying the fourth and final Black Widow, made a few runs through the fog trying to find the runway. On one approach, he could see all the way to the ground in places. The minutes ticked by and gallons of fuel were burned. Finally, Dames was able to bring his fighter down through the fading mist. His tanks were nearly dry.

In May, the 549th took over the job of night combat air patrol entirely, as the 548th began preparations to move forward to the island of Ie Shima, near Okinawa. So when Japanese aircraft attacked on the nights of 21 May and 31 May, 549th aircraft attempted to intercept. The frustration of the grounded 548th flyers, lying in shallow drainage ditches instead of up in the inky skies chasing Japanese bombers, was apparent when the historian wrote, "It was heart-sickening for this detachment to sit on the ground and watch Jap aircraft both times successfully get over and bomb the island. During the entire period of this squadron's operations on Iwo Jima, not one single Jap had ever reached the island."[131]

The report went on to say that, "No enemy aircraft were destroyed or intercepted by night fighter craft, though AA [anti-aircraft] units shot down two on the first raid. It was with extreme surprise that they watched the tremendous amount of concentrated AA firepower that could be poured into the Iwo skies, making a Fourth of July celebration look sick by comparison. Bombs did material damage both times, and in each raid both deaths and casualties were suffered by island personnel."[132]

THE SHOOT-DOWN

While the 548th was no longer involved in combat air patrols, they did fly from Iwo Jima occasionally until mid-June. One of the night fighter's strangest adventures involved a 548th aircraft, *Midnite Miss*, aloft in the daytime, on 9 June. Major Arthur Shepherd and his crew were running a check of their fighter's radar, using B-29s returning from Japan. More than 100 miles north of Iwo Jima, they encountered an emergency signal from an aircraft and closed on a fast-moving B-29.

The crew of *Midnite Miss*, a 548th Night Fighter Squadron aircraft, was credited with shooting down an abandoned American B-29 Superfortress. Left to right, Lieutenant Arthur Shepherd, pilot, Lieutenant Arvid Shulenberger, radar observer, and Master Sergeant Donald Meech, gunner/observer. The terrier was named Rags. With his own sleeping bag and oxygen mask, Rags often came along on combat missions from Iwo Jima. His human companions said that the little dog loved everything about flying—except when the Widow's four 20-mm cannons were fired. (Air Force Historical Research Agency)

They pulled alongside K-37, a Boeing Superfortress of the 330th Bomb Group, based on Guam. There was no answer as the Black Widow crew tried to raise the bomber on the radio. The P-61 moved to the opposite side of the apparently undamaged bomber.

They were amazed at what they saw as the port side of the B-29 came into view—the entire left side the plane's cockpit was missing. There was a hole as big as a grand piano ripped in the nose of the bomber. The unbelieving Black Widow crewmen were looking into the flight deck of the bomber as if in cross section. The pilot, his instrument panel, and control

Sometimes, the cameras caught a Black Widow night fighter out of its element—during the daylight hours. Iwo Jima's radar-equipped P-61s were assigned escort and search missions during the day, as well as night patrols. (U.S. Army Air Forces via National Archives)

yoke were gone. There, in the mangled mess, sat the copilot, the wind whipping at his bloodied flight suit.

K-37's amazing story had begun hours earlier, in the skies over Osaka. Before bombs were dropped, the B-29 took a direct hit from a 90-mm anti-aircraft shell. There was a tremendous explosion as the sidewall of the nose tore away. Captain Arthur Behrens was killed instantly. The left arm of the copilot, Lieutenant Bob Woliver, was shattered and his left eye blinded.

The flight deck was destroyed—all of the pilot's instrument panel was carried away in the blast, and Woliver squinted to see that only the magnetic compass on his side of the cockpit was functioning. Blood and hydraulic fluid were being whipped everywhere by the wind. The pilot's yoke was sawed off a foot from the floor, and Woliver had to pull back hard on his to keep the bomber flying level.

The navigator gave the copilot a guess at a heading that would get them near Iwo Jima and the mangled bomber limped out to sea. For four hours, the bleeding Woliver struggled with the blasted plane, being periodically spelled by the flight engineer and the bombardier when he became too weak to fly.

The plane's instruments were ravaged, so the crew guessed at power settings, speed, altitude, and fuel consumption. If Shepherd and his P-61 crew had not been nearby to find them, the Superfortress would have missed Iwo Jima by 100 miles.

Through the giant hole, Shepherd used hand signals to tell the copilot to follow and he banked his fighter toward Iwo Jima. The men called Agate Base, told them of the situation, and warned other aircraft out of the way.

There was no way they were going to land. The crew would have to bail out—preferably over the island. Most of the crew "hit the silk" on the first pass. On the second run, the bombardier pulled Woliver to the nose wheel well, pushed the copilot out, and then jumped himself. K-37 flew on, back towards Japan, with the autopilot activated and Shepherd's P-61 still trailing.

After brief consideration, Iwo Control told Shepherd and his crew to "splash" the unmanned Superfortress. The P-61 pulled up and made a firing pass on the B-29, blasting away with all four .50-calibers and four 20-mm cannons. As they pulled away, the Black Widow crewmen were amazed to see that K-37 lumbered along, straight and level, as if untouched.

After a second pass, a fire developed near the big bomber's left outboard engine. As the engine began to lose power, K-37 initiated a slow, gentle turn back toward Iwo Jima. Shepherd had to hold his fire as the unmanned B-29 again cruised over the island. By now, hundreds of men below

The copilot's area, to the right on the flight deck, was all that remained in the blasted nose of mortally wounded 330th Bomb Group Superfortress. Shepherd and his Black Widow crewmen could hardly believe the big bomber was still flying. (Harry Hadlock and Loren Cockrell)

Men of Iwo Jima's 386th Air Service Group load ammunition into the four .50-caliber machine guns mounted on the fixed top turret of a P-61 Black Widow. The streamlined fairing that covered the guns in flight can be seen sitting near the feet of the man in the center of the photo. (U.S. Army Air Forces via National Archives)

had come out of their tents or stopped their work on the flight line to watch the show.

The P-61 lit into the Superfortress again as soon as it moved out to sea. The .50-calibers stitched hundreds of neat, small holes as the 20-mm shells ripped gaping chunks out of the plane's skin. The B-29 still carried its entire load of explosives, but that was unknown to the fighter's crew. They tried to concentrate on the wings and the engines, but several rounds crashed into the fuselage, tail, and bomb bay as well.

Shepherd's supply of ammunition was nearing its end, and the Boeing bomber simply flew on. The flyers thought briefly about what an embarrassment it would be, disgraced by an unmanned aircraft in full view of everyone on Iwo Jima. Finally, the B-29's circular flight path seemed to tighten and the plane began a slow spiraling descent toward the sea. Shepard would later admit that the plane was not truly shot down—it *flew* into the water. The relieved flyers had used 564 .50-caliber rounds and 320 rounds of 20-mm to bring K-37 down.

Days later, the 548th Night Fighter Squadron P-61s took off from Iwo Jima to their new base of operations, Ie Shima. This left the 549th as the sole night fighter unit on the island. The following months were relatively quiet, with long night patrols punctuated by a few minutes of action. The cat-and-mouse games with Japanese bombers continued, with the night fighters usually able to chase them away from the island—but hardly ever, it seemed, able to close within firing distance. The 549th ended the war with one confirmed air-to-air victory.

THE FLOATING AIR DEPOT

Soon after the fighters and bombers began landing on Iwo Jima in great numbers, a modified Liberty ship steamed north from Saipan and dropped anchor near Sulphur Island. The ship was built as the *Rebecca Lukens*, but it had been recently re-named the *Major General Herbert A. Dargue* for its special mission—code-named Project IVORY SOAP.

As the United States military moved from island to island across the Pacific, Army fighters and bombers came in right behind the frontline troops. Iwo Jima was a classic example. In this ugly battlefield environment, aircraft were going to be subjected to damage—there was no doubt about it. And though the Army's service squadrons could sometimes perform miracles while they were dug in near the airfields, there were certain large and complex jobs that they simply couldn't do.

That's where the *Dargue* fit in. The ship had been converted into a massive floating machine shop and repair and maintenance depot. Manned by an assortment of 344 men from the Army, Navy, and Merchant Marine, the *Dargue* and five other ships were officially classified as Aircraft Repair Units, Floating (ARUs).

To ferry parts, supplies, and workmen to and from the host island, the ARU had two motor launches and two DUKW ("duck") amphibious trucks. But what caught the attention of the soldiers on Iwo Jima was the ARU's pair of helicopters.

The Sikorsky R-4B choppers were something entirely new for most men on the island. Operating from a platform near the bow of the ship, the strange "eggbeaters" searched for downed planes, rescued flight crews, ferried shipwrights and mechanics, and hauled parts. They always seemed to gather a crowd (after the dust settled) when they landed on Iwo Jima.

The *Dargue* was virtually a permanent fixture off Iwo Jima's shores after mid-March. The ship left only briefly, heading for open sea when a typhoon passed near the island on 15 May. The Navy gunners aboard the repair ship, firing 20-mm and 40-mm anti-aircraft guns, were even credited with shooting down a raiding Japanese Betty bomber near the island.

ON PATROL

The damaged B-29, *Dinah Might*, wasn't the first four-engine aircraft to land on Iwo Jima. On the same day, 4 March, hours before the famous Superfortress arrived, a Navy Consolidated PB4Y-2 patrol bomber from VPB-118 braved the falling mortars at airfield number one and came in to land. Aboard the aircraft were the senior patrol plane officer and the commander of all Navy land-based planes on Tinian. They had come to see if Iwo Jima's first airfield was suitable to be used by Navy Consolidated PB4Y-1 Liberators and PB4Y-2 Privateers.

The idea of Navy patrol planes using Iwo Jima was simple and logical. Marianas-based aircraft could extend their patrol sectors almost to Japan's shoreline if, on the return leg, they landed at Agate Base to refuel before continuing south. The "Iwo connection" made it possible for the patrol bombers to fly north for two additional hours, allowing the snooping American airplanes within sight of Tokyo to the north, over parts of Honshu, off the coasts of Shikoku and Kyushu, and to the smaller islands of Tanega and Amami to the south.

The entire flying time on one of these Iwo Jima connections was between 16 and 20 hours—around 14

At the base of Mount Suribachi, a float-equipped Sikorsky R-4 Hoverfly lifts off to shuttle a load of aircraft parts to a repair vessel offshore. The helicopters were used for transport of men and smaller-sized airplane components and local search and rescue missions. (U.S. Army Air Forces via National Archives)

Soldiers can't help but wander over and look at the strange "eggbeater" that has descended onto Iwo Jima's black soil. It's probably the first time many of the men have seen a helicopter. As one Army reporter accurately predicted, "The damn thing is here to stay." (U.S. Army Air Forces via National Archives)

hours from Tinian to Japan and then back to Iwo Jima and about four hours from Iwo Jima back to Tinian. Several patrol squadrons—VPB-118, VPB-116, VPB-106, and VPB-102, flying Privateers and Liberators—used Iwo Jima regularly to refuel.

On these patrols, the Navy land-based aircraft undertook a number of important missions. The type of mission the bombers became involved with often simply depended on what targets of opportunity the crews found during their long hours in the air.

The bombers frequently engaged Japanese picket boats that dotted the seas. The vessels were small, well-gunned, highly maneuverable craft that were difficult and dangerous to attack. They were able to not only give warning to the Empire of American surface ship activities in the area, but could also report on the fleets of attacking U.S. aircraft cruising north from the Marianas and Iwo Jima nearly every day.

The patrol bombers also watched for larger Japanese merchant and military ships, bombing them when possible or reporting the ship's positions to nearby Allied submarines and surface vessels. Some flew routine patrols while others ranged ahead of Allied warships, alerting them to any threats, unusual activities, or golden opportunities that revealed themselves to their "eyes on the sky."

Returning to Iwo Jima was always an adventure. In the early days, though there were still snipers and falling mortars, the planes often gathered a crowd of Marines when they parked. Many leathernecks had never seen a tall-tailed Privateer up close, and others simply came for the handouts. The patrol crews were popular because they often shared their spare sandwiches and leftover canteens of water with the dirty fighting men who climbed from their holes to greet them. Upon return to Tinian, some of the patrol bombers took wounded but ambulatory Marines with them.

Soon after, portions of VPB-102, VPB-116 (operating Liberators), and VPB-106 (flying Privateers) moved to Agate Base. The squadrons only deployed part of their complement of aircraft on Iwo Jima at one time, working on a rotational basis. Other parts of the squadrons continued to fly from the Marianas. By 8 April, patrol bombers from all three squadrons were flying from Iwo Jima. The forward-stationed PB4Ys cut the long haul to the Empire in half, allowed for larger bomb loads, deeper penetrations, and

Navy patrol plane *Modest' O-Miss* of VPB-118 returned from Japan on 6 March 1945. Navy ships shelling Iwo Jima paused as the plane, low on gas, came into airfield number one. A soft spot in the runway tore off the Privateer's right main gear. The plane remained on Iwo as a source of spare parts for other visiting patrol aircraft. (U.S. Army Air Forces via National Archives)

more cruising time off the enemy's coast. The aircraft located on Iwo Jima also diminished the need for many of the Iwo connection flights.

A member of VPB-106 happily described life on Sulphur Island like this: "There was never a dull moment on Iwo Jima. Zoomies [fighter pilots and planes], dust, sulphur, and steaming earth by day, trip flares and Japs by night, with an ammo dump blowing up all added to the general confusion. Nerves were calmed and quieted by the sedative of Spam and K rations three times a day."[133]

On a stopover at Iwo Jima, a curious B-29 flyer snapped this image of the nose art painted on the side of a VPB-116 Consolidated PB4Y-2 Privateer near airfield number three. *Cover Girl's* artwork was a favorite among flyers—Milton Caniff's "Dragon Lady" comic strip character. (Harry Hadlock and Loren Cockrell)

CHAPTER 11

SQUIDS AND DUMBOS

During planning sessions for the first VLR mission to Japan, Iwo Jima's Mustang pilots were more concerned with flying 1,400 miles over the ocean than encountering enemy aircraft. While both Army Air Forces and Navy search and rescue units were deployed along the way to help any flyer in trouble, the long flight was risky. (U.S. Army Air Forces via National Archives)

On 6 April 1945, the evening before the first fighters went to Japan, Iwo Jima's P-51 pilots met to discuss the mission. While the men reviewed strip maps of the route, rendezvous times, radio frequencies, and call signs, the generator that fed power to their tent sputtered and died. In the darkness, one Mustang pilot moaned, "That's what my engine's gonna do over Tokyo!"

The joke got a chuckle out of many of the fighter pilots, though to most, it wasn't really all that funny. Men who flew the 1,400-mile missions from Iwo Jima and back say that every little hiccup or strange burble of sound from their Mustang's Packard Merlin engine was cause for concern or even panic. It was almost as simple as if a pilot's engine keeps running, he lives, if his engine dies, he very well may die soon after.

Unlike the many amazing stories of Army flyers fighting over Occupied Europe, who escaped and evaded capture on dry land, there were slim chances for survival after bailing out over the massive and hardly ever passive Pacific Ocean. "No nice haystacks to hide inside or beautiful French girls to smuggle you food," Iwo's flyers scoffed, "just miles and miles of cold water in every direction but up."

One Navy carrier pilot, shot down nearby, was amazingly located and rescued by a destroyer as he floated alone in his one-man raft after five days at sea. When the flyer climbed back aboard his ship, his first words to his buddies were, "All right, you guys, put all that stuff of mine back in my locker." His friends had raided his foot-locker. It was almost a sure bet that, after a flyer had been lost at sea for that long, he was not ever going to make it home.

The dreary reality was that the Pacific hardly ever even surrendered a flyer's lifeless body. For example, the 15th Fighter Group lost more than 45 pilots in combat and still others in accidents. One man, Lieutenant Alex Trodahl, was the only member of the group buried on Iwo Jima during the entire war. Trodahl's

A horrifying scenario for many flyers in the Pacific—sitting alone in a tiny raft, afloat on the vast and empty sea. But things ended happily for this Navy pilot. The weather stayed calm and he was spotted by a searching Navy warship. (U.S. Navy via National Archives)

Lieutenant Alex Trodahl was the only pilot of the 15th Fighter Group to be buried on Iwo Jima. His service and burial took place on 29 April 1945. More commonly, a flyer lost during operations or in combat simply disappeared. (Bob Scamara via the 7th Fighter Command Association)

Mustang crashed and burned 150 feet short of airfield number one's runway as he was returning from a test hop with a malfunctioning engine on 29 April.

Yet, a number of flyers beat the odds and escaped the all-consuming sea. Many survived thanks to Army and Navy rescue personnel stationed on and near Iwo Jima. As the war progressed and American forces became more dominant in the Pacific Theater, rescue efforts became more organized and bold. At the beginning of 1945, it was estimated that the chances of surviving after being lost at sea were one in two. Tales of last-minute rescues, selfless heroics, and heartbreaking tragedies appeared in the last six months of the Pacific war as they always had for U.S. aviators. Doomed flyers came back from the dead to fly again. Improvements in rescue operations, combined with the gradual pullback of the Japanese sphere of influence, raised the odds—near the end of the war, it was three out of every five.

The AAF versions of the amphibious Consolidated Catalina were called "Dumbos" by flyers. They could roam over long stretches of ocean and land at sea once a downed pilot was found. Note the search radar "teardrop" above the flight deck on this worn and dust-streaked OA-10 Catalina of the 4th Emergency Rescue Squadron. (Harry Hadlock and Loren Cockrell)

Over Iwo Jima, an Army Dumbo rescue airplane sets out over the Pacific. Below, dust clouds rise from the never-ending construction on Iwo's runways. (Nick Teresi via the 7th Fighter Command Association)

THE RESCUE NET

Aircraft, surface ships, and submarines had the difficult work of trying to pluck downed flyers from the seemingly endless Pacific during air raids on the Japanese homeland. Overall, the Navy handled most of the task of air-sea rescue. The Army had established its first Emergency Rescue School in late 1943. Some of the first Army rescue squadrons began to deploy in 1944. By 1945, portions of the Army's 4th Emergency Rescue Squadron were based at airfield number one on Iwo Jima. They helped veteran Navy outfits cover the area around the island.

The 4th flew search and rescue missions with two types of aircraft. The first was an Army version of the Consolidated PBY Catalina flying boat built by Canadian Vickers Ltd. in Quebec. Designated the OA-10A, these amphibious "Cats" of the AAF could land on Iwo Jima's airfields or, more importantly, settle into the sea near a raft or drifting airman. Lovingly called "Dumbos" by aviators, the aircraft are credited with saving the lives of hundreds of airmen in the Pacific and off the shores of Europe.

The second type of aircraft employed by the 4th ERS was converted Boeing B-17G Flying Fortress bombers. Redesignated the B-17H "Flying Dutchman," the rescue planes carried an A-1 lifeboat contoured to fit snugly under its belly. Airmen called them "Bulging Bessies." As the war began to wind down and aircrews felt safer, the aircraft often carried an airborne search-radar system in the place of its chin turret armament. The plywood A-1 boat could be dropped over a stranded flyer and descended to the water via parachutes.

The Army's air rescue fleet also included several converted B-29s from the Marianas-based bomb groups. With plenty of range to fly all the way to Japan and back, the planes airmen called "Superdumbos" carried additional radio equipment and droppable rescue kits, rations, radios, and pneumatic rafts. The bombers also retained enough armament to fight it out with any enemy patrol boat or aircraft that came along to harass a flyer in the water.

Navy submarines and destroyers played a critical role of the Pacific's rescue net. Supporting a typical strike mission to Japan, aircraft and vessels were spread out along the route between Iwo Jima and Japan at intervals—to quickly rush to the scene of any incident along the way. Life-saving planes were dispersed along the route to reach any point in 20 to 30 minutes. Rescue vessels, commonly a mixture of submarines and destroyers, were likewise spread along the path to arrive at any location required in less than four hours.

An Iwo-based 4th Emergency Rescue Squadron "Flying Dutchman" cruises off the shores of Chichi Jima with a squadron mate during a rescue operation. The plane has already dropped its lifeboat and the attachment rigging can be seen on the belly of the converted bomber. (U.S. Army Air Forces via National Archives)

Code names were assigned to the vessels and geographical locations so they could be discussed on the radio without revealing information to the enemy. Names were chosen that were thought to be difficult for English-speaking Japanese to pronounce; "Nellie's Nipple," "Hairbreadth Harry," or "Fleas Knees." There were code words for aircraft types too; "chicken" for fighter, "boxcar" for heavy bomber, and "monster" for B-29s. Finally, there were codes for a flyer's condition: "Goodyear" meant the airman was in a raft, "yellow jacket" for in a life jacket, and "Davy Jones" for without a life jacket. "Evergreen" meant a dye marker was being used.

Together, a typical distress call might be, "18 Hairbreadth Harry 170 chicken Goodyear evergreen," meaning a fighter pilot was down 18 miles from a certain location on a heading of 170. The flyer was in a raft and his position was indicated by a dye marker.

On the lookout for a telltale flare, dye marker, piece of wreckage, or glint of light, a crewman aboard a 4th Emergency Rescue Squadron scans the seas. Finding a downed airman in miles and miles of nothing was akin to spotting a needle in a haystack—from hundreds of feet in the air. (U.S. Army Air Forces via National Archives)

A Mustang flyer's strip map for an attack on the Nagoya area shows the locations of rescue aircraft and vessels, code-named Boxkite and Darkeyes, arrayed along the fighters' entrance and exit routes. A point of land, called "Burlesque Queen," allowed pilots to talk about their location without revealing information to the enemy. (John Wilson via the 7th Fighter Command Association)

At a stateside factory, a worker checks stacks of inflated one-man life rafts for a telltale air leak. It was critical to supply airmen with rescue equipment that was in perfect working order. (U.S. Navy via National Archives)

In the shadow of the Japanese home islands, the USS *Quillback* races in to put itself between a downed Seventh Air Force pilot and the shoreline. In the summer of 1945, brave AAF and Navy rescuers often worked right under the noses of the rapidly weakening Japanese military forces. (Naval Historical Center)

The submarine farthest north in the rescue net commonly loitered 20 to 30 miles from the Japanese coast and moved in as close as five miles during the actual attacks. In the last months of the war, understandably jumpy but amazingly brave submarine crews even managed to snatch a handful of American flyers from the immensely dangerous waters of Tokyo Bay. During operations so close to shore, submarines often made their gutsy efforts to reach downed airmen with two Superdumbos flying shotgun overhead.

On one occasion, a B-29 crewman, Tech Sergeant Jack Cannon, came down by parachute within sight of the Japanese shoreline. He watched helplessly from his life raft as a Navy submarine and two Superdumbos fought it out with seven Japanese fighters and eight small boats in an attempt to bring him home. After a harrowing six hours, the Americans won the battle for possession of Cannon, wresting him and six other flyers from the grasp of the enemy.

One day in July, the USS *Quillback* was the northernmost submarine in the net. Though on her maiden patrol, she wasted no time getting into combat. An Army fighter pilot, Captain Roy Jacobson, parachuted into the sea just 3,000 yards off Kyushu's shore and the *Quillback* ran straight through minefields and into range of shore batteries to get him. Dodging torpedo attacks and blasting a suicide motorboat with the sub's deck gun, the crew of the sub maneuvered between the exhausted pilot and the shore, dragging Jacobson aboard. After the daring rescue, sailors aboard the submarine claimed that their captain had told them, "We were going to get that pilot even if we had to put wheels on to reach him."[134]

OVER JAPAN

Aviators tried to stay with their planes as long as possible. Bailing out over Japan was certainly no guarantee of safety. By 1945, Japanese civilians and military personnel were regularly subjected to devastating firebomb attacks by U.S. heavy bombers and more concentrated raids on key targets by Army fighters and Navy carrier planes. With the Japanese homeland in jeopardy and many loved ones lost, there was no telling what might happen to a U.S. airman—the so often unreachable harbinger of death and disaster—should he float down on Japanese soil.

A fighting man captured alive was viewed as a terrible dishonor in the ways of Japanese culture. In briefings, B-29 airmen were told that Japanese civilians were stoning and pitchforking American flyers they caught on the ground. One joke that B-29 flyers liked to tell wide-eyed groundlings was that if you were taken alive in the Japanese homeland, the best you could hope for was a quick beheading. There was no chance to "blend in" with the local population, so aviators were told to immediately surrender to the military or police. At least they wanted their prisoners alive so that they could interrogate them.

In reality, the best a flyer could hope for was that, though he'd probably be beaten and starved, he might survive long enough to see the end of the war. But the popular phrase among the men in the Pacific was "the Golden Gate in '48," meaning they anticipated returning to the United States at war's end, via San Francisco, in 1948. With the painful thought of three years' captivity in the hands of a vengeful enemy, many flyers turned their battle-ravaged or smoking aircraft towards the open sea rather than risk capture in Japan.

When Mustang pilot Lieutenant Ralph Heintz pulled away after strafing Katori Airfield on 3 August, he noticed coolant gurgling from his engine compartment and watched as the temperature gauges shot up into the red. His damaged fighter crossed the Japanese shoreline into open sea, but five miles later, the engine rumbled, sputtered, and died. His propeller ground to a halt. Prospects looked good as he jumped, with a Dumbo on the way and a submarine not far behind. Once in his tiny one-man raft, Heintz's hopes soared as P-51s circled overhead and the rescue plane dropped a supply packet nearby. But once the American planes ran short of fuel and left him, there was still no sign of a submarine.

Lieutenant Ralph Heintz bailed out of his dying Mustang and spent more than 24 hours drifting in Japanese waters before he washed ashore. (Ralph Heintz via the 7th Fighter Command Association)

Heintz's afternoon air show offshore had certainly attracted the enemy's attention. Two pairs of Japanese Zeke fighters came out to finish him off as he sat in his bright yellow raft. Every time they approached, Heintz dove under water. Though terrified, he was never hit by the bullets that rained down upon his little patch of sea. His floating rescue equipment fared worse. The fighters blasted his supply packet to pieces and deflated his raft with three punctures. As nightfall came, Heintz calmly patched his raft while treading water and climbed back aboard.

The exhausted P-51 pilot drifted near the shore of Honshu for that night and the following day. The next night, Heintz navigated nervously through a sea of mines before he washed up onto the beach. He was hiding in the dunes, trying to figure out what to do, when clam fishermen discovered him. Prudently, Heintz lowered his .45 pistol and let the Japanese take him away. He figured it was his only chance to make it out alive.

He began to regret his decision minutes later when a group of angry villagers tied him to a pole. "I figured that was about it."[135] But at what seemed like the last moments of his life, a Japanese policeman arrived, put Heintz in handcuffs, and pulled him away from the growing mob.

His train to Tokyo was strafed by American Mustangs, but luckily for him, the fighters did only a half-hearted job of it, leaving the coaches and locomotive intact and moving minutes later. Ralph Heintz spent the next few weeks as a prisoner of war before being liberated near the end of August.

"HARD LUCK" HARRIGAN

Lieutenant Thomas Harrigan of the 506th Fighter Group participated in the ill-fated 1 June 1945 mission that cost the Army Air Forces 28 Iwo-based Mustangs. But "Hard Luck" Harrigan wasn't lost to weather or collision, as many other pilots were that day. Poor Harrigan reached up to transfer the flow of gasoline from one fuel tank to another. The fuel selector-valve switch broke off in his hand.

He tried desperately to fix the problem, but was ultimately forced to bail out of his perfectly good Mustang when he ran out of fuel. "Hard Luck" sat alone in his raft for 50 hours, overlooked by a veritable parade of American aircraft—a Navy patrol plane, a B-29 with two Mustangs in tow, and another B-29 bomber all buzzed close to his tiny raft. He shot flares and signaled with his mirror but no one seemed to notice. Finally, on 3 June, after a long staring contest with a frigate bird who had come to visit him, Harrigan was able to attract the attention of an alert B-24 Liberator crew as they passed overhead. A destroyer, the USS *Fanning*, arrived on the scene soon after.

Harrigan had a lot to teach the other flyers about search and rescue when he returned to Iwo Jima. One important, albeit strange, result of Harrigan's adventure was that many flyers began carrying a pair of pliers or a wrench among their 85 pounds of flight gear, just in case the fuel selector valve broke off in *their* hands while they were flying so far from home.

"Hard Luck" Harrigan apparently used up all of his luck during his unexpected cruise. Over Japan on 8 July, his new Mustang failed him when a coolant line was hit. The engine

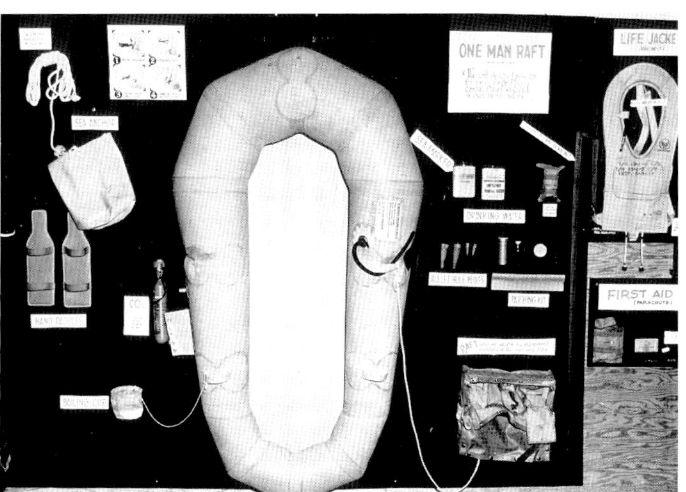

A public relations display at a California Army air base shows the some of the rescue supplies carried by fighter pilots in the Pacific, including bullet hole plugs, hand oars, sea anchor, and patching kit. (U.S. Army Air Forces via National Archives)

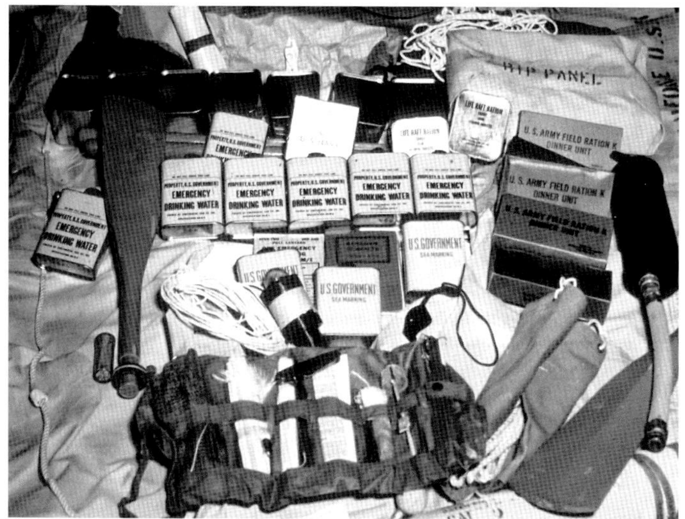

Long flights over water required an upgrade in the survival equipment carried by Iwo Jima's flyers. Flyers complained about sitting on the lumpy mass of materials in their seat packs on long flights but were grateful for all the components should they have to bail out. (U.S. Army Air Forces via National Archives)

The concept of the Josephine air-dropped raft was beautifully simple. It was a halved drop tank shell, some strapping, and a cord to pull the entire package apart once it had been separated from the aircraft. (U.S. Army Air Forces via National Archives)

died while he was over southwest Tokyo. He had to bail out again—which, the pilots agreed, was not the safest of endeavors. Harrigan was never seen again.

BAILING OUT

During missions over the Pacific, many pilots were killed jumping from their aircraft. In a Mustang, the prescribed method of leaving the fighter was to roll it over on its back and drop out. Many men disappeared after falling from their plane—no parachute, no raft—they were simply gone. Pilots speculated that perhaps airmen were hitting the tail as they fell away from their stricken aircraft.

On the second mission to Japan, 12 April 1945, Major James Tapp's wingman encountered trouble. Lieutenant Fred White followed closely behind Tapp as he swooped in on a Japanese Tony fighter and shot it down. Tapp speculates that Fred White's radiator may have ingested spent shells from Tapp's .50-caliber guns. White's airplane began losing coolant, the death knell for Mustangs, and it soon became clear that he would have to bail out.

Fred White rolled his P-51 onto its back and jettisoned his canopy. He then fell from the airplane. The other pilots

Over Hawaii, Major James Tapp experiments with an invention he developed—a fighter-dropped life raft. Code-named Josephine, the raft was hauled along on many trips to attack "the Jimas," but it caused too much drag to be taken to Japan. (David Beyl via the 7th Fighter Command Association)

watched as White plummeted from 3,000 feet. No one saw a parachute.

The losses troubled the squadrons on Iwo Jima. Even on occasions when a pilot's parachute opened, by the time a rescue vessel had arrived on the scene, the flyer was dead or simply gone. One of Iwo Jima's flight surgeons, Lieutenant Colonel Joseph Walther, was picked to conduct an experiment. A dummy would be dropped from a Boeing B-17 flying 200 miles from Iwo Jima. A Catalina carrying Walther would locate the "downed pilot" and he would parachute into the water and proceed to "rescue" the dummy.

With a carefully packed chute, Walther jumped from the aircraft and counted to 10. "At that point, I pulled the ripcord and immediately lost consciousness."[136]

The shroud lines from his blossoming parachute had whipped up and struck Walther in the right temple with a hammer blow. Plunging into the cold water revived him. He immediately attempted to inflate his Mae West life preserver. Only one of the two carbon-dioxide bottles worked, which allowed him to float with his nose just slightly above the rolling waves. He started vomiting within minutes from the rough seas and his bash to the head. After considerable effort, he climbed aboard a one-man raft dropped from the B-17.

"I felt so miserable that I had lost most of my interest in the dummy but fortuitously, I drifted directly toward it and pulled it in the raft." Walther said. The helicopter that was scheduled to come and pluck him from the sea never appeared on the scene and he floated, exhausted, for nearly three hours. A destroyer steaming though the area happened upon Walther and his quiet companion, the dummy, and pulled the pair aboard. "The captain told me I looked like hell," Walther said. "I told him I felt worse than that."[137]

Afloat in a sea of black sand, a 21st Fighter Group pilot trains to use his one-man raft should he have to bail out between Iwo Jima and Japan. Specifically, the men are discussing the use of a hand pump, used to keep the small vessel inflated over long periods of time. This image was taken on 19 April 1945. (U.S. Army Air Forces via National Archives)

Joseph Walther's dunking changed several things. Personnel checked all carbon dioxide bottles and over 40 percent of them were empty. And "an immediate Army regulation was published indicating that on bailing out, a person should place both hands on the sides of his head" to avoid being knocked silly by the parachute shroud lines, Walther wrote.[138]

SQUIDS TO THE RESCUE

Lieutenant Walter Kreimann was what veteran pilots called a "Yardbird." He had joined the 15th Fighter Group only months before they left for Iwo Jima. He was a new pilot, fresh from advanced training. His status as a newbie kept him at home on the first long-range mission to Japan on 7 April. But later, his position allowed him to fly on the wing of some of the most experienced and successful pilots of the Seventh Air Force. He was flying with Major Jim Tapp on the 12 April mission to Japan. That day Tapp shot down his fifth enemy aircraft and became the Seventh Air Force's first ace.

On Kreimann's second trip to the Empire on 25 May, he was flying with Captain Robert Moore. The fighters were assigned to attack Matsudo Airfield near Tokyo. Near the target, the 36 American Mustangs spread into a line abreast and dove in for the attack perpendicular to the airfield's runway. The pickings were slim, and the anti-aircraft fire from the ground was intense. All that was left were "dummies"—mock airplanes parked on the runway made from wood and cloth, carefully oriented to give the gunners nearby excellent lines of fire.

After a few minutes of shooting and dodging anti-aircraft fire in this "flak-trap," Kreimann tucked in behind his leader and headed back to the rally point, followed by four others. The Mustangs suddenly stumbled onto a mass of approximately 60 orbiting Japanese fighters. "They were just flying like a bunch of chickens, all straight out. I never saw them break ranks." said Kreimann.[139]

Moore dove toward a Zero at the end of one long line and Kreimann dutifully followed. "Normally," Kreimann explained, "a wingman doesn't ever get to shoot because of the ricocheting bullet danger." But as Moore's Mustang pulled off to the left, young Kreimann found himself directly behind a slower-flying Japanese plane. "So, I pulled the trigger. I couldn't resist."[140]

"The plane that I was firing at suddenly exploded and covered my windshield with oil. I thought I was going to hit it. It was that close."[141] Seconds later, it was over. The high-speed blast of air cleared Kreimann's windshield and he caught up with Moore as they headed for home.

On the way back to Iwo Jima, Walt used hand signals to congratulate Moore on becoming an ace—it got a rare smile out of what he described as his normally "unassuming and unemotional" leader. Then, he indicated to Moore that he too

P-51 pilot Lieutenant Walter Kreimann—downed, alone, and badly burned. (U.S. Navy via National Archives)

had blasted an enemy fighter. "I got no reaction! I said, 'Well, my gun camera film will straighten that one out'."[142] As he settled in for the long flight back to Iwo Jima, Kreimann's thoughts turned to the nice rubdown at the new spa.

About halfway home, the Mustangs passed over a lifeguard station. On a routine scan of his instruments, "I saw a very high temperature indicated and I knew something was going on."[143] Kreimann figured his strafing pass over the Japanese airfield resulted in damage from small arms fire. For two hours, coolant slowly seeped from his P-51.

He hoped to stay with the plane, to shorten the distance to Iwo Jima and get nearer to the next lifeguard station but it was not to be. "Waiting was a big mistake. I should have immediately bailed out before it got too hot."[144] Flames began to spew from the cowling of his plane as he drifted away from formation, rolled the Mustang over, and put the dying fighter into a stall. Kreimann pulled the handle to release the canopy but nothing happened. As the stricken fighter began to fall, Walt struggled to crank the canopy back by hand, release his harness, and stand up. Flames were being sucked into the open cockpit as the P-51 was picking up speed, headed for the water below. Standing on the seat, Kreimann was trapped, his chute pack was caught on something. He struggled to shake it loose.

"I couldn't get in and I couldn't get out." Seconds were ticking away and he knew he must be getting very close to the water. His right combat boot brushed against the stick. It was rock-solid, indicating his fighter was plummeting toward the ocean at over 300 miles per hour. "I rammed that stick as hard as I could and pulled the ripcord," he said[145]

Kreimann is still unsure how he got loose. "My immediate next sensation was being under water." He inflated his Mae West life vest and then his one-man raft and climbed aboard. Then Kreimann realized he had been badly burned—he had second- and third-degree burns on his legs, neck, face, and one arm. After a few minutes in the heavy swells, the young pilot also became violently sea sick. But, overjoyed to have survived his brush with almost certain death, he described it as "one of the most euphoric and jubilant moments of my life!"[146]

As evening settled over the Pacific, Kreimann began to feel awfully cold, hungry, and most of all, alone. It seemed too late for help to arrive that evening and he knew that by morning the currents would have moved him miles from his bailout point. As the sun began its slide to the horizon and his heart sank too, he heard a strange sound behind him. A metallic sound—"a clink." He turned to see a shape looming near him in the gathering dusk. "It could have been a Jap fishing boat or anybody and I would have been happy to get out of that raft at that point. A voice in English said, 'I have a rope. Can you catch it?'"

Life aboard the American submarine USS *Tigrone* seemed like heaven. After a warm shower, a dose of brandy, a wonderful steak served with real silverware and china, ice cream, and a first-run movie, Kreimann was ready to enlist in the United States Navy. "The Squids," as many airmen called submariners, were treating him exceptionally well.

His meeting with the sub's skipper soured his mood. Commander Hiram Cassady showed him his parachute—burned and melted, it was only half there. And when he informed the young flyer about where the *Tigrone* was headed, Kreimann felt even worse. In the last months of the war, Japanese shipping in the Pacific had become sparse. The *Tigrone* had been assigned the dangerous task of sneaking through the submarine nets and harassing shipping in Japan's Inland Sea. "I felt like I had gone from the frying pan into the fire."[147] Cassady told Kreimann that he was expected to stand watch like any other member of the sub's crew—he was going to become a Squid! All this bad news made Walt's burns hurt a little more.

The next day wasn't much better. Kreimann awoke to the sound of the *Tigrone's* deck gun blasting away and machine gun bullets spattering the hull near his bunk. Enclosed in the submarine, it was only years later that Walt saw the *Tigrone's* log and discover what had happened. The submarine had attacked a small Japanese boat called a "lugger," leaving the vessel engulfed in flames in the high seas.

Crewmen from the USS *Tigrone* haul their first catch from the Pacific—Lieutenant Walter Kreimann. The sub was headed for Japan's Inland Sea, but the men aboard had too much good luck in the rescue racket. Over the next few days, 28 other flyers would join Kreimann in the cramped confines of the Balao class submarine. (U.S. Navy via National Archives)

Badly damaged in a failed takeoff, one of Iwo Jima's 4th Emergency Rescue Squadron aircraft lies stranded at sea with its own crew and the men from a downed B-29. The USS *Tigrone* came to the rescue, taking them all aboard on 29 May 1945. Interestingly, "official" versions of this image, used in publications, were retouched to eliminate the name painted near the waterline and the damaged radar housing above the propeller-smashed flight deck area. (The Museum of Flight/Moon Collection)

Over the next few days, the USS *Tigrone* had astounding success as a lifeguard. First, a Navy bomber located the sub and ditched 500 yards away. They rescued five flyers. Next, the *Tigrone* came to the scene of an aircraft accident. A Catalina of the 4th Emergency Rescue Squadron had been damaged while taking off with 11 airmen from a stricken B-29 bomber. The submarine took in all the men—16 total. The pilot of the rescue airplane died from injuries he sustained in the accident while the *Tigrone* was still at sea. Next, the crew of another American bomber was added to the already overloaded vessel. With the food supply aboard the *Tigrone* rapidly dwindling, the mission to the Inland Sea was scrubbed, "which we all thought was a great idea!" said Kreimann.[148] Kreimann and 27 other grateful airmen were dropped off on Iwo Jima on 3 July 1945.

After a record-setting rescue patrol in the waters off Japan, the submarine USS *Tigrone* returns to Iwo Jima to drop off their full load of happy flyers. Here, 23 of the 29 Army Air Forces and Navy flyers pulled from the sea pose for photos before being ferried ashore. Suffering from burns, Lieutenant Walter Kreimann is not among the men pictured. (U.S. Navy via National Archives)

In the shores immediately off Iwo Jima, an Army DUKW ("duck") amphibious truck practices rescue drills. On the side of the vehicle/boat, the crew has painted symbols—one for each flyer pulled from the water. (U.S. Army Air Forces via National Archives)

MISSION TO CHICHI

Not all rescue stories had such a happy ending. The same day Kreimann returned to Iwo Jima, 3 July, the 78th Fighter Squadron left the island to attack Japanese boats near the neighboring island of Chichi Jima. During one of the strafing runs, Lieutenant Richard Schroeppel's Mustang caught fire. He was immediately forced to bail out near the shore of the Japanese-held island.

The remaining pilots of the 78th went straight to work to protect their downed comrade. A pair of aircraft climbed into the skies to radio Iwo Jima while the other Mustangs set up to strafe the island near where Schroeppel had splashed into the water.

As machine gun bullets and mortar rounds crashed around him, Schroeppel paddled furiously to pull his one-man raft out into the open ocean. In the air above, the P-51s of the

The P-51 pilots of Iwo Jima waged a furious battle with Japanese soldiers on the shore of Chichi Jima in an attempt to rescue downed flyer Lieutenant Richard Schroeppel. Dozens of Mustangs ran strafing attacks and rescue aircraft bravely dodged heavy enemy gunfire in order to give Schroeppel a chance to make it into a rescue boat. (Jim Vande Hey via the 7th Fighter Command Association)

The "Flying Dutchman's" lifeboat dropped into the sea attached to three large parachutes. Once down, the 27-foot long all-plywood boat could be propelled by two small five-horsepower motors or a mainsail affixed to a 20-foot mast. (U.S. Army Air Forces via The Boeing Company Archives)

78th wheeled and dived, continually pounding the rocks from where a mass of Japanese soldiers gathered to take pot-shots at the floating pilot.

Low on gas and running out of ammunition, the 78th needed to return to Iwo Jima. The 45th Fighter Squadron, tasked with bombing and strafing nearby Haha Jima, jettisoned their bombs and took over at the scene. As the 45th arrived, the pilots could see that Schroeppel was losing his battle with the sea and being slowly pulled toward the cliffs, still alive with Japanese gunfire. While the downed pilot took cover among the rocks, the 45th Mustangs continued to hose down anything that moved with their .50-caliber guns.

A lifeboat-equipped B-17 from the 4th Emergency Rescue Squadron arrived on the scene and bravely made a low pass near the shore of the island, collecting a massive barrage of gunfire. Just as the B-17 pilot, Lieutenant Claude Bodin, Jr., radioed that he was unable to spot the downed airman, Schroeppel sprang from his hiding place and tossed a dye marker into the water just off shore. With this information, the B-17's crew dropped their motorized lifeboat 100 yards from the water's edge, near the pilot's location.

Young Richard Schroeppel, stripped down to his underwear, crashed out into the water a few moments later, and swam and climbed over the reefs to reach the lifeboat amid a hail of gunfire. The Mustang pilots overhead doubled their efforts to hammer the shoreline as it appeared this long ordeal might possibly end well.

Schroeppel reached the boat and climbed in as machine guns and mortar fire rippled the water nearby. The boat didn't move. It simply sat there, with its waterlogged parachutes holding it in place. His fellow pilots of the 78th arrived back on scene refueled and rearmed, along with an OA-10A Dumbo from the 4th ERS. The Dumbo's pilot, Captain Robert Richardson, asked Iwo Jima's command for permission to conduct a dangerous landing near the boat and Schroeppel—right into range of the Japanese guns and mortars still peppering the water from the shoreline.

Permission was granted, and again the fighter pilots orbiting above intensified their fire on the shoreline again as the big Catalina thudded into the water nearby and gunned its engines to hop over the reefs along the way. The Dumbo made several passes near the lifeboat, taxiing amid heavy gunfire. Then, they took off blind—a mortar blast had hit close enough to cover their windshield with spray. Word came over the radio from the Dumbo crew about what they had found: Schroeppel was dead. He had been hit in the head and chest and had a catastrophic wound to one leg.

The Mustang pilots made a few more final runs through the gunfire off the shore of Chichi Jima to strafe and sink the lifeboat with their dead comrade inside. "It was better that way," 78th pilot Lieutenant Jerry Yellin told *Brief* magazine. "Those fellows were Dick's best friends—they didn't want his body washed ashore with those sons of bitches."[149]

CHAPTER 12

THE FINAL PHASES

Just a few feet from where American fighting men planted the Stars and Stripes, the Army erected major components of Iwo Jima's radar system. Mount Suribachi and the rest of the island became "the most radar-filled eight square miles in the world." (U.S. Army Air Forces via National Archives)

Iwo Jima was brimming with radar units. Soon after the Marines raised the flag on Suribachi, a medium-range radar set was hauled up the mountainside on the backs of Army Air Forces GIs. Later, nearly every type of available offensive and defensive radar was brought in. With two units per square mile, reporters claimed that Iwo Jima was the most heavily equipped radar site in the world

One summer night, Captain Hamlin Williston of the 302nd Fighter Control Squadron saw something unusual on one of Iwo Jima's radar screens. It was a bogey, perhaps more than one, and it was heading south from Japan. The mystery aircraft was flying at 30,000 feet and seemed to be moving fast. If he had to guess, he would have called it a lost B-29—but he wasn't supposed to guess. Williston looked for the plane's flight plan and found nothing, so he called an air raid.

The fast-moving aircraft passed 50 miles to the west of Iwo Jima, but was gone before the night fighters could "pour on the coals" and get into position to intercept him. The intruder zoomed on, unmolested, headed toward the Marianas.

Williston's superior officer was fuming and Williston was unsure why. The boss said only that Williston should have checked with him before sounding the alarm. Though Williston didn't know it at the time, he was witnessing the beginning of the end. Months later, he put all the pieces together—the mystery aircraft was the *Enola Gay*, or a sister ship, making a practice bomb run over Japan.

Packed onto the flight deck of the escort carrier USS *Casablanca*, the square-wingtipped P-47Ns of Iwo Jima's 414th Fighter Group are delivered to the Pacific. The planes arrived on Iwo in late July 1945. (U.S. Navy via National Archives)

THE LATECOMERS

The Thunderbolt fighters of the 414th Fighter Group began arriving at Iwo Jima on 27 July. A variation of the venerable attack plane used by American pilots with such success against German forces in Europe, the P-47N fighters of the 414th were slightly larger, heavier, and could fly farther than their predecessors.

Naturally, the new planes were informally compared by pilots with the Mustangs that inhabited the island. The P-47s were heavy, taking much of the runway to get airborne with a full VLR load of gas, ammunition, and rockets. In mock dogfights, the Mustang was still king, easily outmaneuvering the newcomer. The P-47 held an advantage only in a dive.

In the skies over Japan, the chances of encountering an enemy aircraft were becoming rarer every day, making the Thunderbolt's disadvantage in aerial fighting somewhat insignificant. The P-47, a hearty attack plane, could carry rockets and eight .50-caliber machine guns compared to the P-51's six, which gave the plane a bit more "punching power" when attacking ground targets. The Thunderbolt's air-cooled Pratt & Whitney radial engine also offered a somewhat greater safety factor in absorbing ground fire when compared to the Mustang's liquid-cooled Merlin.

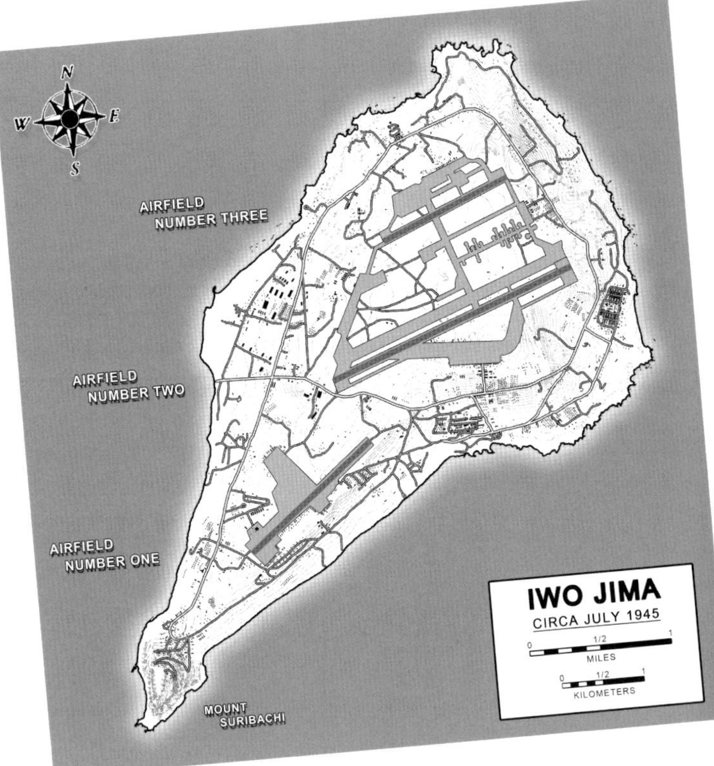

The men of the 414th settled in on Iwo Jima with only the usual complaints about the primitive conditions of the island. The pilots flew their first mission from Iwo Jima two days after their arrival, on 29 July. A flight of nine 414th fighters lifted off from the runway at 1241 and headed for Chichi Jima. Seven planes were slated to attack a radar installation. Of the remaining two, one would act as high cover, and the last fighter—a lifeguard—carried a Josephine belly tank life raft.

The newcomers encountered the typical weather in the Central Pacific; clouds covered their target. The pilots cruised over the northern part of the island, straining to find a hole. Finally, the flyers spotted two radio antennas and buildings, which they determined was "radio and power station number seven" on their maps.

The shiny new P-47s dropped through the hole in the clouds from 8,500 feet, launching rockets and firing their guns. No direct hits were observed from their unguided

The P-47s of the 414th Fighter Group were rushed into service so fast that flyers and ground crewmen had to paint the squadron markings on their aircraft between missions. Below, a 437th Fighter Squadron aircraft has checkers on its cowling, but has yet to receive its distinctive checked tail. On the left, Lieutenant Henry Jones works to shoot blue paint onto the tail of his 456th Fighter Squadron Thunderbolt. (Air Force Historical Research Agency)

Lieutenant Ben Drew pilots *Detroit Miss II* during the last month of the war. Similar to Iwo Jima's other fighter groups, the 414th pounded Chichi Jima before moving on to the longer missions to Japan. (Ben Drew via the 7th Fighter Command Association)

rockets, though a number of them blasted the ground around the "radio shack." Unharmed, all the Thunderbolts returned to Iwo Jima.

On this day and the next, P-47 fighters were involved in experiments with fuel consumption. On July 29, four aircraft took off with two 165-gallon tanks, a 110-gallon belly tank, six rockets, and 3,200 rounds of ammunition. They stayed aloft for 10 hours. The second day's experiment was less successful. The planes carried an identical load except that the belly tank was replaced with a 500-pound bomb. They returned to Iwo Jima after only six and a half hours of flying.

Thunderbolts were big consumers of fuel. Here, one of Iwo's 414th Fighter Group aircraft is configured with two 165-gallon wing tanks and a 110-gallon centerline tank. Note the mounting points for 10 five-inch rockets. (Air Force Historical Research Agency)

On the first day of August, the 414th fighters took off for their inaugural mission to Japan. Soon after they arrived over the Empire, Lieutenant Scott Coley's P-47 went missing in the overcast. He was never seen again.

The remaining 20 fighters attacked Okazaki Airfield first, shooting up the barracks and maintenance lines. They then flew to nearby Nagoya East Airfield and worked over the hangars and shops. Flak was "inaccurate, meager, light at both targets," said the group.[150] The fighters returned to Iwo Jima after nine hours and 58 minutes in the air.

Captain James Butler, Jr. poses at the checkered tail of his P-47 *Baby Dumpling* on Iwo Jima. Due to personnel shortages, Butler and many other pilots painted the squadron markings on the aircraft themselves. The Thunderbolts were equipped with same "Uncle Dog" homing system as Iwo's Mustangs. Here, the double antenna can be seen. (Air Force Historical Research Agency)

The appearance of a different fighter plane over the Empire may have caused questions among the Japanese military. On the morning of 4 August, Iwo Jima's radar reported two bogeys approaching. Three flights of 414th Thunderbolts where vectored to investigate.

One unknown aircraft moved swiftly away from the area, but the P-47s caught and cornered the other at 31,000 feet. It was a Dinah—a twin-engine Japanese photo-recon plane. Two flights of P-47s made firing passes on the lone aircraft almost simultaneously. The plane went into a left spin, one engine belching smoke. The Americans followed it down, still firing. The dying plane pulled up sharply and did a wing-over into the water some 12 miles from Suribachi.

THE BOMB

Sometime before August, Colonel Paul Tibbets, Jr. and members of his crew flew north from Tinian and landed on Iwo Jima. The men had come because they wanted to look at "the hole"—a concrete-reinforced pit that had been sunk into ground in a fenced off area on Iwo Jima's airfield.

"Washed out" in a landing accident, this filthy P-47 is unceremoniously loaded onto one of Iwo Jima's flatbeds. On both Mustangs and Thunderbolts, the canopy needed to be removed for crane operators to access the center lift point. (George Lonering via the 7th Fighter Command Association)

have been to drop one or two of them. It definitely would have destroyed so many of the Japs that were on the island. In that case, you could have eliminated the 25,000 [sic] casualties we had. But anyway, it wasn't done, and it wasn't dropped in Japanese waters. But I don't think there was anything wrong with the idea."[152]

As Lewis watched, Sulphur Island passed beyond the horizon. The *Enola Gay* flew north into the history books.

Named after Colonel Paul Tibbets' mother, the *Enola Gay* would become one of the most famous aircraft of World War II. On his history-making flight to Japan, Tibbets flew close to Iwo Jima—in case there was trouble. (Harry Hadlock and Loren Cockrell)

Very few understood the hole's purpose. It was there in case their B-29, the *Enola Gay*, failed them. Though Tibbets and his men would be embarking on arguably the most important flight of the war, something could still go wrong. If there was a bad oil pressure reading, hydraulics problems, weather difficulties, or a rough-running engine, the *Enola Gay* and its heavy, bulky, top secret cargo would make a beeline for Iwo Jima.

There, its mystery load would be lowered into the hole and another bomber, already waiting nearby, would be rolled into position. (For the 6 August atomic bomb mission, the spare B-29 at Iwo Jima was nicknamed *Top Secret*, piloted by Captain Chuck Knight.) The atomic bomb was going to Japan. Which plane, or even which crew delivered it, was of little importance to America's military leaders and President Harry Truman.

On 6 August at 0245, the *Enola Gay* took off hefting the secret bomb and headed north to Iwo Jima. Like any other American bomber flying from the Marianas, "We always flew pretty close to Iwo Jima," said Sergeant Joseph Stiborik, the *Enola Gay's* radar operator. "If anything went wrong, that's where we would land."[151] Arriving over Suribachi at 0552, the bomber circled at 9,300 feet. Soon two other B-29s, a photo aircraft and instrument aircraft, joined up. With the *Enola Gay* leading, the three bombers turned to compass heading 327 and began to climb.

From his seat on the flight deck, Captain Robert Lewis, the *Enola Gay's* copilot, looked toward Iwo Jima and wondered what it would have been like had the bomb been ready for use months earlier. "I wanted to see it used on Iwo Jima," Lewis later said. "It seemed a shame. What an ideal spot Iwo would

GLOOMY AUGUST

"The stunning news of the atomic bomb, of the Russian surge into Manchuria, of the doom of Hiroshima, of the preliminary requests for peace and the sparring for face and terms—all this came in August, while we still fought the war," wrote the 506th Fighter Group's historian.[153]

The idea of flying over hundreds of miles of water to blast cars, fishing boats, and few derelict airplanes seemed even more futile once the airmen learned that America had the ability to erase entire cities with a single bomb. But the flyers on Iwo Jima were still ordered into the air.

The day after the bombing of Hiroshima, 7 August, all three Mustang groups over Japan flew their usual missions of escort and attack. During these final days, the American pilots continued to fight, dodge blasts of anti-aircraft fire, and a few never came back.

Even in the last month of the war, heartbreaking accidents still took place. During a shakedown mission, Lieutenant Walter Cecot's P-47 lost power and crashed short of the runway at Iwo Jima. The pilot was the first loss for the 414th Fighter Group on the island. (U.S. Army Air Forces via National Archives)

Captain Jack Ort, of the 21st Fighter Group, crashed in a rice paddy near Osaka and was taken prisoner. Mystified by the Hiroshima blast, frustrated Japanese officials questioned Ort and other flyers about the atomic bomb. Captain Ort, of course, had very little to share with his captors, even if he had wanted to. He and four other airmen were executed.

On 8 August, the 414th Fighter Group flew its second VLR mission to the Empire. Major Paul Wignall's P-47 was hit by flak while strafing small vessels near Takamatsu Airfield. Wignall later wrote, "Great indeed was the relief I felt when I found that, by exercising great care, I could avoid crashing into the water a few feet below me. In fact, I later found it possible to climb a bit."[154]

Wignall nursed his dying airplane out to sea, where an American rescue submarine code-named Juke Box 772 awaited his arrival. When Wignall came into view, the sub was occupied with snagging a Mustang pilot, already in the water. Wignall circled in his faltering P-47, readying himself to jump. Finally, he rolled the plane over and fell out. His parachute opened perfectly and the airman drifted down into the cold Pacific. He was in his raft by the time the rescue sub came knifing alongside.

Wignall enjoyed his time aboard the submarine, becoming an understudy to the captain. They would spend their days submerged off Japan's coastline, looking for shipping that never appeared. "Then the evenings when we surfaced," said Wignall, "once again to reestablish radio contact with the outside world hoping to learn that the world was again at peace."[155]

On the same day Wignall began his brief career as a submariner, another 414th pilot sweated out the return trip to Iwo Jima. "Fortunately, one of those lovely navigation B-29s was around," said Lieutenant Frank Collyer, "and it succeeded in leading me over a destroyer while I still had 15 gallons of fuel left."[156]

The USS *Downes*, Bird Dog 63, was stationed about 100 miles north of Iwo Jima when Collyer's P-47 arrived. He positioned his plane upwind of the ship and began to prepare for bailout. "First I unfastened my oxygen mask, mike plug, and earphones. Then I jettisoned the canopy."[157]

At 3,000 feet, Collyer's engine coughed and he knew it was time to leave. "I chose the right side, and made the leap while the plane was in a straight and level altitude [sic]. I was pleased to find that I had cleared the plane, and realized that I was falling end over end through a cloud. When I finally broke out of the cloud I was at about 2,000 feet up."[158]

After pulling the ripcord, Collyer floated down to the water below. "I hit the water in exactly the same spot where my plane had hit! It occurred to me that I was fortunate to have landed after the plane."[159]

He inflated his Mae West life jacket and then his one-man raft and climbed aboard. Collyer spread dye marker on the water and sent up two flares. He wanted to make sure that the destroyer would have no trouble locating him. The ship arrived on the scene within 15 minutes.

Aboard the *Downes*, Collyer was treated very well. The ship's personnel were "excellent hosts." He spent five days at sea before reaching port. The crewmen of the *Downes* told him he was the thirty-fifth flyer the destroyer had rescued from the Pacific.

THE LAST DAYS

The following morning, 9 August, another B-29 flew close to Iwo Jima, carrying a second atomic bomb northward. Due to cloud cover over Agate Base, the aircraft of the strike group flew to an island off the southern tip of Japan to rendezvous. Again, the spare B-29 stationed at Iwo Jima—*Full House*, with Captain Ralph Taylor as pilot—was not needed.

Prior to takeoff, the flight engineer assigned to *Bockscar*, the B-29 carrying the atomic bomb, noted that a fuel-transfer pump was not functioning, preventing the bomber from using 600 gallons of its gasoline. The airmen decided to fly anyway. *Bockscar* would have to land at Iwo Jima on the way home and take on more fuel.

At the rendezvous, one of the strike aircraft failed to appear. After 40 precious minutes of waiting, the remaining aircraft flew toward Kokura—the primary target for the mission. They found the city mostly covered by clouds. Three attempts to drop the bomb visually were aborted and more fuel was sucked from the bomber's dwindling supply.

Over Nagasaki, the secondary target, the flyers found better weather and made their bomb run. Flying away from Japan, one look at the fuel gauges told the crew they didn't even have a chance to make it back to Iwo Jima. *Bockscar* turned toward Okinawa, slightly closer, and barely made it, landing only moments before one engine died due to fuel starvation.

Iwo Jima's flyers of the 15th and 506th went up to Japan again on 10 August to escort bombers in the Tokyo area. The planes of the 506th Fighter Group got into a rare air-to-air skirmish with a number of Japanese fighters which rose to harass the B-29s.

Captain Abner Aust and his wingman, Lieutenant Jackie Horner, chased one Zeke in a group of three that were approaching the bombers from the rear at 23,000 feet. Aust's gunfire tore the left wing off the Japanese fighter, which went down in flames. The pilot was observed bailing out of the burning plane.

Next, Aust and Horner encountered another Zeke and made several firing passes on the plane, hitting the wing root, canopy, engine, and external gas tank. "This enemy aircraft disappeared into a cloud at 500 feet in a flat, slow glide, trailing smoke and apparently without power," reports later said.[160]

Soon after, the pair spied a silver Zeke at 500 feet, north of Tokyo. After two passes, the Japanese fighter retreated over the grounds of an airfield. To dodge the anti-aircraft fire flying up at them, Aust and his wingman climbed into a cloud and waited for the Zeke to continue a wide turn which would bring the enemy aircraft right under the Mustangs.

Nose Art

Like most AAF aircraft of World War II, Iwo Jima's fighting machines were adorned with cartoon characters, clever names, and images of women. Aircraft based in the Pacific had some of the raciest nose art—far from the eyes of most civilians. However, a crackdown by the top brass on artwork with nudity or lude sayings, primarily focused on the B-29 Superfortress bombers based in the Mariana Islands, seems to have had an effect on Iwo Jima's population of flyers as well. Most imagery painted on the cowlings of the dusty fighters was fairly subdued.

The Enchantress *was flown by Lieutenant William Saks of the 506th Fighter Group, 457th Fighter Squadron. This image and many of the others in this section were taken by a pair of curious B-29 flyers stranded on Iwo Jima in late July and early August. (Harry Hadlock and Loren Cockrell)*

Flying with the 506th Fighter Group, 457th Fighter Squadron, the pilot of this P-51 has shot down three enemy fighters, signified by the Japanese flag symbols. The plane's crew chief has kept a tally of participation in escort missions to the Empire (middle) and bombing missions to "the Jimas" (below). (Harry Hadlock and Loren Cockrell)

A wartime slogan encouraging the conservation of gasoline in stateside automobiles has been applied to this Mustang—giving it a whole new meaning. Like many American flyers during World War II, Iwo Jima's pilots privately wondered if their efforts were worth the risks, danger, and death. And, like most, they continued to fly and fight for their nation. (Military History Institute/Milne Collection)

Before redeployment to Iwo Jima, this AAF man had a chance to paint the bushmaster snake emblem on the side of a 15th Fighter Group, 78th Fighter Squadron P-51 Mustang. The photo was taken on Saipan. (U.S. Army Air Forces via National Archives)

My Achin' (Ass) *was Major Harry Crim's good-natured commentary on the long, uncomfortable flights to Japan. Crim, ace of the 21st Fighter Group, shot down six enemy aircraft before the end of the war. (Harry Hadlock and Loren Cockrell)*

Staff Sergeant James Lindsay was the artist behind the 15th Fighter Group, 47th Fighter Squadron Mustangs. Each aircraft carried the name and likeness of Dogpatch *characters from* Li'l Abner, *Al Capp's cartoon strip. (W. H. Sparks via the 7th Fighter Command Association)*

Hairless Joe *and another Mustang crashed just five minutes and 50 feet apart during takeoff for a mission from Iwo Jima's airfield number one. Captain Joseph Brunette flying the 15th Fighter Group, 47th Fighter Squadron aircraft, walked away from the accident. (U.S. Army Air Forces via National Archives)*

Lieutenant Charles Seale poses in the cockpit of Shawnee Princess. *The image of "a prancing, black thoroughbred horse" and "jagged, red lightning flash" was the emblem of the 506th Fighter Group, 462nd Fighter Squadron. Seale parachuted from the* Princess *and was rescued on a mission to Chichi Jima. (Ed Bahlhorn via the 7th Fighter Command Association)*

Dropping from above, Aust's .50-caliber blasts set the plane on fire. It dove into the ground near the airfield, exploding on impact. Captain Abner Aust's two confirmed victories that day (along with one damaged) made his official tally five enemy planes destroyed. He became the 506th Fighter Group's first and only ace.

"Everyone knew it was the last mission," the 506th historian wrote of 14 August flight to Japan. "The Nips had sued for peace." The same writer described the final VLR, involving all four fighter-groups based on Iwo Jima, as "a final tap on the noggin."[161] The 414th called it a "persuader mission."[162] If there was a peace agreement while the flyers were in the air, the code word, "Utah," would be flashed to the navigational B-29s and be passed along to Iwo Jima's fighters.

"Since the run was obviously a gesture and would contribute nothing toward winning the war, the foremost thought in the minds of everyone was, 'will all these men get home safely on this last trip'," said the 506th report.[163]

But it was not to be. While no Japanese aircraft came up to tangle with the Mustangs and Thunderbolts, the anti-aircraft fire was as heavy as ever as the flyers went in low and did their best to locate and hammer the meager targets they found—locomotives, power plants, airfields, and even single automobiles. Several flyers were hit and bailed out, including two members of the 15th Fighter Group. One pilot was rescued by a lifeguard destroyer and was pulled aboard by the USS *Tigrone*, which was still roaming near Japan on its final war patrol. Major Ed Markham, the commanding officer of the 15th Fighter Group's 78th Squadron, was the *Tigrone's* thirty-first and final rescued airmen.

Tragically, one flyer never made it home. On the 414th's third combat mission over Japan, Lieutenant Harold Regan's P-47 was hit by the omnipresent anti-aircraft fire over Akenogahara Airfield. Regan fought to return, but the engine of his Thunderbolt failed just 225 miles northeast of Iwo Jima.

A lifeguard destroyer, *Playmate 61*, soon found the downed flyer in the cold sea. Regan had broken both of his legs against the tail surfaces of his stricken fighter when he jumped. He died five days later, on 19 August.

VICTORY

At 0900 on the morning of 15 August, President Truman announced the Japanese capitulation. The message came via Iwo Jima's radio station and the word spread quickly through every man on the island. There was little "civilian style" hysterical jubilation, said one Army publication. "Those who could drop their work took off and hit the sack. They were tired. Never—even on the island whose hallmark had been suspense—had the strain been so terrific as during those days of desperate Japanese stalling."[164]

Some of the most exhausted were Iwo Jima's radio crew, who had been repeating the same thing to the troops for more than 24 hours straight—no news as of yet. When peace finally came, it "was essentially an indwelling experience for Iwo men," said a reporter. "They had bitched and bitched, a bitching that was just short of neurotic in a war that thrived on bitching. They hoped more desperately for the end of the war than men on other islands where life was somewhat easier."[165]

Further dampening the mood was the voice of the provost marshal over Iwo Jima's public address system, "There will be no firing, repeat, no firing of weapons." Many men recalled their night crouching in a hole or huddled under a truck during the false V-E Day fiasco back in March. No gunfire was just fine with them.

There were, of course, some celebrations. The Navy craft anchored around Iwo Jima let loose with their horns and whistles, shooting flares into the air. The men of the 414th, perhaps because they had been on Iwo Jima the shortest amount of time, were less sedated than most. "The officers of the squadron sent down 65 quarts of whiskey to the 'Enlisted Men's Service Club'," said the 437th Fighter Squadron history. "There are few incidents the enlisted men can recall after uncorking the first bottle. Sergeant George Shawe tried walking down the club steps using his beard instead of his feet. His beard is curly now. Private Walter Traugh walked through the shower walls … or thought he did. They held fast but 'Wally' didn't. Thursday, 16 August came much too soon for us all. With splitting headaches and aching bones, we went back to work at noon."[166]

While some ambitious military projects were abandoned on the island, there was still work to be done. The fighters kept flying and the airfields stayed open. The biggest fear among the pilots was that they would die in some silly operational accident and never make it home. As a result, it seemed most pilots chose to stick a bit closer to the island when they went up flying. The airspace around Iwo Jima became very busy and downright dangerous.

The B-29s from the Marianas kept streaming in. No longer carrying explosive payloads, the bombers worked to gather information about the weather, get a more complete picture of Japan's damaged cities and ports via photo reconnaissance, and deliver food, medicine, and clothing to Allied prisoners at camps in Japan, China, Manchuria, Formosa, and Korea. As always, Iwo Jima took in stragglers with mechanical problems or too little fuel to make it home.

All this activity seemed secondary to the real question—when were the men of Iwo Jima going home? There were parades, inspections, VIPs, and all the typical military non-combat "nonsense" to keep everyone busy, but mostly, "we sat on Iwo Jima, and sat, and sat, and sat."[167]

The artwork on the cowling of Lieutenant "Herkie" Powell's P-47 was inspired by his sweetheart. But then a "Dear John" letter arrived at APO 86—Iwo Jima—and Powell felt he needed to adjust the imagery on his aircraft. (Air Force Historical Research Agency)

A Superfortress unloads packs of food over a POW camp in Japan. Even after the fighting had ceased, Iwo Jima was still a safety valve for returning B-29s low on fuel or suffering from mechanical failures. (U.S. Army Air Forces via National Archives)

The captured Allied airmen freed from Aomori POW Camp near Yokohama celebrate their release and the end of the war on 29 August 1945. P-51 Mustang pilot Lieutenant Gordon Scott can be seen just behind the man holding the Dutch flag (on the right). Scott says that some of the plumper-looking men in the photo were the crew of a recently shot down B-29 Superfortress. (Naval Historical Center)

Soldiers who had been preparing their squadron's equipment for one final beachhead airfield during what would be the last battle, the invasion of the Empire, were re-packed for a ride on a Navy ship. They would happily head in the opposite direction. But the waiting was almost worse than the fighting.

A few "rock-happy" flyers found ways to fill the void for excitement left when combat flying disappeared. On 27 August, the skipper of a Navy patrol bomber unit on Iwo Jima, Lieutenant Commander Walter Michaels, called for volunteers among his ranks of bored and listless men. He had no trouble creating a crew.

Then, he asked the island's commissary officer for 1,000 pounds of rations. The commissary man said Michaels could have the food—but only if he, too, could come along on the secret mission. With the rations and one Iwo Jima stowaway loaded aboard his Consolidated PB4Y-2 Privateer patrol bomber nicknamed *Peace Feeler*, Michaels took off and flew straight to Atsugi Airfield near Tokyo.

The victory symbols on *Peace Feeler* show the bomber's crew has had some success on the long runs to Japan. This VBP-116 Privateer is the Lieutenant Commander Walter Michaels flew to Atsugi Airfield on 27 August 1945. (Harry Hadlock and Loren Cockrell)

Those who asked were told the Privateer was going to Japan to help drop supplies to Allied prisoners in the area. But Michaels had another intention. He'd studied the aerial photos of Atsugi and memorized the runways, including where bombs had ripped up the landing mats.

Over Japan, he feigned an oil leak problem over the radio—just to have an excuse. Then Michaels' big Navy patrol bomber came in and made a bumpy landing at Atsugi. His was the first U.S. Navy plane to land on the Japanese mainland since the beginning of the war.

Michaels awaited the arrival of an entourage of cars that started out to meet him while a mechanic made a good show of working on an oil fitting in the plane's wing. But before the cars could reach him, Michaels noticed a group of trucks, heading out to block his takeoff path.

Mission accomplished as far as he was concerned, Michaels told the crew, "Let's go while we still can." They piled into the plane and got into the air before they could be stopped, probably leaving the Japanese on the ground scratching their heads in puzzlement.

ONE LAST MISSION

There was one last VLR mission. The pilots on Iwo Jima were sure the top brass were out-and-out trying to kill them. Despite almost unanimous complaining, grumbling, and, as soldiers say, "bitching," some fighters from Iwo Jima made one more trip to Japan on 30 August 1945.

The fighters, along with B-29 flyers from the Marianas and Navy aviators, were ordered to participate in a "Show of Power" above General Douglas MacArthur's landing at Atsugi Airfield.

When the P-47s of the 414th arrived on station, "A happy, crazy air carnival was in progress everywhere," according to the operations report. "Tremendous B-29 formations droned overhead as Navy fighters darted about over hundreds of warships in Tokyo Bay participating in landing operations. Air power was overwhelming, and the Field Day complete."[168]

The fighter pilots were fascinated to see Tokyo's destruction from close up. Cruising along at 1,500 to 900 feet, they saw how huge portions of the city had been completely obliterated by American firebombs.

After returning from the last mission over Japan, Lieutenant Dave Fitton of the 414th Fighter Group is photographed during a final debriefing on Iwo Jima. (Air Force Historical Research Agency)

While departing the area, Lieutenant Robert Flint's P-47 developed an oil leak and was forced to land at Atsugi Airfield. Unlike Michaels' "oil leak" three days before, this malfunction appears to have been legitimate. He came in at 1045, about the time General MacArthur's plane was expected to land, so he made his approach on an auxiliary metal strip. He later said the runway was so rough that it even made Iwo Jima's landing fields feel as smooth as silk.

He watched the general arrive and examined several Japanese Jack and Frank aircraft up close. Flint said the planes "appeared to be of poor construction, built of cheap materials."[169] Later, Flint convinced a B-25 mechanic and an armorer to help him try to fix his fighter.

A postwar photo of Atsugi Airfield shows a large number of Japanese aircraft in various states of disrepair. It was here that stranded P-47 pilot Lieutenant Robert Flint got the chance to examine Frank and Jack fighters up close. (U.S. Navy via National Archives)

The stranded pilot "was refused food and water by an American Major, but a crew chief smuggled some out. After sleeping overnight in the cockpit of his plane, he finally managed to hitch a ride back to Iwo in the tail of a B-29."[170]

THE END OF THE LINE

Everyone wanted to leave, but the Army's wheels of bureaucracy turned slowly. Pilots with the most seniority, via a system of points, departed first. Others anxiously waited.

To save weight and fuel, many of Iwo Jima's aircraft had most of their armament removed. For example, the P-47s of the 414th began to fly with two machine guns instead of the regular eight. The others were packed in Cosmoline, a preservative, and readied for shipping back to the States.

While all the men eventually went home, not all the aircraft did. Tired, corroded, and worn out aircraft were ordered destroyed on the spot. No one is quite sure what happened to them. Some say they were taken out to sea and dumped. Others contend that many Mustangs were unceremoniously bulldozed into a ravine and covered over with Iwo Jima's black sand.

The end to World War II came late for at least a few men based on Iwo Jima. On a January morning, years after the surrender, two 20th Air Force corporals were headed to the base motor pool in their jeep when they encountered a pair of hitchhikers.

Activity on the island had picked up a little recently because the United States had struck a deal to allow Chinese workers to recover much of the battlefield debris that littered the island. The GIs figured their visitors to be Chinese scrap men who had decided to walk the island's loop road and stopped to give them a lift.

As they bumped down the road, the Americans got a closer look at their guests. Each of the men was wearing a dirty U.S. Army field jacket that looked many sizes too big. They didn't speak English, so there was not much to say as the four rode into the Air Force base headquarters. At the motor pool, the GIs walked inside and the hitchhikers wandered among the Quonset huts.

Later that day when the pair of corporals came back into the base for lunch, everyone was talking about a supply sergeant who had captured two Japanese soldiers. The subsequent investigation cleared up a lot of mysteries for the Air Force men who had been living on Iwo Jima. The 24-year-old former Japanese navy machine gunners had been living off materials stolen from the base. They decided to turn themselves in after discovering a discarded American magazine that showed a photo of U.S. occupation troops in Japan.

They had lived in a cave and kept out nosy GI souvenir hunters by stretching barbed wire entanglements across its entrance. Americans came to respect barbed wire on Iwo Jima as a warning of danger. Inside the cave, investigators discovered mounds of stolen food containers, trash, and hundreds of flashlight batteries. The Air Force men had always wondered who was going through cases of their batteries.

Among the trash was one item that solved another mystery the Americans had been pondering for more than a week. They'd found out what had happened to their stolen canned ham. The missing ham was supposed to have been the centerpiece to their meal on Christmas Eve, 1948.

AFTERWORD

In the years after the war, Iwo Jima's long runways and remote Pacific location continued to serve the United States' military. Radio, weather, and radar stations remained in service.

Iwo Jima also may have been a storage facility for U.S. nuclear weapons beginning in the early 1950s. Military planners theorized that an all-out nuclear conflict with Russia would destroy much of Japan (now America's ally) and the airfields on Okinawa within hours. Iwo Jima and Chichi Jima were designated as "recovery and reload" centers—refueling and rearming American submarines and aircraft that were still operational after the initial attacks.

By 1968, there were only a handful of American men still stationed on the island they had nicknamed "the Black Pearl." Around 40 members of the Air Force were stationed on what used to be known as airfield number two. Another 38 were Coast Guardsmen operating a LORAN radio navigation tower.

In June 1968, the last Americans departed, and the island of Iwo Jima was returned to the Japanese people.

COLOR SECTION

Recently recovered Grumman F6F Hellcats are readied to be moved to the hanger deck after air strikes against Japanese targets. In the background, a General Motors TBM Avenger comes in for landing. Avengers were nicknamed "turkeys" by the carrier crewmen because of their ungainly look with their long, wide track landing gear extended. (U.S. Navy via Stan Piet)

Before a strike, a TBM Avenger is raised to the flight deck. The big torpedo bombers weighed over five tons when empty and could carry an additional 2,000 pounds of bombs. They were generally well liked by Naval aviators, partly because Avengers were able to absorb a remarkable amount of battle damage and stay in the air. (U.S. Navy via Stan Piet)

Lieutenant Paul Dechary of the 318th Fighter Group was photographed on combat air patrol near Saipan at 30,000 feet. *Dottie*, a streaked and stained Republic P-47D Thunderbolt, carries a 110-gallon centerline tank and a load of ammunition, standing guard to fight off any air attack the Japanese might launch from Iwo Jima or Pagan Island. (Earl Bach via the 7th Fighter Command Association)

Right: Lieutenant Jim Weir poses in front of the 318th Fighter Group P-38 *Diller's Killer*. The red-painted prop spinners are wearing through, showing the yellow markings of the former owners—the 21st Fighter Group—underneath. (Jim Weir via the 7th Fighter Command Association)

The 318th Fighter Group acquired twin-engine Lockheed P-38 Lightnings from the Hawaii-based 21st Fighter Group in late 1944. The planes had a longer range than their P-47s and could escort bombers and reconnaissance aircraft all the way from Saipan to Iwo Jima and back. (Stan Piet)

Vought OS2U Kingfisher observation aircraft were the eyes of the Navy fleet during the invasion of Iwo Jima. Catapulted from battleships and cruisers, the planes helped direct the roaring salvos of gunfire directed at the island's hidden defenses. (U.S. Navy via Stan Piet)

The bomber bases in the Mariana Islands were a tempting target for Japanese flying units on Iwo Jima. Through much of late 1944, American fighter and bomber groups worked to eliminate the threat by pounding Iwo Jima's airfields repeatedly. This image shows Boeing B-29 Superfortress aircraft of the 9th Bomb Group on Tinian. By the time this photo was taken, most of the enemy aircraft on Iwo were destroyed. (Stan Piet)

An F6F Hellcat passes over the fantail of the carrier USS *Randolph* with flaps, tail hook, and gear down. Aircraft from the *Randolph* retired from the Tokyo area on 17 February, hit Chichi Jima, and steamed to Iwo Jima for D-Day. The carrier's aircraft flew in support of Iwo's invasion activities until 23 February 1945. (U.S. Navy via Stan Piet)

Left: A Curtiss SC-1 Seahawk scout plane is towed on a recovery sled beside the battle cruiser USS *Alaska*. The plane was spotting for the *Alaska's* 12-inch guns near Iwo Jima on 6 March 1945. The ship carried a total of four scout aircraft that could be launched from two catapults. (Naval Historical Center)

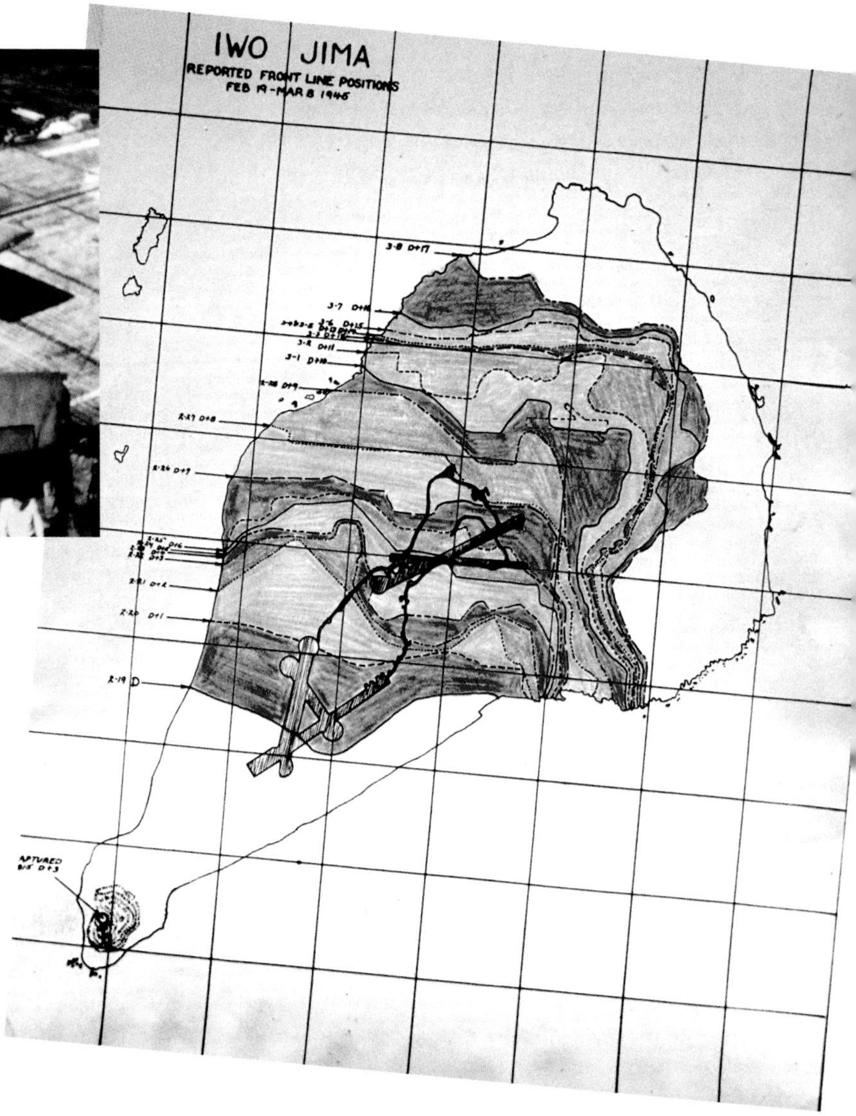

Bleached and exhaust-stained FM-2 Wildcats line up for takeoff aboard the USS *Makin Island* for a strike on Iwo Jima. After the larger carriers had departed, the fighters and bombers from small escort carriers took on the job of hammering points of Japanese resistance ahead of the advancing Marines. (U.S. Navy via Stan Piet)

Right: As Navy pilots worked to soften Japanese defenses in front of the Marines, it was important for them to know exactly where the front lines were so as to minimize "friendly fire" accidents. This map of the reported front line positions was for the flyers aboard the USS *Makin Island.* (U.S. Navy via National Archives)

A North American P-51D Mustang from the 15th Fighter Group makes the long flight back to Iwo Jima. This plane was assigned to the 78th Fighter Squadron. (Paul Martin via the 7th Fighter Command Association)

Five 15th Fighter Group Mustangs arrive over Mount Suribachi. One of the aircraft has begun his turn into the landing pattern for airfield number one. (Paul Martin via the 7th Fighter Command Association)

Ready to fly, 15th Fighter Group pilot Lieutenant Paul Martin poses with his chute, helmet, oxygen mask, and Mae West life preserver on the steps of the parachute shack on Saipan. The young pilot would later fly Mustangs from Iwo Jima. (Paul Martin via the 7th Fighter Command Association)

Below: As time went on, the accommodations on Iwo Jima changed from holes in the ground, to squad tents, to finally Quonset huts with plywood floors. Among the 15th Fighter Group pilots who lived in this room was Lieutenant Walter Kreimann—the P-51 pilot who was rescued after bailout by the submarine USS *Tigrone*. (Paul Martin via the 7th Fighter Command Association)

Iwo Jima's east beaches, photographed long after the invasion. Buildings and roads have sprung up everywhere—even a wide drive up to the crest of Suribachi. Which was, according to the Japanese, an impossibility. Note the 110-gallon aircraft drop tank being used for water storage at the bottom of the photo. (Stan Piet)

The aprons of airfield number one lie stuffed with 15th Fighter Group Mustangs. On the left is a row of Douglas A-26 Invader medium bombers—passing through on their way to Okinawa. (Paul Martin via the 7th Fighter Command Association)

Photographed from the cockpit of a 15th Fighter Group P-51, the island of Iwo Jima is overgrown with American facilities late in the war. The massive B-29 maintenance apron attached to airfield number two, just to the right of the clouds. (Paul Martin via the 7th Fighter Command Association)

A new Republic P-47N Thunderbolt fighter awaits deployment on the island of Guam. The plane was most likely headed to a combat unit based on Iwo Jima or Ie Shima, near Okinawa. (Harold Gronenthal via the 7th Fighter Command Association)

This rare photo shows a variety of aircraft on the island of Guam. A new North American P-51D and a Republic P-47N long-range fighter are parked in the foreground. Next, an older 318th Fighter Group P-47D. Lastly, a pair of Curtiss Commando transport aircraft flanking a smaller Douglas C-47-type cargo plane. (Harold Gronenthal via the 7th Fighter Command Association)

Late in the war, a 21st Fighter Group P-51 Mustang stands parked on Guam. Also seen in the photo are a B-17 emergency rescue squadron aircraft, a B-24, and a 504th Bomb Group B-29. (Harold Gronenthal via the 7th Fighter Command Association)

ENDNOTES

1. Phoebe Burns, *History of the Seventh Air Force (unclassified)* (Pacific Air Force, 1955) p. 32.

2. Morris Markey, *Well Done!*, (New York: D. Appleton-Century Company, 1945), p. 111.

3. Clark Reynolds, *The Fighting Lady*, (Missoula, MT: Pictorial Histories Publishing Company, 1986), p. 143.

4. Ibid.

5. Aircraft Action Report, USS *Hornet*, June 1944, National Archives.

6. Morris Markey, *Well Done!*, (New York: D. Appleton-Century Company, 1945), p. 120.

7. Ibid. p. 126.

8. Clark Reynolds, *The Fighting Lady*, (Missoula, MT: Pictorial Histories Publishing Company, 1986), p. 146.

9. Saburo Sakai with Martin Caidin and Fred Saito, *Samurai!*, (Garden City, NY: Nelson Doubleday, Inc., 1957), p. 235.

10. Ibid. p. 236.

11. Ibid.

12. Ibid. p. 237.

13. Ibid. p. 240.

14. Ibid. p. 255.

15. USS *Archerfish*, 3rd War Patrol Report.

16. Roger Angell, "Iwo Mission," *New Yorker*, 6 January 1945, p. 45.

17. Ibid. p. 52.

18. 30th Bomb Group History, Air Force Historical Research Agency, Maxwell AFB.

19. Richard Dugan, "Iwo Alarm Clocks," *Brief* magazine, 20 February 1945, p. 5.

20. Unknown, *AAF Evaluation Board Report Number Seven*, The Pacific Ocean Area, Air Force Historical Research Center, Maxwell AFB. p. 32.

21. 318th Fighter Group History, Air Force Historical Research Agency, Maxwell AFB.

22. Ibid.

23. Ibid.

24. Ibid.

25. 30th Bomb Group History, Air Force Historical Research Agency, Maxwell AFB.

26. Unknown, "The Japs Hit Back," *Impact* magazine, January 1945. p. 32.

27. 318th Fighter Group History, Air Force Historical Research Agency, Maxwell AFB.

28. Ibid.

29. Robert Frederick, "Escort in Reverse," *Brief* magazine, 23 January 1945, p. 8.

30. Ibid.

31. 318th Fighter Group History, Air Force Historical Research Agency, Maxwell AFB.

32. Unknown, "Borrowed Paradise," *Brief* magazine, 29 February 1945, p. 13.

33. 30th Bomb Group History, Air Force Historical Research Agency, Maxwell AFB.

34. Unknown, *AAF Evaluation Board Report Number Seven*, The Pacific Ocean Area, Air Force Historical Research Center, Maxwell AFB. p. 71.

35. 30th Bomb Group History, Air Force Historical Research Agency, Maxwell AFB.

36. 318th Fighter Group History, Air Force Historical Research Agency, Maxwell AFB.

37. Action Report, USS *Pensacola*, March 1945, National Archives.

38. Ibid.

39. Unknown, *AAF Evaluation Board Report Number Seven*, The Pacific Ocean Area, Air Force Historical Research Center, Maxwell AFB. p. 47.

40. 30th Bomb Group History, Air Force Historical Research Agency, Maxwell AFB.

41. Richard Newcomb, *Iwo Jima*, (New York; Henry Holt and Company, 1965) p. 103.

42. G. Roger Chambers, interviewed by Cory Graff, 11 September 2003, tape recording.

43. Ibid.

44. Ibid.

45. Ibid.

46. Ibid.

47. Ibid.

48. Ibid.

49. William Huie, *From Omaha to Okinawa* (New York: E.P. Dutton & Company, Inc., 1945) p. 47.

50. William Y'Blood, *The Little Giants*, (Annapolis: Naval Institute Press, 1987) p. 343.

51. Richard Dugan, "Quick, Henry—the DDT," *Brief* magazine, 15 May 1945, p. 7.

52. Mike Michalski, *Recollections of Iwo Jima*, published on the Internet.

53. Unknown, *AAF Evaluation Board Report Number Seven*, The Pacific Ocean Area, Air Force Historical Research Center, Maxwell AFB. p. 51.

54. Robert Krueger, interviewed by Cory Graff, 4 July 2003, tape recording.

55. Ibid.

56. John Lambert, *The Pineapple Air Force*, (St. Paul, MN: Phalanx Publishing Company, Ltd., 1990) p. 116.

57. Unknown, "Hop-Scotch through Hell," *Brief* magazine, 17 April 1945, p. 13.

58. Ibid.

59. Richard Newcomb, *Iwo Jima*, (New York: Henry Holt and Company, 1965) p. 246.

60. Gene Gurney, *B-29 Story*, (Greenwich, CT: Fawcett Publications, 1963) p. 80.

61. Lynn Kessler, *Never in Doubt*, (Annapolis: Naval Institute Press, 1999) p. 139.

62. Bud Nelson, "One Damned Island After Another," *Brief* magazine, 3 April 1945, p. 16.

63. Ibid.

64. Bud Nelson, "Iwo Airbase," *Brief* magazine, 3 April 1945, p. 3.

65. Bud Nelson, "One Damned Island After Another," *Brief* magazine, 3 April 1945, p. 16.

66. Jerry Yellin, *Of War and Weddings*, (Fairfield, IA: Sunstar Publishing, Ltd., 1995) p. 126.

67. Ibid.

68. Leon Sher, interviewed by Cory Graff, 5 July 2003, tape recording.

69. 15th Fighter Group History, Air Force Historical Research Agency, Maxwell AFB.

70. Alan Hartman, "Iwo Looked Beautiful," *Brief* magazine, V-J Issue, p. 7.

71. 15th Fighter Group History, Air Force Historical Research Agency, Maxwell AFB.

72. Ibid.

73. Gordon Scott, interviewed by Cory Graff, 3 July 2003, tape recording.

74. Paul Chism, interviewed by Cory Graff, 3 July 2003, tape recording.

75. 506th Fighter Group History, Air Force Historical Research Agency, Maxwell AFB.

76. John Lambert, *The Pineapple Air Force*, (St. Paul, MN: Phalanx Publishing Company, Ltd., 1990) p. 121.

77. 21st Fighter Group History, Air Force Historical Research Agency, Maxwell AFB.

78. Unknown, "Banzai!," *Air Force Magazine*, July 1945, p. 41.

79. Ibid.

80. Ibid.

81. 21st Fighter Group History, Air Force Historical Research Agency, Maxwell AFB.

82. Ibid.

83. Ibid.

84. Ibid.

85. Unknown, "Banzai!," *Air Force Magazine*, July 1945, p. 41.

86. 21st Fighter Group History, Air Force Historical Research Agency, Maxwell AFB.

87. *The Global Twentieth vol 3*, ed. Chester Marshall, Lindsey Silvester, and Scotty Stallings (Memphis, TN: Global Press, 1988) p. 366.

88. James Tapp, interviewed by Cory Graff, 4 July 2003, tape recording.

89. Ibid.

90. Ibid.

91. Ibid.

92. Unknown, *Fighter Notes*, Volume 1, Number 1, July 1945, p. 16.

93. Andy Doty, *Backwards into Battle*, (Palo Alto, CA: Tall Tree Press, 1995) p. 101.

94. Ibid.

95. Unknown, "Slop Chute Premiere," *Brief* magazine, 17 April 1945, p. 8.

96. 549th Fighter Squadron History, Air Force Historical Research Agency, Maxwell AFB.

97. Unknown, "Mustang Millinery," *Brief* magazine, 21 August 1945, p. 14.

98. Ibid.

99. Unknown, "U of Iwo," *Brief* magazine, 29 May 1945, p. 19.

100. 506th Fighter Group History, Air Force Historical Research Agency, Maxwell AFB.

101. John Lambert, *The Pineapple Air Force* (St. Paul, MN: Phalanx Publishing Company, Ltd., 1990) p. 154.

102. 506th Fighter Group History, Air Force Historical Research Agency, Maxwell AFB.

103. Ibid.

104. Ibid.

105. 21st Fighter Group History, Air Force Historical Research Agency, Maxwell AFB.

106. 506th Fighter Group History, Air Force Historical Research Agency, Maxwell AFB.

107. Ibid.

108. Gordon Scott, "*A Fish Eyes View of Kasumigaura Air Field, Honshu, Japan*," unpublished.

109. Ibid.

110. Gordon Scott, "*The Capture, the Trial, the Firing Squad, the Trip, the Prison*," unpublished.

111. Ibid.

112. Ibid.

113. Ibid.

114. Gordon Scott, interviewed by Cory Graff, 3 July 2003, tape recording.

115. Wyatt Blassingame, *The U.S. Frogmen of World War II*, (New York: Random House, 1964), p.110.

116. Unknown, "The B-29ers," *Impact* magazine, September/October 1945, p. 69.

117. Harry Hadlock, interviewed by Cory Graff, 8 September 2003, tape recording.

118. Frank Saffarrans Jr., *My Reminisces of WWII*, published on the Internet.

119. Dick Veach, "Two Missions from Tinian," *40th Bomb Group Association Memories*, June 1995.

120. Joe Majeski, *Majeski's Memories*, published on the Internet.

121. Arnie Bader, interviewed by Cory Graff, 20 August 2003, tape recording.

122. Ibid.

123. Ibid.

124. Ibid.

125. 548th Night Fighter Squadron History, Air Force Historical Research Agency, Maxwell AFB.

126. Ibid.

127. Unknown, "Black Widow Opener," *Brief* magazine, 17 April 1945, p. 8.

128. 549th Night Fighter Squadron History, Air Force Historical Research Agency, Maxwell AFB.

129. Paul Slocumb, "Foggy Morning on Iwo," *Brief* magazine, 15 May 1945, p. 16.

130. Ibid.

131. 548th Night Fighter Squadron History, Air Force Historical Research Agency, Maxwell AFB.

132. Ibid.

133. Robert Hastings, *Patrol Bombing Squadron One Hundred Six*, (Unknown) p. 67.

134. Gordon Britten, "USS *Quillback*," *Stories of Adventure*, 3 November 2002.

135. John Lambert, *The Long Campaign* (Manhattan, KS: Sunflower University Press, 1982) p. 146.

136. Joseph Walther, *Unrecognized Father of Air-Sea Rescue*, unpublished.

137. Ibid.

138. Ibid.

139. Walter Kreimann, interviewed by Cory Graff, 5 July 2003, tape recording.

140. Ibid.

141. Ibid.

142. Ibid.

143. Ibid.

144. Ibid.

145. Ibid.

146. Ibid.

147. Ibid.

148. Ibid.

149. Alan Hartman, "Death at Chichi," *Brief* magazine, 7 August 1945, p. 4.

150. 414th Fighter Group History, Air Force Historical Research Agency, Maxwell AFB

151. Joseph Stiborik, interview transcript, The Museum of Flight Collection

152. Robert Lewis, interview transcript, The Museum of Flight Collection

153. 506th Fighter Group History, Air Force Historical Research Agency, Maxwell AFB.

154. Paul Wignell, "The Air Force and a Sub," *413th Fighter Squadron* "Yearbook," Air Force Historical Research Agency, Maxwell AFB.

155. Ibid.

156. Frank Collyer, "Bail Out!," *413th Fighter Squadron* "Yearbook," Air Force Historical Research Agency, Maxwell AFB.

157. Ibid.

158. Ibid.

159. Ibid.

160. 457th Fighter Squadron History, Air Force Historical Research Agency, Maxwell AFB.

161. 506th Fighter Group History, Air Force Historical Research Agency, Maxwell AFB.

162. 414th Fighter Group History, Air Force Historical Research Agency, Maxwell AFB.

163. 506th Fighter Group History, Air Force Historical Research Agency, Maxwell AFB.

164. Alan Hartman, "Iwo Looked Beautiful," *Brief* magazine, V-J Issue, p. 6.

165. Ibid.

166. 437th Fighter Squadron History, Air Force Historical Research Agency, Maxwell AFB.

167. 414th Fighter Group History, Air Force Historical Research Agency, Maxwell AFB.

168. Ibid.

169. Ibid.

170. Ibid.

INDEX